NIKOLAI GOGOL. The son of a small landowner, Nikolai Gogol was born in 1809 on
the family estate in the province of Poltava.
He was educated at the Niezhin gymnasium where he
started a magazine and acted in student theatricals. In
1828 he went to St. Petersburg, obtained a government clerkship, and devoted himself to writing. In
1831-32 he published two volumes of *Evenings on a
Farm Near Dikanka,* a collection of stories based
on Ukrainian folklore, which were enthusiastically
received. He next planned to write a history of Russia
in the Middle Ages; the work never materialized but
the planning of it served to win him a chair of history
at the University of St. Petersburg which he resigned
in 1835. Meanwhile he published "Taras Bulba"
and a number of short stories including "The Overcoat." On April 19, 1836, his famous comedy *The
Inspector General* was produced. The play stirred up
strong controversy and the critics hailed its author as
the head of the "naturalist" school. Gogol spent the
next twelve years abroad, living mainly in Rome.
During his voluntary exile, he completed *Dead Souls,*
a panorama of Russian life. The book was published
in 1842 and was an immediate success. The next ten
years Gogol spent writing and rewriting a sequel
which was doomed never to see publication. He
burned it a few days before his death in February
1852.

The Diary of

NEWLY TRANSLATED BY
Andrew R. MacAndrew

WITH AN AFTERWORD BY
Leon Stilman

NIKOLAI GOGOL

a Madman

And Other Stories

A SIGNET MODERN CLASSIC
NEW AMERICAN LIBRARY
TIMES MIRROR
NEW YORK AND SCARBOROUGH, ONTARIO
THE NEW ENGLISH LIBRARY LIMITED, LONDON

SIGNET CLASSIC TRADEMARK REG. U.S. PAT. OFF. AND FOREIGN COUNTRIES
REGISTERED TRADEMARK—MARCA REGISTRADA
HECHO EN CHICAGO, U.S.A.

SIGNET, SIGNET CLASSICS, MENTOR, PLUME AND MERIDIAN BOOKS
are published *in the United States* by
The New American Library, Inc.,
1301 Avenue of the Americas, New York, New York 10019,
in Canada by The New American Library of Canada Limited,
81 Mack Avenue, Scarborough, 704, Ontario,
in the United Kingdom by The New English Library Limited,
Barnard's Inn, Holborn, London, E.C. 1, England.

7 8 9 10 11 12 13 14 15

PRINTED IN THE UNITED STATES OF AMERICA

Contents

The Diary of a Madman

An extraordinary thing happened today. I got up rather late, and when Marva brought my boots, I asked her the time. Hearing that ten had struck quite a while before, I dressed in a hurry. I must say I'd as soon have skipped the office altogether, knowing the sour look the Chief of my Division would give me. For a long time now he has been telling me: "How come, my man, you're always in such a muddle? Sometimes you dart around like a house on fire, and get your work in such a tangle the Devil himself couldn't put it straight; you're likely to start a new heading with a small letter and give no date or reference number." The vicious old crane! He must envy me for sitting in the Director's room and sharpening his quills. So I wouldn't have gone to the office if not in hopes of seeing the cashier and trying to get even a small advance on my salary out of the Jew. What a creature he is! The Last Judgment will come before you'll get a month's pay out of him in advance. Even if there's a dire emergency, you can beg till something bursts inside you; he won't give in, the hoary monster. Yet at home his own cook slaps him around. Everyone knows that. I see no advantage in working in our department. No side benefits whatever. It's not like working, say, for the City Administration or in the Justice Department. There you may see someone nesting in a corner and scribbling away. He may be wearing a shabby coat and have a snout that you'd want to spit at. But then, just take a look at the summer house he rents! And don't even think

7

of offering him a gilt china cup: this, he'd say, may be all right for a doctor. But he—he must have a pair of horses maybe, or a carriage, or a beaver fur—300 rubles' worth or so. And he looks so quiet and sounds so deferential and polite: "Would you," he'll say, "be so kind as to lend me your penknife to sharpen my quill, if you please." But he'll strip a petitioner naked, except perhaps for his shirt. On the other hand, though, to work in our department carries more prestige. The people of the City Administration have never dreamt of such cleanliness. Then we have red mahogany tables and our superiors always address us politely. Yes, if it weren't for the prestige, I confess I'd have left the department long ago.

I put on my old overcoat and, as it was pouring rain, took my umbrella. The streets were quite deserted except for some peasant women, their skirts thrown over their heads, a few merchants under umbrellas, and a coachman here and there. As for decent people there was only our kind, the civil-service clerk, squelching along. I saw him at a street crossing. And as soon as I saw him I said to myself: "You're not on your way to the office, my man. You're after that one trotting ahead over there and it's her legs you're staring at." What a rogue your civil servant is! When it comes to such matters, he can take on an army officer any day. He'll try to pick up anything under a bonnet. I was passing by a store, thinking about all this, when a carriage stopped in front of it. I recognized it at once: it belonged to the Director of our Department, himself. But, I thought, he cannot possibly need anything here—it must be his daughter. I pressed myself against the wall. The footman opened the carriage door and she fluttered out like a little bird. Ah, how she looked around, first right, then left, how her eyes and eyebrows flashed past me! . . . Oh God, I'm lost, lost forever. And why did she have to drive out in the pouring rain? Try and deny after that, that women have a passion for clothing. She did not recognize me. Besides, I was trying to hide myself; my coat was quite stained and out of fashion too. Nowadays, they are wearing long collars on their coats while I had two very short ones, one on top of the other. Her lap dog was too slow to get into the store while the door was open and had to stay in the street. I know this little dog. She's called Madgie. Then, a minute or so later, I heard a thin little voice: "Hello, Madgie." I'll be damned! Who's that talking? I turned around and saw two ladies walking under their umbrellas: one old, the other young and pretty. But they had already passed when I heard again, just next to me: "You ought to be ashamed, Madgie!" What on earth was going on? I saw Madgie and a dog that had been following the two ladies sniffing at one another. "Maybe I'm drunk," I said to myself, "but it's not likely. It doesn't happen to me very often." "No, Fidele, you're wrong." With my own eyes I saw Madgie forming the words, "I was, bow-wow, I was, bow-ow-ow, very sick." Talk about a lap dog! I must say I was quite surprised to hear her talking. Later, however, when I had properly sized up the situation, I was no longer surprised. As a matter of fact, the world has seen many similar occurrences before. I've heard that, in England, a fish broke surface and uttered a couple of words in such an outlandish language that scholars have been trying to work out their meaning for three years—so far in vain. Then, too, I read in the newspapers about two cows who went into a store and asked for a pound of tea. But I'll confess that I was much more bewildered when Madgie said: "I *did* write you, Fidele. Perhaps Fido didn't give you my letter." Now, I'd be willing to forfeit a month's pay if I've ever heard of a dog that could write. Only a gentleman can write correctly anyway. Of course, one finds some scribbling shopkeepers—even serfs—but that sort of writing is mostly mechanical; no commas, periods, or spelling. So I was surprised. I'll confess that recently I have been seeing and hearing things that no one else has ever seen or heard. "Let's," I said to myself, "follow this little dog and find out who she is and what her thoughts are." I opened my umbrella and followed the ladies. We crossed Pea Street, from there on to Tradesman's Avenue, turned into Carpenter's Lane, and finally stopped before a large building near Cuckoo Bridge. "I know this house," I said to myself, "it's the Zverkov house." What a house! Who isn't to be found there! There are so many cooks, so many Poles! And it teems with my fellow civil servants; they sit there on top of one another, like dogs. I have a friend there who can play the trumpet quite well. The ladies went up to the fifth floor. "Fine," I thought, "I won't go in now. I'll make a note of the place and wait for the first opportunity."

Today is Wednesday and that's why I was in our Director's study at his home. I purposely came in early, settled down and sharpened all the quills. Our Director must be a very brilliant man. His study is crammed with bookcases. I looked at some of the titles: such erudition all over the place—cuts an ordinary person off completely; they're all in French or German. And just look into his face, good gracious! What a lot of importance shines in his eyes! I've never heard him utter an unnecessary word. Except, perhaps, when one hands him some documents, he may ask: "How's the weather outside?" "It's quite damp, sir." Yes, he's different from our kind. A public figure! Nevertheless, I feel that he has taken a special liking to me. If only his daughter . . . Ah, what a rogue I am! Never mind, never mind . . . Quiet! . . . I was reading the *Bee*. Aren't the French a stupid race? Whatever can they be driving at? I'd like to take them all and give each one of them a good thrashing. In the same journal I also read a very nice description of a ball by a landowner from Kursk. Kursk landowners certainly write well. . . . Whereupon I noticed that it was striking twelve-thirty and our Director still hadn't left his bedroom. But then, around one-thirty, a thing happened that no pen can adequately describe. The door opened; I thought it was the Director and jumped up from my desk holding the documents in my hand; but it was her, in person! Holy Fathers, the way she was dressed! Her dress was white, all fluffy, like a swan, and when she looked at me, I swear it was like the sun! She nodded to me and said: "Hasn't Papa been in here?" What a voice! A canary, an absolute canary. "Ma'am," I was on the point of saying, "don't have me put to death. But if you do decide that I must die, let it be by your own aristocratic little hand." But my tongue would not obey me and I only muttered, "No, ma'am." Her glance slid from me to the books and she dropped her handkerchief. I rushed like mad, slipped on the blasted parquet and almost smashed my nose. But somehow I recovered my balance and picked it up. Holy

Saints, what a hanky! Such fine, delicate linen, and amber, sheer amber. It exuded aristocracy. She said, "Thank you" and smiled, but so faintly that her divine lips hardly moved, and then she left. I remained seated there and, after another hour, a footman came in and told me: "You may go home, the master has gone out." The flunky is the one thing I cannot stand. They're always sprawled out in the entrance hall, not even bothering to acknowledge my existence with a little nod. Once, one of those lumps actually offered me snuff, and without even getting up. Don't you know, you stupid flunky, that I am a civil servant and that I come from a respectable family? Still, I picked up my hat and pulled on my overcoat unaided since those gents wouldn't think of helping you, and left. At home, I lay on my bed most of the time. Then I copied an excellent poem:

> Without you one hour crept
>   Slowly like a year.
> "Is my life worth while," I wept,
>   "When you are not near?"

Sounds like Pushkin. In the evening, I put on my overcoat and walked over to the Director's house and waited by the gate for quite a while to see whether she wouldn't come out and get into her carriage. But she didn't.

November 6

Something has got into the Chief of my Division. When I arrived at the office he called me and began as follows: "Now then, tell me. What's the matter with you?" "What do you mean? Nothing," I said. "Come, try to understand; aren't you over forty? Time to be a bit wiser. What do you fancy you are? Don't imagine I can't see what you're up to. I know you're trailing after the Director's daughter. Just look at yourself—what are you? Just nothing. You haven't a penny to your name. Look in the mirror. How can you even think of such things?" The hell with him! Just because he's got a face like a druggist's bottle and that quiff of hair on his head all curled and pomaded, and because he holds his head up in the air like that, he thinks he can get away with anything. I see through his indignation. He's envious; perhaps he's noticed the marks of favor bestowed upon me. A lot I care what he says. So he's a Divisional Chief, so what! So he hangs out his gold watch chain and has custom-made boots at thirty rubles. Let him be damned. Perhaps he imagines I had a shopkeeper or a tailor for a father. I'm a gentleman! And I can be promoted too. I'm only forty-two, an age when one's career is really just beginning. Wait, my friend, I'll go higher than you yet, and, God willing, very, very much higher. Then I'll have a social position beyond your dreams. Do you imagine you're the only one to have dignity? Give me a fashionable new coat, let me wear a tie like yours, and you won't be worthy to shine my shoes. My lack of means—that's the only trouble.

November 8

Went to the theater. The play was about the Russian fool Filatka. Laughed a lot. They had a vaudeville show as well, full of amusing verses lampooning lawyers, so outspoken that I wondered how it got past the censor; as to the merchants, it says plainly that they swindle the people, that their sons wallow in debauchery and elbow their way into society. There was also an amusing couplet which complained about the way newspapermen criticize everything and asked the audience for protection from them. Playwrights write very amusing plays nowadays. I love going to the theater. As soon as I get hold of a few pennies, I can't help myself, I go. But civil servants are such swine . . . you won't catch clods like them going to the theater, not even if they're given free tickets. One actress sang really well. . . . It made me think of . . . What a rogue I am! Never mind, never mind . . . silence!

November 9

Left for the office at eight. The Divisional Chief pretended he hadn't noticed me come in. And I also acted as though nothing had happened between us. I went through the papers and sorted them out. Left at four. On the way home, passed by the Director's house but didn't see anyone. After dinner, mostly lay on my bed.

Today, I sat in the Director's study and sharpened twenty-three quills for him, and four quills for . . . . oh-oh . . . her. He likes to have as many quills to hand as possible. My, how brainy he must be! Usually he doesn't say much but I guess he must be weighing everything in that head of his. I'd like to know what he has on his mind most of the time, what's cooking up there. I'd like to have a closer look at these people, how they live, with all their subtle innuendoes and courtly jokes; I wish I knew how they behave and what they do among themselves. I've often tried to engage the Director in conversation but I'm damned if it's ever come off. I've managed to say it's warm or cold outside and that is absolutely as far as I've got. One day I'd like just to step into their drawing room. The door is ajar sometimes and from there I can see another door, leading to another room. That drawing room! You should see how it's decorated. All those mirrors and fine pieces of porcelain. I'd also like to see the part where her rooms are. That's where I'd really like to go! I'd like to peep into her boudoir, and see all those little jars and bottles of hers standing there amidst the sort of flowers one doesn't even dare breathe on; to have a glimpse at the dress she has thrown off, lying there looking more like air than a dress. It would be wonderful to glance into her bedroom. . . . Miracles must happen there. It's a paradise surpassing the heavenly one. What wouldn't I give to see the little stool upon which her delicate foot descends when she gets out of bed and watch how an incredibly fine, immaculate stocking is pulled up her leg. . . . Oh, the roguish thoughts! . . . Never mind . . . never mind . . . silence!

But today something suddenly became clear to me when I recalled the conversation between the two dogs I'd overheard on Nevsky Avenue. Fine, I said to myself, now I'll find out everything. I must get hold of the letters exchanged between those nasty mutts. I'm sure to find out something. Now I'll confess that, at one point, I almost called Madgie and said to her: "Listen, Madgie, we are alone now. If you wish, I'll even lock the door so that no one'll see us. Tell

me everything you know about your mistress: what she's
like and all that. And don't worry, I swear I'll not repeat
a thing to anyone." But the sly little mutt just sort of
shrank into herself, put her tail between her legs, and left
the room in silence, as though she hadn't heard a thing.
For a long time I've suspected that dogs are much more
intelligent than men; I was even certain that they could
speak and simply chose not to out of a peculiar stubbornness. A dog is an extraordinary politician and notices
everything, every step a human takes. Still, whatever happens, tomorrow I'll go to the Zverkov house and question
Fidele and, if possible, I'll lay my hand on Madgie's letters
to her.

November 12

At 2:00 P.M. I went out determined to find Fidele and
question her. I can't stand the smell of cabbage which
comes pouring out of all the greengrocers along Tradesman's Avenue. This, and the infernal stench from under
the gates of every house, sent me scurrying, holding my
nose. And all the soot and smoke that they let pour out
of the vile workshops make it a quite unsuitable place for
a person of breeding to take a stroll. When I reached the
sixth floor and rang the bell, out came a girl with little
freckles and not too bad-looking at that. I recognized her
at once. She was the one I had seen walking with the old
woman. She blushed a little and I immediately saw through
her: what you need, my dear, is a husband. "What do you
want?" she asked. "I want to have a talk with your
doggie."

The girl was stupid. I could see from the start how
stupid she was! At that moment the mutt ran in yapping
furiously and as I was trying to grab her, the repulsive
creature almost caught my nose between her teeth. But
then I saw her basket in the corner—which was just what
I was looking for! I went over to it and felt under the
straw and, to my great joy, I found a small bundle of
papers. Seeing what I was doing, the nasty little cur first
took a bite out of my calf; then, when upon further sniffing she found that I had taken her letters, she began

whining and making up to me, but I told her, "Oh no, my dear. See you later!" And off I went. I believe the girl mistook me for a madman—she seemed very frightened indeed.

Once home, I wanted to get down to work immediately, to have those letters sorted before dark, since I can't see too well by candlelight. But for some reason Marva decided to scrub the floor just then. Those stupid Finns always succumb to their obsession for cleanliness at the worst moments. So I went out for a walk to think it all over. Now, finally, I'll find out everything about these intrigues and plots; I'll understand all the little wheels and springs and get to the bottom of the matter. These letters will explain. Dogs are a clever race. They know all about intrigue and so it's all bound to be in their letters: all there is to know about the Director's character and actions. And she, she too is sure to be mentioned . . . but never mind that . . . silence! I came home toward evening. Most of the time, I lay on my bed.

November 13

Let's see now. This letter looks quite legible, though there *is* something canine about the handwriting:

> *Dear Fidele, I still find it difficult to get accustomed to the commonness of your name. Couldn't they find a better one for you? Fidele, like Rose, is very ordinary, but all that's beside the point. I'm very glad we have decided to write to each other.*

The spelling is very good. It's even punctuated correctly. This is considerably better than our Divisional Chief can do, although he claims to have gone to some university or other. Let's see further on:

> *I believe that sharing feelings and impressions with another is one of the main blessings in life. . . .*

Hm! The thought is stolen from a work translated from the German. The author's name escapes me now.

*I speak from experience although I've never been much
further than the gates of our house. But then, isn't my life
full of blessings? My young mistress, whom her papa calls
Sophie, is crazy about me.*

Ouch! Never mind, never mind. Silence!

*Papa often pets me too. I drink tea and coffee with cream.
I must tell you, my dear, that I am not in the least tempted
by the half-gnawed bones which our Fido chews on in the
kitchen. I only like the bones of game and, even then, only
if the marrow hasn't been sucked out by someone else. A
mixture of sauces is nice as long as they contain no capers
or vegetables. What I hate is people who give dogs the little
pellets they knead out of bread. Some person sitting at the
table, who has previously touched all sorts of filthy things,
begins to knead a piece of bread with those same hands,
then calls you and thrusts the pellet into your mouth. It
is awkward somehow to refuse and, disgusted, you eat it
up. . . .*

What's that all about? What rubbish! As though there
weren't more interesting things to write about. Let's see
the next page. There may be something less stupid.

*Now, I'll tell you with pleasure what goes on in this house-
hold. I have mentioned the main character, whom Sophie
calls Papa. He's a very strange man. . . .*

At last! I knew they had very shrewd judgment, whatever the subject. Let's see what Papa's like.

*. . . a very strange man. He's usually silent. He speaks
very little, but a week ago he never stopped saying to himself: Will I get it or not? Once he even asked me: What do
you say, Madgie, will I get it or won't I? I could make no
sense out of it so I smelled his shoe and left the room. Then,
a week later, Papa came home overjoyed. All that morning
formally dressed people came and congratulated him. At
dinner Papa was gayer than I'd ever seen him before, and
after dinner, he picked me up and held me level with his
chest, saying: Look, Madgie, what's this? I saw some sort
of a ribbon. I sniffed at it but it had no fragrance whatever.
Finally, discreetly, I gave it a lick: slightly salty.*

Hm. The mutt really goes too far . . . she needs a good

whipping . . . So he is that vain is he? I must take it into account.

Good-bye, my dear, I must run along . . . blah-blah-blah-blah . . . will finish this letter tomorrow. Hello, I am back with you. Today my mistress, Sophie . . .

Aha! Let's see what she says about Sophie. I really *am* a rogue! But never mind, never mind. Let's go on.

. . . my mistress, Sophie, was in a terrific to-do. She was getting ready for a ball and I intended to take advantage of her absence and write to you. Sophie is always very happy when she's about to leave for a ball but is always very irritable while she's getting dressed for it. You know, my dear, I personally can see no pleasure in going to a ball. Sophie usually returns home from balls at 6 A.M., and I can tell by her pale and emaciated features that the poor thing hasn't been given a bite to eat. I confess I could never lead such a life. If I had to go without game in sauce or chicken-wing stews, I don't know what would become of me. A sauce is not at all bad with porridge. But nothing can make carrots, turnips, and artichokes palatable. . . .

The style is very jerky. You can see that it's not written by a man. She starts off all right and then lapses into dogginess. Let's see another letter. Looks rather long . . . hm . . . no date . . .

Oh, my dear, how strongly I feel the approach of spring. My heart beats as though it were waiting for something. In my ears, there's a constant buzz. Very often I listen so intently behind doors that I raise my front paw. And, confidentially, I have plenty of suitors. I often sit by the window and watch them. If only you could see some of them, they're so ugly. There is a horrible mongrel with stupidity written all over him, who swaggers along the street and imagines he is a person of breeding and that everyone is bound to admire him. I paid no attention to him, as though I hadn't even noticed him. Then you should have seen the terrifying Great Dane that stopped in front of my window! If that one stood up on his hind legs, which, incidentally, the clod is incapable of doing, he would be a head taller than Sophie's Papa, who's quite tall himself and fat besides. Moreover, the lump seems to be very arrogant. I growled at him but it didn't put him off in the least. He just hung his tongue out, drooped his huge ears, and kept staring at my window, the oaf! But, my dear, you don't really imagine, do you, that my heart is indifferent to all the hopefuls? . . . You should have seen the dashing young lover that came jumping over the fence into our courtyard. His name is Treasure and he has such a nice face. . . .

Ah, damn it all! What rubbish! How much of her letters is she going to fill with such stupid stuff? I'm after *people*, not dogs! I need spiritual food and I am served these inanities. . . . Let's skip a page, perhaps we'll find something more interesting. . . .

. . . Sophie was sitting at the table sewing something. I was looking out of the window; I like to watch people in the street. Suddenly the manservant came in and announced someone. "Show him in!" Sophie said. She hugged me hard and murmured, "Oh Madgie, darling, if you only knew who that is. He's a Guards officer, his hair is black and his eyes are so dark and so light at the same time . . . like fire." And Sophie rushed out. A minute later a young officer with black side whiskers appeared. He went to the mirror and smoothed his hair; then he looked around the room. I growled a little and settled down by my window. Soon Sophie came back, greeted him gaily, while I pretended to be busy looking out of the window. In fact, however, I turned my head sideways a little, so that I could catch what they said. You cannot imagine, Fidele dear, the silliness of that conversation. They spoke about some lady who, during a dance, kept doing a certain step instead of the one she was expected to do, then about somebody called Bobov, who looked like a stork and almost fell over, then about one Lidina, who thought she had blue eyes when they were really green, and so on and on. Oh no, I said to myself, this officer doesn't compare to Treasure. Heavens, what a difference! To start with, the officer has a wide face, quite bald except for his side whiskers which, in fact, look like a black kerchief tied around it, whereas Treasure's face is narrow and fine and he has a sweet white patch on his brow. Treasure's waist is incomparably slenderer than the officer's, and his eyes, his gestures, and his ways are vastly superior. Really, a tremendous difference! I wonder what she finds in her officer. What on earth can she admire in him? . . .

Yes, here I tend to agree. Something seems wrong. It is

quite unbelievable that this officer should have swept her off her feet. Let's see:

> *If she likes the officer, I think she'll soon be liking the civil-service clerk who sits in Papa's study. That one, my dear, is a real scarecrow. He looks a bit like a turtle caught in a bag. . . .*

Which clerk can that be? . . .

> *He has a funny name and he's always sitting sharpening quills. The hair on his head is like straw. Papa sends him on errands like a servant. . . .*

The filthy cur seems to be trying to get its own back! Why is my hair like straw?

> *Sophie can hardly control her laughter when she sees him.*

You wretched, lying dog! What a filthy, poisonous tongue! As if I didn't know it's all your jealousy. I know whose tricks these are. I recognize the hand of the Divisional Chief here. For some reason, that man has sworn undying hatred for me and he is trying to harm me, to harm me every minute of the day and night. Still, let's see one more letter. It may make it clear.

> *My dear Fidele, forgive me for not writing to you all this time. I've been going around in absolute ecstasy. I agree, without reservation, with the philosopher who said that love is a second life. Moreover, a lot of things are changing in our household. The officer comes every day now. Sophie is madly in love with him. Papa is very gay. I even heard our Gregory, who always talks to himself while sweeping the floors, say that the wedding is close at hand, because Papa always wanted to see Sophie married to a high official or to an army officer with a brilliant career ahead of him. . . .*

Hell! . . . I can't go on. . . . High officials, senior officers, they get all the best things in this world. You discover a crumb of happiness, you reach out for it and then along comes a high official or an officer and snatches it away. Goddammit! I would like so much to become a high official myself and not just to obtain her hand in marriage either. No, I'd like to be a high official just so that I could watch them jump around for my benefit; I'd listen for a

while to their courtly jokes and innuendoes and then tell
them what they could do with themselves. It hurts, though.
Oh hell! . . . I tore the stupid little dog's letter to shreds.

at stage that he undergoes (handwritten)

December 3

Impossible! Lies! There can't be a wedding. So what if
he has a commission in the Guards? That's nothing but
position, you can't touch it with your hand. A Guards officer does not have a third eye in the middle of his forehead, his nose is not made of gold but the same stuff as
mine or anyone else's and he uses it to sniff not to eat,
for sneezing not for coughing. I've often tried to discover
where all these differences lie. Why am I a clerk? Why
should I be a clerk? Perhaps I'm really a general or a
count and only seem to be a clerk? Maybe I don't really
know who I am? There are plenty of instances in history
when somebody quite ordinary, not necessarily an aristocrat, some middle-class person or even a peasant, suddenly
turns out to be a public figure and perhaps even the ruler
of a country. If a peasant can turn into someone so important, where are the limits to the possibilities for a man
of breeding? Imagine, for instance, me, entering a room in
a general's uniform. There's an epaulet on my right shoulder, an epaulet on my left, a blue ribbon across my chest.
How would that be? What tune would my beauty sing
then? And Papa himself, our Director, what would he say?
Ow, he's so vain! He's a Mason, no mistake about it, although he may pretend to be this or that; I noticed from
the start that when he shakes hands, he sticks out two fingers only. But I can't be promoted to general or governor
or anything like that overnight. What I'd like to know is,
why am I a clerk? Why precisely a clerk?

understands the nature of hierarchy. (handwritten)

at heart a this narrative (handwritten, left margin)

December 5

I read the newspapers all morning. Strange things are
happening in Spain. I can't even make them out properly.

They write that the throne has been vacated and that the ranking grandees are having difficulty in selecting an heir. It seems there's discontent. Sounds very strange to me. How can a throne be vacant? They say that some donna may accede. A donna cannot accede to a throne. It's absolutely impossible. A king should sit on a throne. But they say there is no king. It's impossible that there should be no king. There must be a king but he's hidden away somewhere in anonymity. It's even possible that he's around but is being forced to remain in hiding for family reasons or for fear of some neighboring country such as France. Or there may be other reasons.

progressive ideas

December 8

I was on the point of going to the office but various considerations held me back. I couldn't get those Spanish affairs out of my head. How can a donna possibly become ruler? They won't allow it. In the first place, England won't stand for it. Then we must keep in mind the political setup of the rest of Europe: the Austrian Emperor, our Tsar. . . . I confess I was so perturbed and hurt by these events that I could do nothing all day. Marva remarked that I was very absent-minded during dinner. . . . In fact, I believe I absent-mindedly threw a couple of plates on the floor, where they broke at once. After dinner, I walked the streets, uphill and downhill. Came across nothing of interest. Then, mostly lay on my bed and thought about the Spanish question.

evolution of character's madness gradual movement   next entry

Year 2000, April 43

This is a day of great jubilation. Spain has a king. They've found him. *I* am the King. I discovered it today. It all came to me in a flash. It's incredible to me now that I could have imagined that I was a civil-service clerk. How could such a crazy idea ever have entered my head? Thank

plunge into total commitment to madness (bizarre)

God no one thought of slapping me into a lunatic asylum. Now I see everything clearly, as clearly as if it lay in the palm of my hand. But what was happening to me before? Then things loomed at me out of a fog. Now, I believe that all troubles stem from the misconception that human brains are located in the head. They are not: human brains are blown in by the winds from somewhere around the Caspian Sea.

Marva was the first to whom I revealed my identity. When she heard that she was facing the King of Spain, she flung up her hands in awe. She almost died of terror. The silly woman had never seen a King of Spain before. However, I tried to calm her and, speaking graciously, did my best to assure her of my royal favor. I was not going to hold against her all the times she had failed to shine my boots properly. The masses are so ignorant. One can't talk to them on lofty subjects. Probably she was so frightened because she thought that all kings of Spain are like Philip II. But I carefully pointed out that I wasn't like Philip II at all. I didn't go to the office. The hell with it. No, my friends, you won't entice me there now; never again shall I copy your dreadful documents.

part still recognizes he would escaped from

Martober 86. Between day and night

Today, our Divisional Chief sent someone to make me go to the office. I hadn't been there for over three weeks. I went, just for a lark. The Divisional Chief expected me to come apologizing to him but I just looked at him indifferently, with not too much ire, nor too much benevolence either; then I sat down in my usual place as though unaware of the people around me. I looked around at all that scribbling rabble and thought: If only you had an inkling of who's sitting here among you, oh Lord, what a fuss you'd make. There'd be a terrific to-do and the Divisional Chief himself would bow deeply to me, as he does to the Director. They put some papers in front of me which I was supposed to abstract or something. I didn't even stir. A few minutes later, there was a general commotion. They said the Director was on his way. Several clerks jumped up, hoping he'd notice them. But I didn't budge. When word came that the Director was about to pass through our Division, they all buttoned up their coats. I did nothing of the sort. What kind of a Director does he think he is? Who says I should get up for him? Never! He's an old cork, not a Director. Yes, but an ordinary cork, the kind used for stoppering a bottle. That's all he is. But the funniest thing of all was when they gave me a paper to sign. They expected I'd sign it in the corner: head clerk such and such. Well, let them think again. I wrote in the main space, the one reserved for the Director's signature: Ferdinand VIII. You should have witnessed the awed silence that followed; but I merely waved my hand graciously and said: "Dispense with the manifestation of allegiance!" and walked out of the room. From there, I went straight to the Director's house. He was not at home. The footman tried to stop me from going in but what I said made his arms drop limp at his sides. I went straight to her boudoir. She was sitting in front of her mirror. She jumped up and stepped back, away from me. Still I did not tell her that I was the King of Spain. I simply told her that she couldn't even imagine the happiness awaiting her and that despite all our enemies' intrigues, we would be together. I did not want to say more and left. Oh, women are such perfidious things! Only now did I understand what a woman is like. So far, no one has found out whom Woman is in love with. I was the first to discover it: Woman is in love with the Devil. And I'm not joking either. Physicists write a lot of drivel about her being this, that and the other. She loves only the Devil. Look, do you see over there, in the front tier of the boxes? She raises her lorgnette. You think she's looking at that fat man with the star over there? Nothing of the sort. She's staring at the Devil, the Devil hiding behind the fat man's back. See, now he has hidden himself in the star and he's beckoning to her with his finger! And she'll marry him too. She will for sure. As for all the rest of them, all those who lick boots and proclaim their patriotism, all they really want is annuities and more annuities. Some patriots! They'd sell their mother, their father, and their God for money, the strutting betrayers of Christ! And all this crazy ambition and vanity comes from the little bubble under the tongue which has a tiny worm about the size of a pinhead in it, and it's all the work of a barber on Pea

Street. I can't recall his name but the moving force behind it all is the Sultan of Turkey who pays the barber to spread Mohammedanism all over the world. They say that in France, already, the majority of the people have embraced the Mohammedan faith.

No date. A day without date

Went along Nevsky Avenue incognito. Saw the Tsar riding past. Everybody was doffing his hat, and so did I. I gave no sign that I was the King of Spain. I thought it would be undignified to reveal my identity there, in front of all those people, that it would be more proper to be presented at Court first. What has prevented me so far is the fact that I haven't got Spanish royal attire. If only I could get hold of a royal mantle of some sort. I thought of having one made but tailors are so stupid. Besides, they don't seem to be interested in their trade nowadays and go in for speculation, so that most of them end up mending roads. I decided to make a mantle out of my best coat, which I had only worn twice. But I didn't want those good-for-nothings to mess it all up—I preferred to do it myself. I locked my door so as not to be seen. I had to cut my coat to ribbons with the scissors since a mantle has a completely different style.

Can't remember the day. Nor was there a month. Damned if I know what's been going on

The mantle is ready. Marva really let out a yell when I put it on. Even so, I still don't feel ready to be presented at Court. My retinue hasn't as yet arrived from Spain. The absence of a retinue would be incompatible with my dignity. I'm expecting them at any time.

1st Date

I'm puzzled by the unaccountable delay in the arrival of my retinue. What can be holding them up? I went to the post office and inquired whether the Spanish delegates had arrived. But the postmaster is an utter fool and knows nothing: No, he says, there are no Spanish delegates around here but if you wish to mail a letter, we'll accept it. What the hell is he talking about? What letter? Letter my foot! Let druggists write letters. . . .

Madrid, Februarius the thirtieth

So I'm in Spain. It all happened so quickly that I hardly had time to realize it. This morning the Spanish delegation finally arrived for me and we all got into a carriage. I was somewhat bewildered by the extraordinary speed at which we traveled. We went so fast that in half an hour we reached the Spanish border. But then, nowadays there are railroads all over Europe and the ships go so fast too. Spain is a strange country. When we entered the first room, I saw a multitude of people with shaven heads. I soon realized, though, that these must be Dominican or Capuchin monks because they always shave their heads. I also thought that the manners of the King's Chancellor, who was leading me by the hand, were rather strange. He pushed me into a small room and said: "You sit quiet and don't you call yourself King Ferdinand again or I'll beat the nonsense out of your head." But I knew that I was just being tested and refused to submit. For this, the Chancellor hit me across the back with a stick, twice, so painfully that I almost let out a cry. But I contained myself, remembering that this is customary procedure among knights on initiation into an exalted order. To this day, they adhere to the chivalric code in Spain.

Left to myself, I decided to devote some time to affairs

of state. I have discovered that China and Spain are the same thing and it's only ignorance that makes people take them for two separate countries. I advise anybody who doubts it to take a piece of paper and write the word "Spain" and they'll see for themselves that it comes out "China." I also gave much thought to a sad event that must occur tomorrow at seven o'clock. As foreseen by the famous English chemist Wellington, the Earth will mount the Moon. I confess I was deeply worried when I thought of the Moon's extraordinary sensitivity and fragility. The Moon, of course, is made in Hamburg, and I must say they do a very poor job. I wonder why England doesn't do something about it. It's a lame cooper that makes the Moon, and it's quite obvious that the fool has no conception of what the Moon should be. He uses tarred rope and olive oil and that's why the stench is so awful all over the Earth and we are forced to plug our noses. And that's why the Moon itself is such a delicate ball that men cannot live there—only noses. And that's why we can't see our own noses: they are all on the Moon. And when I thought what a heavy thing the Earth is and that, sitting down on the Moon, it would crush our noses into a powder, I became so worried that I put on my socks and shoes and rushed into the State Council Room to order my police force to stand by to prevent the Earth from mounting the Moon. The Capuchin monks I found in the State Council Room were very clever people and when I said, "Gentlemen, let's save the Moon, the Earth is preparing to mount it," they all rushed at once to execute my royal wish and many tried to climb the wall to reach the Moon. But at that moment, the Grand Chancellor came in. As soon as they saw him, they scattered. Being the King, I remained there alone. But to my surprise, the Chancellor hit me with his stick and chased me into my room. Such is the power of popular tradition in Spain!

January of the same year which happened after Februarius

I still can't make out what sort of a place Spain is. The customs and the etiquette at the Court are quite incredible.

I don't see, I don't grasp it, I don't understand at all! Today, they shaved my head, although I shouted with all my might that I did not want to become a monk. But then they began to drip cold water on my head and everything went blank. Never have I been through such hell. I just can't understand the point of this peculiar custom, so stupid, so senseless. And the irresponsibility of the kings who never got around to outlawing this custom is quite beyond me.

Some indications make me wonder whether I haven't fallen into the hands of the Inquisition. Maybe the man I took for the Chancellor is really the Grand Inquisitor himself? But then, I can't see how the King can be subjected to the Inquisition. True, this could be the work of France, especially Polignac. That Polignac is an absolute beast. He has sworn to drive me to my death. And so he maneuvers on and on. But I know, my fine fellow, that you in turn are being led by the English. The English are great politicians. They sow the seeds of dissension everywhere. The whole world knows that when England takes snuff, France sneezes.

25th Date

Today, the Grand Inquisitor entered my room. I heard his steps approaching while he was still far off and hid under a chair. He looked around and, not seeing me, he began to call out. First he shouted my name and civil-service rank. I remained silent. Then, Ferdinand VIII, King of Spain! I was about to stick my head out but thought to myself: No, they won't get me that way! They may want to pour cold water on my head again. But he saw me and chased me out from under the chair with his stick. His damn stick hurts dreadfully. But my very latest discovery made me feel better: I had found that every rooster has his own Spain and he has it under his feathers. The Grand Inquisitor left very angry, threatening me with some punishment or other. Of course, I completely ignored his helpless fury. I knew he was a puppet. A tool of England.

da 34 te Mnth. Yr. yraurbeF 349

No, I have no strength left. I can't stand any more. My God! What they're doing to me! They pour cold water on my head. They don't listen to me, they don't hear me, they don't see me. What have I done to them? Why do they torture me so? What do they want from me? What can I give them? I haven't anything to give. I have no strength, I cannot bear this suffering, my head is on fire, and everything goes around me in circles. Save me! Take me away from here! Give me a carriage with horses swift as wind! Drive on, coachman, let the harness bells ring! Soar upward, my horses, carry me away from this world! Further, further, where I will see nothing, nothing. There is the sky smoking before me. A star twinkles far away, the forest rushes past with its dark trees and the crescent moon. The violet fog is a carpet underfoot. I hear the twanging of a guitar string through the fog; on one side, the sea, and on the other, Italy. Then Russian huts come into sight. Perhaps that's my house over there, looking blue in the distance. And isn't that my mother sitting by the window? Mother, save your wretched son! Let your tears fall on his sick head! See how they torture him! Hold me, a poor waif, in your arms. There's no room for him in this world. They are chasing him. Mother, take pity on your sick child. . . .

And, by the way, have you heard that the Dey of Algiers has a wart right under his nose?

safe to be mad

create himself.

finally retreats into madness

The Nose

Chapter 1

An incredible thing happened in Petersburg on March 25th. Ivan Yakovlevich, the barber on Voznesensky Avenue (his last name has been lost and does not even figure on the signboard bearing a picture of a gentleman with a soapy cheek and the inscription WE ALSO LET BLOOD HERE), woke up rather early and detected a smell of newly baked bread. He raised himself a little and saw that his wife, a quite respectable woman and one extremely fond of coffee, was taking fresh rolls out of the oven.

"Praskovia Osipovna," he said to his wife, "no coffee for me this morning. I'll have a hot roll with onions instead."

Actually Ivan Yakovlevich would have liked both but he knew his wife frowned on such whims. And, sure enough, she thought:

"It's fine with me if the fool wants bread. That'll leave me another cup of coffee."

And she tossed a roll onto the table.

Mindful of his manners, Ivan Yakovlevich put his frock coat on over his nightshirt, seated himself at the table, poured some salt, got a couple of onions, took a knife and, assuming a dignified expression, proceeded to cut the roll in two.

Suddenly he stopped, surprised. There was something

whitish in the middle of the roll. He poked at it with his knife, then felt it with his finger.

"It's quite compact . . ." he muttered under his breath. "Whatever can it be? . . ."

He thrust in two fingers this time and pulled it out. It was a nose.

He almost fell off his chair. Then he rubbed his eyes and felt the thing again. It was a nose all right, no doubt about it. And, what's more, a nose that had something familiar about it. His features expressed intense horror.

But the intensity of the barber's horror was nothing compared with the intensity of his wife's indignation.

"Where," she screamed, "did you lop off that nose, you beast? You crook," she shouted, "you drunkard! I'll report you to the police myself, you thug! Three customers have complained to me before this about the way you keep pulling their noses when you shave them, so that it's a wonder they manage to stay on at all."

But Ivan Yakovlevich, at that moment more dead than alive, was immune to her attack. He had remembered where he had seen the nose before and it was on none other than Collegiate Assessor Kovalev, whom he shaved regularly each Wednesday and Sunday.

"Wait, my dear, I'll wrap it in a rag and put it away somewhere in a corner. Let it stay there for a while, then I'll take it away."

"I won't even listen to you! Do you really imagine that I'll allow a cut-off nose to remain in my place, you old crumb! All you can do is strop your damn razor and when it comes to your duties, you're no good. You stupid, lousy, skirt-chasing scum! So you want me to get into trouble with the police for your sake? Is that it, you dirty mug? You're a stupid log, you know. Get it out of here. Do what you like with it, you hear me, but don't let me ever see it here again."

The barber stood there dumfounded. He thought and thought but couldn't think of anything.

"I'll be damned if I know how it happened," he said in the end, scratching behind his ear. "Was I drunk last night when I came home? I'm not sure. Anyway, it all sounds quite mad: bread is a baked product while a nose is something else again. Makes no sense to me. . . ."

So he fell silent. The thought that the police would find

the nose on him and accuse him drove him to despair.
He could already see the beautiful silver-braided, scarlet
collars of the police and started trembling all over.

Still, in the end he stirred and went to get his trousers and
his boots. He pulled on these sorry garments, wrapped the
nose in a rag, and left under Praskovia Osipovna's unen-
dearing barrage of recriminations.

He wanted to get rid of the nose, to leave it under a
seat, stick it in a doorway, or just drop it as if by accident
and then rush down a side street. But he kept meeting acquaintances who immediately proceeded to inquire where
he was going or whom he was planning to shave so early
in the morning, and he missed every opportunity. At one
point he actually dropped the nose, but a watchman pointed
to it with his halberd and informed him that he'd lost something. And Ivan Yakovlevich had to pick up the nose and
stuff it back into his pocket. Things began to look completely hopeless for him when the stores began opening
and the streets became more and more crowded.

Then he decided to try throwing the nose into the Neva
from the Isakievsky Bridge. . . .

But, at this point, we should say a few words about
Ivan Yakovlevich, a man who had a number of good points.

Like every self-respecting Russian tradesman, Ivan Yakovlevich was a terrible drunkard. And although he shaved
other people's chins every day, his own looked permanently
unshaven. His frock coat (he never wore an ordinary coat)
was piebald. That is to say, it had been black originally but
now it was studded with yellowish-brown and gray spots.
His collar was shiny and three threads dangling from his
coat indicated where the missing buttons should have been.
Ivan Yakovlevich was a terrible cynic.

While being shaved the collegiate assessor often complained:

"Your hands always stink, Ivan Yakovlevich!"

He would answer: "How can they stink?"

"I don't know how, man, but they stink!" the other
would say.

In answer Ivan Yakovlevich would take a pinch of snuff
and proceed to soap Kovalev's cheeks and under his nose
and behind his ears and under his chin, in fact, anywhere
he felt like.

By and by, this worthy citizen reached the Isakievsky

Bridge. He glanced around and then, leaning over the parapet, peered under the bridge as if to ascertain the whereabouts of some fish. But actually he discreetly dropped the rag containing the nose. He felt as if a three-hundred-pound weight had been taken off his back. He let out a little laugh and, instead of going back to shave the chins of government employees, he decided he had to recuperate. He was setting out for an establishment which operated under the sign MEALS AND TEA, to treat himself to a glass of punch, when all of a sudden he saw a police inspector of most imposing appearance—handlebar mustache, three-cornered hat, saber and all. He froze in his tracks. The policeman beckoned to him and said:

"Just step over here, fellow!"

Having great respect for this particular uniform, Ivan Yakovlevich pulled off his cap while he was still a good distance away, trotted toward the policeman and said:

"Good morning, officer."

"Instead of good morning, you'd better tell me what you were doing in the middle of the bridge over there."

"I was on my way to shave people, officer, and I wanted to see whether the current was fast——"

"You're lying, man. You won't get away with it. You'd better answer my question."

"Officer, I'll give you two . . . no, three free shaves every week . . . what do you say, officer?" said Ivan Yakovlevich.

"Not a chance. I have three barbers to shave me as it is. And they consider it a great honor, too. So you get on with it and explain what you were doing."

Ivan Yakovlevich turned ashen. . . . But here the incident becomes befogged and it is completely unknown what happened after this point.

Chapter 2

That morning Collegiate Assessor Kovalev had awakened rather early. He went brrr . . . brrr with his lips as he always did upon waking, although he himself could not explain why. He stretched himself and asked his man for the small mirror that stood on his dressing table. He needed it to examine a pimple that had broken out on his nose the day before. But he was bewildered to find that instead of his nose there was nothing but a bare smooth surface. Horrified, he asked for water and rubbed his eyes with a towel. There was no doubt about it: his nose was not there. He felt himself all over to make sure he was not asleep. It seemed he wasn't. Collegiate Assessor Kovalev jumped up then and shook himself. Still no nose. He called for his clothes and rushed directly to the police inspector.

But, in the meantime, a few things should be said about Kovalev to show what sort of collegiate assessor he was. Collegiate assessors who reach their positions by obtaining academic degrees cannot be compared with the collegiate assessors that used to be appointed in the Caucasus. They are two completely unrelated species. The collegiate assessors equipped with learning . . .

But Russia is a strange place and if we say something about one collegiate assessor, all of them, from Riga to Kamchatka, will take it personally. The same is true of all vocations and ranks.

Kovalev was a Caucasus-made collegiate assessor. Moreover, he had been a collegiate assessor for only two years. In order to feel distinguished and important he never referred to himself as a collegiate assessor but employed the equivalent military rank of major.

"Look here, my good woman," he used to say when he met a woman selling shirt fronts in the street, "I want you to deliver them to my place. I live on Sadovaya Street. Just ask for Major Kovalev's, anybody'll show you."

And if he met someone pretty, he would whisper to her discreetly: "You just ask for Major Kovalev's apartment, deary."

As a rule, Major Kovalev went out for a daily walk along Nevsky Avenue. The collar of his shirt was always clean and well starched. He had whiskers such as are still to be found on provincial surveyors, and architects if they happen to be Russian, among persons performing various police functions, and, in general, on men who have full faces, ruddy cheeks, and play a strong hand at certain games of chance. Whiskers of this type flow straight across the middle of the cheek up to the very nostrils.

Major Kovalev always carried with him a great quantity of seals, both seals engraved with coats of arms and others on which were carved WEDNESDAY, THURSDAY, MONDAY, and that sort of thing. He had come to Petersburg on business, namely, to find a position commensurate with his rank. He hoped, if lucky, to get a Vice-Governorship; otherwise, he would consider a post as executive in some administration. Nor was Major Kovalev averse to matrimony, as long as the bride happened to have a capital of about two hundred thousand rubles.

And now that all this has been said about the major, it can be imagined how he felt when, instead of a quite acceptable-looking, medium-sized nose, he found an absurd, smooth flatness.

And, to make things worse, there was not a cab to be seen in the street and he was forced to walk all the way wrapped in his cloak, his face covered with a handkerchief, pretending he was bleeding, and repeating to himself:

"Maybe it's just imagination. How could I possibly have lost my nose so stupidly? . . ."

He entered a tearoom simply to have a look in a mirror. Fortunately the place was empty except for waiters sweeping the floor and moving chairs around and some others who, with sleepy eyes, were carrying trays with hot buns somewhere. Yesterday's newspapers spotted with coffee were strewn around on tables and chairs.

"Well, thank heaven there's no one here," he said. "I'll be able to have a look."

Gingerly he approached the mirror and looked.

"Filth," he said, spitting, "goddammit. If only there was something to take the nose's place! But it's completely blank!"

He bit his lip in anger and, leaving the tearoom, decided that, contrary to his usual custom, he wouldn't look at the people he met or smile at anyone. Suddenly he stopped dead near the entrance door of a house. An incredible sequence of events unrolled before his eyes. A carriage stopped at the house entrance. Its door opened. A uniformed gentleman appeared. Stooping, he jumped out of the carriage, ran up the steps and entered the house. A combination of horror and amazement swept over Kovalev when he recognized the stranger as his own nose. At this eerie sight, everything swayed before his eyes. But although he could hardly stand on his feet, he felt compelled to wait until the nose returned to the carriage. He waited, shaking as though he had malaria.

After two minutes or so, the nose emerged from the house. He wore a gold-braided, brightly colored uniform, buckskin breeches, a three-cornered hat, and a saber. The plumes on his hat indicated the rank of state councilor. From everything else it could be inferred that he was setting off on some sort of official visit. He looked left, then right, called out to the coachman to bring the carriage up to the very door, got in and was off.

This almost drove poor Kovalev insane. He could no longer think coherently about the whole affair. No, really, how was it possible that the nose, until yesterday on his face, utterly incapable of walking or driving around, should show up like this today and, what's more, wearing a uniform! And Kovalev ran after the carriage, which, luckily for him, did not have far to go. It stopped before Kazan Cathedral.

Kovalev reached the spot and, rushing after the nose, had to elbow his way through a throng of old beggar-women who used to make him laugh because of the way they kept their faces completely wrapped in rags, leaving only slits for their eyes. He entered the cathedral. There were a few worshipers around, all standing near the entrance. Kovalev was in such a depressed state that he could not possibly muster the strength to pray and instead his eyes scrutinized every recess in search of the gentleman. Finally he discovered him standing in a corner. The nose's face was completely concealed by his high, stand-up collar and he was praying with an expression of the utmost piety.

"How shall I address him?" Kovalev wondered. "From his uniform, his hat, everything about him, he must be a state councilor. Damned if I know what to do. . . ."

He approached and cleared his throat. But the nose never even changed his pious posture and remained absorbed in his worship.

"Excuse me, sir . . . " Kovalev said, scraping up all his courage.

"Yes?" the nose said, turning around.

"I don't know how to put it, sir . . . I would say . . . it seems . . . it seems you ought to know where you belong, and where do I find you? Of all places, in church. You must surely agree——"

"Pardon me, but I can make neither head nor tail of what you're saying. Just what do you want?"

Kovalev tried to think how he could explain to the nose what he had in mind and, taking a deep breath, said:

"Of course, sir, for my part . . . but, after all, I am a major, you know, and it's most improper, in my position, to walk around without a nose. Some old woman selling peeled oranges by the Voskresensky Bridge might be able to get along without a nose. But for someone who is almost certain of a high administrative appointment . . . you can judge for yourself, sir. I really fail to understand . . ." At this point Kovalev shrugged. "You'll excuse me, but if this affair were handled according to the code of honor and duty . . . You can see for yourself——"

"I don't see anything," the nose said. "Kindly come to the point."

"Sir," Kovalev said with dignity, "I don't know how to interpret your words. The matter is quite clear, I believe. Unless you are trying . . . Don't you realize that you are my nose?"

The nose looked at the major and frowned slightly.

"You're mistaken, sir. I'm all on my own. Moreover, there couldn't possibly have been close relations between us. Judging by your dress, you must be employed by the Senate, or possibly by the Ministry of Justice, whereas my field is science."

And having said this, the nose turned away and resumed his prayers.

Kovalev was now completely at a loss. Then he heard the pleasant rustle of a feminine dress. He saw a middle-aged lady covered with lace and, with her, a pretty, slender thing in a white dress which set off a very moving waistline, and with a straw hat as light as whipped cream. Behind them walked a tall man with side whiskers and a very complicated collar.

Kovalev worked his way toward them, pulled up the spotless collar of his shirt front to make sure it showed, straightened the seals that hung on a golden chain, and concentrated his attention on the young lady who, like a spring blossom, raised her white hand with its half-transparent fingers to her forehead. And Kovalev's smile spread twice as wide when, under the hat, he made out a chin of a tender whiteness and a cheek touched by the early spring coloring of a rose. But then he jumped back as though burned. He had remembered that instead of a nose he had absolutely nothing, and the tears sprang to his eyes.

He turned to the gentleman dressed as a state councilor to tell him that he was nothing but a fraud and a crook, nothing but his, Kovalev's, personally owned nose.

But the nose was nowhere to be seen. He must have driven off on another official visit.

Kovalev was in despair. He retraced his steps, stopped for a while under the colonnade, and looked intently around him in the hope of catching sight of the nose. He remembered that the nose had had a plumed hat and a gold-braided uniform, but he hadn't noticed his greatcoat, or the color of his carriage, or his horses, or even whether he had had a footman up behind him and, if so, what livery he wore. And then there were so many carriages rushing back and forth, all going so fast that he would have had difficulty in picking one out and no way of stopping it anyway. It was a lovely sunny day. Nevsky Avenue was thronged with people; from the central police station to Anichkin Bridge, ladies poured over the sidewalks in a colorful cascade. There went an acquaintance of his, a court councilor, whom he addressed as Lieutenant-

Colonel, especially in the presence of outsiders. Then Kovalev saw Yaryzhkin, head clerk in the Senate, a good friend who always lost whenever they played cards together. And there was another major, another Caucasus-made collegiate assessor, beckoning . . .

"Goddammit," Kovalev said, "what the hell does he want from me Cabbie! To the police commissioner's!"

He got into the cab and kept exhorting the cabbie again and again: "Come on, let's go! Quick! Now turn into Ivanovskaya Street."

"Is the Commissioner in?" he called out, as soon as he entered the house.

"No, sir," the doorman answered. "He left only a minute ago."

'That's really too much. . . ."

"Yes, sir," the doorman said. "If you'd come a minute earlier, you'd have caught him."

Kovalev, still holding his handkerchief to his face, got back into the cab and shouted in a desperate voice:

"Get going."

"Where to?"

"Straight ahead."

"Straight ahead? But this is a dead end. Shall I go right or left?"

Kovalev was caught off balance and forced to give the matter some thought. In his position, he ought first to go to the National Security Administration, not because it was directly connected with the police, but because its orders would be acted on more rapidly than those of others.

Certainly it was no use taking his grievance to the scientific department where the nose claimed to have a post. At best, it would be unwise, since, judging by his statement that he had never seen Kovalev before, it was obvious that he held nothing sacred and he might lie whenever he found it convenient. So Kovalev was about to tell the cabman to drive him to the National Security Administration when it occurred to him that the crook and impostor, who had just behaved so unscrupulously toward him, might very well try to slip out of town, in which case finding him would be quite hopeless or would take, God forbid, a whole month perhaps. Finally, he had what seemed like a divine inspiration. He decided to go straight to the

Press Building to have an advertisement put in the papers with a detailed description of the nose in all his aspects, so that anyone who met him could turn him over to Kovalev, or at least inform him of the nose's whereabouts. So, having decided this, he told the cabman to take him to the Press Building and, during the entire ride, he kept pommeling him on the back with his fist and shouting:

"Faster, damn you! Faster!"

"Really, sir!" the cabman said, shaking his head and flicking the reins at his horse, which had hair as long as a lap dog's.

At last the cab came to a stop, and Kovalev, panting, burst into the small outer office where a gray-haired, bespectacled employee in an ancient frock coat was seated at a table, his pen clenched between his teeth, counting out the change someone had paid in.

"Who handles advertisements here?" shouted Kovalev. "Ah," he said, "good morning!"

"Good morning, sir," the gray-haired employee said, raising his eyes for a moment and lowering them again to the little piles of coins before him.

"I want to insert——"

"Excuse me. Would you mind waiting just a moment, please," the employee said, writing down a figure with his right hand while his left hand moved two beads on his abacus.

A footman, whose gold-braided livery and whole appearance testified to his service in an aristocratic house, stood by the old employee holding a piece of paper in his hand and, to prove his worldliness, started chattering away:

"Believe me, I'm quite sure the mutt isn't worth eighty kopeks. In fact, I wouldn't give eight kopeks, if you ask me. But the Countess loves that cur—she has to if she's willing to give a hundred rubles to the person who finds it. Since we are among people who understand, I'll tell you one thing: it's all a matter of taste. I can understand a dog lover. But then, go and get a deerhound or maybe a poodle. Then, if you want to spend five hundred or a thousand on it, it's only natural. But, in my opinion, when you pay you are entitled to a *real* dog. . . ."

The elderly employee was listening to this speech with an important expression and was counting the number of letters in the text of the advertisement the manservant had handed him. The room was full of old women, shopkeepers, and doormen, all holding pieces of paper on which advertisements had been written out. In one a coachman, sober and dependable, was for hire; another announced that a carriage with very little mileage, brought from Paris in 1814, was for sale; a nineteen-year-old girl, a washerwoman's assistant, but suitable for other work too, wanted employment; also for sale were an excellent hansom cab (one spring missing) and a young, seventeen-year-old, dappled-gray horse, as well as a consignment of turnip and radish seeds straight from London, a summer house with a two-carriage coach house and a piece of land very suitable for planting a lovely birch wood. Another advertisement invited persons desirous of buying secondhand shoe soles to present themselves in a certain salesroom between 8 A.M. and 3 P.M.

The reception room in which all these people waited was quite small and the air was getting stuffy. But the smell didn't bother Collegiate Assessor Kovalev because he kept his face covered with a handkerchief and also because his nose happened to be God knew where.

"Excuse me, sir . . . I don't want to bother you, but this is an emergency," he said impatiently at last.

"Wait, wait . . . two rubles, forty-three kopeks, please. One minute, please! . . . One ruble, sixty-four, over there . . ." the old employee said, shoving sheets of paper under the noses of porters and old women. "Now, what can I do for you?" he said finally, turning to Kovalev.

"I wanted," Kovalev said, "to ask you to . . . a fraud, or perhaps a theft, has been committed. I'm still not clear. I want you to run an advertisement simply saying that whoever delivers that robber to me will get a handsome reward."

"Your name, please."

"My name? What for? I can't tell you my name. I have too many acquaintances, such as Mrs. Chekhtareva, the wife of a civil servant, and Palageya Grigorievna Podtochina, who's married to Captain Podtochin, an officer on the Army General Staff. . . . Suppose they found out, God forbid. Write simply 'a collegiate assessor' or, better still, 'a major.' "

"And the runaway, was he a household serf?"

"A household serf. That wouldn't be half so vicious a crime. The runaway is my nose . . . yes, my own nose. . . ."

"Hm . . . odd name. And now may I inquire the sum, the amount, of which this Mr. Nose has defrauded you?"

"No, no, you don't understand. I said nose. My own nose, which has disappeared God knows where. I am the victim of some foul joke. . . ."

"But how could it disappear? I still don't understand, sir."

"Well, I can't explain how, but the main thing is that he mustn't go all over town impersonating a state councilor. That's why I want you to advertise that anyone who catches him should contact me as quickly as possible. Besides, imagine how I feel with such a conspicuous part of my body missing. It's not just a matter of, say, a toe. You could simply stick your foot into your shoe and no one would be the wiser. On Thursdays, I usually visit Mrs. Chekhtareva, the wife of a state councilor. . . . And Mrs. Podtochina, the wife of the staff officer, has an extremely pretty daughter. They are close friends of mine, you see, and now tell me, what am I to do? . . . How can I show myself to them?"

The employee was thinking hard, as could be seen from his tightly pressed lips.

"I am sorry, sir, but I cannot accept your advertisement," he said, after a long silence.

"What's that! Why?"

"I just can't. A newspaper could lose its good name if everybody started advertising vagrant noses. . . . No, sir, as it is, too many absurdities and unfounded rumors manage to slip into print."

"Why is it absurd? I don't see anything so unusual about it."

"It may look that way to you. But just let me tell you . . . Last week, for instance, a government employee came to see me just as you have now. I even remember that his advertisement came to two rubles, seventy-three kopeks. But what it all boiled down to was that a black poodle had run away. You'd think there was nothing to it, wouldn't you? But wait. Turned out to be deliberate libel because the poodle in question happened to be the treasurer of I can't recall exactly what."

"But listen, I'm not advertising about a poodle but about my own nose which is the same as myself."

"Sorry, I can't accept the advertisement."

"But I have lost my nose!"

"If you have, it is a matter for a doctor. I've heard that there are specialists who can fit you with any sort of nose you want. But I'm beginning to think that you are one of these cheerful people who likes to have his little joke."

"But I swear to you by all that's holy! And if it comes to that, I'll show you."

"Why take the trouble," the employee said, taking a pinch of snuff. "But then, after all, if you really don't mind," he added, making a slight movement indicating curiosity, "why, I wouldn't mind having a look."

Kovalev removed the handkerchief from his face.

"My! It *is* strange!" the employee said. "Why, it's as flat as a fresh-cooked pancake, incredibly smooth!"

"Well, now you won't refuse to run my advertisement, will you? It simply must be published. I will be very much obliged to you, and I'm very happy that this accident has given me a chance to make your acquaintance. . . ."

The major, it can be seen, had decided that he'd better make up to him a bit.

"Certainly, running it is no great problem," the employee said, "but I don't see that it would do you any good. However, if you absolutely want to see it in print, why not entrust it to someone who can really write and ask him to present it as a rare natural phenomenon and have it published in the *Northern Bee*"—here he took another pinch of snuff—"for the edification of the young"—here he wiped his nose—"or just as a matter of general interest."

The collegiate assessor was taken aback. He lowered his eyes and his glance happened to fall on the theatrical announcements at the bottom of the page of a newspaper. His face was just about to break into a smile at the sight of the name of a very pretty actress and his hand had already plunged into his pocket to see whether he had a five-ruble bill on him, since, in his opinion, an officer of his rank should sit in the stalls, when he remembered the nose and everything was ruined.

The employee, too, seemed touched by Kovalev's awkward position. To alleviate his distress, he thought it would be appropriate to express his sympathy in a few words:

"I'm very sorry that such a painful thing should have happened to you. Perhaps you'd feel better if you took a pinch of snuff. It eases people's headaches and cheers them up. It's even good for hemorrhoids."

As he said this, the employee offered Kovalev his snuff-box, rather deftly folding back the lid which had a picture on it of some lady in a hat.

At this unintentional provocation, Kovalev's patience snapped.

"I simply don't understand how you can make a joke of it," he said angrily. "Can't you see that I am missing just what I would need to take a pinch of snuff with? You know what you can do with your snuff! I can't even look at it now, especially not at your cheap Berezinsky brand. You might at least have offered me something better. . . ."

Incensed, he rushed out of the Press Building. He decided to take his case to the borough Police Commissioner.

At the moment when Kovalev entered the office of the Commissioner, the latter had just finished stretching himself and reflecting:

"I might as well treat myself to a nap. A couple of hours or so."

Thus it would have been easy to predict that the major's visit was rather poorly timed. Incidentally, the commissioner, though a great lover of the arts and of commerce, still preferred a bill put in circulation by the Imperial Russian Bank over anything else. His opinion on the matter was as follows:

"It has everything: it doesn't have to be fed, it doesn't take up much room, and, in any case, can always be fitted into a pocket. If you drop it, it doesn't break."

The Commissioner was rather cold with Kovalev. Right after a meal, he said, was not the proper time for investigations. Nature itself, he said, dictated rest when one's belly was full. From this, the collegiate assessor was able to gather that the Commissioner was rather familiar with the maxims of the wise men of antiquity.

"Moreover," the Commissioner said, "they don't tear noses off decent citizens' faces."

Bull's-eye! We must note here that Kovalev was quick to take offense. He could forgive anything that was said about himself personally, but he couldn't stand anything that he considered a slur on his rank and position. He even held the view that, in dramatic works, while a disparaging reference to subaltern ranks was permissible, it became intolerable when applied to officers above the rank of captain. He was so disconcerted by the reception given him by the Commissioner that he shook his head slightly, shrugged, and, on his way out, said in a dignified tone:

"Well, I must say . . . after your offensive remarks I have nothing further to add."

He reached home hardly able to feel his feet beneath him. It was getting dark. After his futile search, his place looked sad and repulsive. As he walked in, he saw Ivan, his manservant, lying on his back on the old leather divan in the entrance hall spitting at the ceiling—very successfully it must be said. Ivan was hitting the same spot again and again. But such indifference enraged Kovalev. He hit him on the head with his hat and said bitterly:

"Swine! You think of nothing but trivialities."

Ivan jumped up and started anxiously to help Kovalev off with his coat.

The major went into his room and let himself fall into an armchair, sad and exhausted. He let out a few sighs, after which he said:

"Good heavens! Why is all this happening to *me*? What have *I* done wrong? It would have been better to have lost an arm or a leg. It would have been bad enough without ears, yet still bearable. But without a nose a man is not a man but God knows what—neither fish nor fowl. He can't even be a proper citizen any more. If only I had had it lopped off during a war or in a duel or if *I* had been responsible for the loss. But I lost it for no reason and for nothing; I haven't even got a kopek out of it! No, it's impossible," he added after a pause, "it is impossible that the nose could have disappeared. Incredible! It is probably a dream or just a hallucination . . . maybe, by mistake, I drank a glassful of the vodka with which I rub my face after shaving? That fool Ivan must have forgotten to put it away and I must have swallowed it inadvertently."

To prove to himself that he was really drunk, the major pinched himself so hard that he let out a moan. The pain convinced him that he was quite sober. Then, slowly, as though stalking something, he approached the mirror, his eyes half closed, in the vague hope that, who knows, perhaps the nose would be in its proper place. But immediately he jumped away.

"What a slanderous sight!"

It was really quite bewildering. Many things get lost: a button, a silver spoon, a watch, or some such object. But to disappear just like that. . . . And what's more, in his own apartment! Having weighed the matter, Major Kovalev came to what seemed to be the most likely explanation: the culprit behind it all was Mrs. Podtochina, who wanted him to marry her daughter. He rather enjoyed the girl's company himself but he was just not ready for a final decision. And when Mrs. Podtochina had told him plainly that she wanted him to marry her daughter, he had quietly beaten a polite retreat, saying that he was still very young and that he ought to devote another five years or so to his career, after which he would be at least forty-two. So, probably, that was when Mrs. Podtochina had decided to maim him and had hired witches or something for the purpose, because by no stretch of the imagination could it be assumed that the nose had been cut off; no one had entered his bedroom; Ivan Yakovlevich, the barber, hadn't shaved him since Wednesday and during the rest of that day and even on Thursday, his nose, all in one piece, had been on his face. He was absolutely certain of it. Moreover, had the nose been cut off he would have felt pain and the wound could never have healed so fast and become as smooth as a pancake. . . .

All sorts of plans clashed in his head: should he take the lady to court or would it be better to go directly to her and denounce her to her face? But his thoughts were interrupted by light seeping in through the cracks in the door, indicating that Ivan had lit a candle in the entrance hall. Soon Ivan appeared carrying the candle high above his head, lighting up the entire room. Kovalev's first thought was to grab the handkerchief and cover the place where, only yesterday, the nose had sat, so that this stupid man should not stand there gaping, noticing the peculiar state of his master's face.

But no sooner had Ivan left than he heard an unknown voice coming from the apartment door ask:

"Does Collegiate Assessor Kovalev live here?"

"Come in. Major Kovalev is in," Kovalev shouted, jumping up and rushing into the hall.

It was a police officer, a quite handsome man with whiskers neither too light nor too dark and with rather full cheeks. In fact it was the same one who, at the beginning of this story, had been standing by the Isakievsky Bridge.

"Did you happen to lose your nose, sir?"

"Yes, I did."

"It has been found."

"Is it possible?"

Joy paralyzed the major's tongue. He stared at the police officer standing in front of him, the reflection of the candlelight shining on his damp, full lips.

"How did it happen?" he managed to say at last.

"By sheer coincidence. Your nose was caught as he was getting on the stagecoach for Riga. He had a passport made out in the name of a government official and the strange thing is that, at first, I myself took him for a gentleman. But luckily I had my glasses with me, so I put them on and recognized immediately that he was a nose. The thing is, I am very shortsighted, sir, and with you standing right in front of me there, I can make out your face but I can't discern your beard, or your nose, or anything else. My mother-in-law, that's the mother of my wife, can't see a thing either."

Kovalev was beside himself with excitement.

"Where is he? Where? I'll run over there now. . . ."

"Don't trouble, sir. I thought you might need it, so I brought it along. But you know, the funny part about it is that the main suspect in the affair is the barber from Voznesensky Avenue, a crook who's now being held at the police station. I've had my eye on him for some time because I suspected him of being a thief and a drunkard. As a matter of fact, he lifted a box of buttons in a store the other day. By the way, your nose is exactly as before, sir."

Saying this, the police officer put his hand in his pocket and extracted the nose wrapped in a piece of paper.

"That's it! That's it!" Kovalev shouted. "No doubt about it! Do come in and have some tea with me, won't you?"

"It would be a great honor, sir, but I am afraid I can't. I must stop over at the house of correction—prices are going up, sir. . . . My mother-in-law, I mean the wife's mother, is living with me . . . we have children too. The eldest

son is particularly promising, a very clever boy, but we
have no money for his education. . . ."

When the police officer had left, the collegiate assessor
remained for some minutes in an indeterminate state, just
barely able to see and feel. It was his immense joy that
had plunged him into his half-consciousness. Very carefully
he held his just-recovered nose in his cupped hands and
once again looked it over.

"Yes, that's it, that's it all right. And here, on the left
side, is the pimple that sprang up the other day."

The major almost shouted with pleasure.

But there is nothing long-lived in this world and one's
joy in the minute that follows the first is no longer as vivid.
It further weakens during the third and finally dissolves
into one's everyday state just as the circles produced on
the surface of a pond by the fall of a pebble dissolve into
the smooth surface. Kovalev began to ponder and realized
that his troubles were not quite over: the nose had been
found. That was fine; but it still had to be put back, fixed
in its old place.

"And what if it doesn't stick?"

As he asked himself this question, the major turned
white.

With inexpressible anxiety he leapt toward his dressing
table and pulled the mirror closer, fearing that he would
stick the nose on crooked. His hands trembled. Finally,
with infinite hesitations and precautions he pressed the nose
into place. Oh, horror! It wouldn't stick! He brought it
close to his mouth and warmed it slightly with his breath.
Then he placed it again on top of the smooth area between
his two cheeks. But the nose would not stay on.

"Come on! Come on now! Stick—you fool!" Kovalev
told the nose again and again. But the nose felt as if it
were made of wood and kept falling off. And as it hit the
dressing table it produced a queer light sound, like a cork.
The major's face twisted spasmodically. Panic pervaded
him.

"Can it possibly *not* stick?"

He repeatedly pressed the nose against the approximate
spot, but his efforts were futile. Then he decided to send
Ivan to fetch the doctor who occupied the best apartment
in the house where the major lived.

The doctor was a fine figure of a man. He had pitch-black whiskers and a quite fresh and healthy wife. Furthermore, he ate fresh apples in the morning and kept his mouth in a state of incredible cleanliness, rinsing it for about three-quarters of an hour at a time and then brushing his teeth with five different kinds of toothbrush.

The doctor arrived within the minute. Having asked the major how long ago the misfortune had struck, he grabbed him by the chin and tweaked him so hard on the former site of his nose that Kovalev recoiled violently and banged the back of his head against the wall. The doctor said that it was quite all right and, advising him to move a bit further away from the wall, ordered him to bend his head to the right, felt the spot vacated by the nose with his fingers and said, "Hmmm . . ." Then he asked him to bend his head to the left, touched the spot again and said, "Hmmm. . . ." Finally the doctor delivered another tweak with his thumb and forefinger, making Kovalev toss up his head like a horse whose teeth are being inspected.

Having thus completed his examination, the doctor shook his head and declared:

"No. Can't be done. You'd better stay as you are or your condition might deteriorate even further. Of course, it is possible to stick it on. I could have stuck it on now. But, take my advice, that would make it worse for you."

"That's fine! And how can I stay without a nose? And how could I be worse off than I am? It is absolutely disgusting! And where can I show myself in this obscene condition? I have an active social life. Why, even today I was invited to two important parties. And I have many connections . . . Mrs. Chekhtareva, the wife of a state councilor, Mrs. Podtochina, the wife of a senior army officer . . . although after this business I don't want to have anything to do with her, except through the police. . . ."

And Kovalev added imploringly:

"Do me a great favor, Doctor, can't you think of a way? Make it stick somehow. It doesn't matter if it doesn't hold too well—just as long as it stays on somehow. I could even support it with my hand in case of emergency. I don't even dance, you know, and so couldn't jeopardize it by some inadvertent jerk. As to my appreciation of your services, please rest assured that in the measure of my resources——"

"Believe it or not," the doctor said neither too loudly nor too softly but with persuasiveness and magnetic force, "I never dispense my services out of material considerations. It would be contrary to my principles and to professional ethics. True, I do charge for my visits but only in order not to offend people by refusing to accept a fee. Of course I could stick your nose back on, but I assure you, on my honor, if you won't take my simple word for it, that it will be much worse. You're better off letting things take their natural course. Wash often with cold water and I assure you that you'll feel just as healthy without a nose as you felt with one. As to the nose, you can put it in a jar of alcohol or, better still, add two soupspoonfuls of vodka and warmed-up vinegar to it. I'll bet you could make money out of it. In fact, I'd purchase it myself if it weren't too expensive."

"No, no! I'll never sell it," shouted the desolate major, "I'd rather it disappeared again!"

"Forgive me," the doctor said, "I was simply trying to help. Well, I can do no more. At least you see that I tried."

The doctor departed with dignity. Kovalev had not even looked at his face; dazed as he was, he was only aware of the spotless white cuffs sticking out of the black sleeves of the doctor's frock coat.

The next day Kovalev decided to write to Mrs. Podto-china asking her to restore to him voluntarily what was rightfully his and saying that otherwise he would be forced to lodge a complaint. The letter he composed read as follows:

Dear Madam,

I am at a loss to understand your strange action. Rest assured that you will achieve nothing by acting this way, and you certainly won't force me to marry your daughter. Please believe me, Madam, that I am fully aware of exactly what happened to my nose as well as of the fact that you, and nobody else, are the prime instigator of this affair. Its sudden detachment from its assigned place, its desertion, and its masquerading first as a state councilor and then in its natural shape is nothing but the result of witchcraft practiced by you or by those specialized in such pursuits. For my part, I deem it my duty to warn you that if the above-mentioned nose is not back in its proper place this very day, I shall be forced to avail myself of my rights and ask for the protection of the law.

> *I remain,*
> *Faithfully yours,*
> *Platon Kovalev.*

To which the lady sent an immediate reply:

My dear Platon,
    I was very surprised by your letter. To be perfectly frank, I never expected anything of this kind from you, especially your unfair reproaches. For your information, I have never received the state councilor you mention at my house, either in disguise or in his natural shape. However, I did receive Philip Ivanovich, but, despite the fact that he asked me for my daughter's hand and was a man of irreproachable character, sober habits, and great learning, I never held out any hopes for him. You also mention your nose. If you mean it symbolically, that I wanted you to stop nosing around my daughter, i.e., that I had decided to refuse you her hand, I am surprised at your saying such things when you are fully aware of my feelings on the subject, namely that, if you asked for her hand formally tomorrow, I would be prepared to grant your request forthwith, since it has always been in agreement with my wishes and in hope of which,
    I remain,
    Always at your service,

> *Alexandra Podtochina.*

"She," Kovalev said, after he had read the letter, "is certainly not involved. Someone guilty of a crime couldn't write such a letter."

And the collegiate assessor knew what he was talking about because he had taken part in several judicial investigations back in the Caucasus.

"But then, how the devil did it happen, after all? How'll I ever get it straight?" he said, dropping his arms to his sides.

In the meantime, rumors about the extraordinary occurrence spread all over the capital and, as was to be expected, not without all sorts of embellishments. At that time people were prone to fall for supernatural things: only a short time before, experiments with magnetism had caused a sensation. Also, the story about the dancing chairs of Stables Street was still fresh, and people soon began to repeat that Collegiate Assessor Kovalev's nose was to be seen taking a daily walk on Nevsky Avenue at 3:00 P.M. sharp. And every day a multitude of the curious gathered there. Then someone said that the nose was in Junker's Department Store, and, as a result, such a melee developed there that the police had to interfere. A shady character with side whiskers, who nevertheless looked very respectable, and who sold all sorts of dry cakes at the entrance to the theater, got hold of some special wooden benches, perfectly safe to stand on, and invited the curious to do so for a fee of eighty kopeks per person. A highly respected colonel, who had left his home especially early for this purpose, managed to make his way through the dense throng with great difficulty only to see in the display window not a nose but an ordinary woollen sweater and a lithograph of a girl pulling up her stocking with a well-dressed gentleman wearing a waistcoat with lapels and a small beard, a lithograph that had rested there, in the identical spot, for more than ten years. As the colonel left, he declared:

"It shouldn't be allowed—befuddling people with such stupid and improbable rumors!"

Then a rumor spread that Major Kovalev's nose was taking promenades, not on Nevsky Avenue, but in the Tavrichesky Gardens, and that it had been doing so for some time now. In fact, even when Khosrov Mirza lived there he used to marvel at this freak of nature. Students from the School of Surgeons went there. One socially prominent lady wrote a special letter to the director of the park suggesting that he show this rare object to children, if possible with explanations and instructions that would edify the younger generation.

All this was quite welcome to those who never miss a party and like to display their wit before the ladies; without it topics of conversation would have been exhausted. But there was also a dissatisfied and displeased minority among respectable people. One gentleman said he could not understand how it was possible in our enlightened age for such preposterous lies to be believed and that he was flabbergasted at the passivity of the authorities. Apparently this gentleman was one of those who desire the government to interfere in everything, including his daily fights with his wife.

Following these events . . . but here again, things become beclouded and what followed these events has remained completely unknown.

Chapter 3

The world is full of absolute nonsense. Sometimes it is really unbelievable. Suddenly, the very nose that used to go around as a state councilor and caused such a stir all over the city turned up, as though nothing had happened, in its proper place, namely between the cheeks of Major Kovalev. This happened on April 7. Waking up and chancing to glance in the mirror, what did he see but his nose! He grabbed it with his hand—no doubt about it—it was his nose, all right!

"Aha!" Kovalev said.

And in his infinite joy he would have performed a jig, barefoot as he was, had not Ivan come in at that moment. He ordered Ivan to bring him some water to wash with and, while washing, looked again into the mirror: he had his nose. Drying himself with his towel, he looked again—the nose was still there!

"Here, Ivan, look, I think I have a pimple on my nose," he said, all the while thinking anxiously: "Wouldn't it be terrible if Ivan came out with something like, 'No, sir, not only is there no pimple on your nose, there is no nose on your face.'"

But Ivan simply said:

"Nothing, sir, I see no pimple, the nose is clear."

"Feels good, dammit!" the major said to himself and snapped his fingers gaily.

At that moment, through the partly opened door, there appeared the head of Ivan Yakovlevich, the barber, wearing the expression of a cat that had just been smacked for the theft of a piece of suet.

"Your hands clean?" Kovalev shouted out to him.

"They're clean, sir."

"Liar!"

"I swear they're clean."

"You know, they'd better be."

Kovalev sat down. The barber wrapped a towel around his neck and in one instant transformed the major's whiskers and a part of his cheek into whipped cream of the kind that is likely to be served at a birthday party in the house of a rich merchant.

"Well, I'll be damned!" Ivan Yakovlevich muttered under his breath, looking at the nose. Then he turned the major's head and looked at the nose from the other side and muttered. "Well, well, well . . . who would have thought . . ." and he stared at the nose for a moment.

Then, with a daintiness that can only be imagined, he lifted two fingers to catch the nose by its tip. Such was Ivan Yakovlevich's shaving style.

"Look out, look out, careful!" Kovalev shouted and Ivan Yakovlevich dropped his hand and stood there frozen and embarrassed as never before. Finally he snapped out of it and started carefully tickling the major under his chin with the razor. And although it felt quite awkward and unusual for him to shave someone without holding him by the olfactory organ of the human body, he managed, somehow, by resting his rough thumb on Kovalev's cheek, then on his lower gum, to overcome all the obstacles and complete the shaving operation.

When he was through being shaved, Kovalev hurried to get dressed, rushed out, took a cab and drove to the tearoom. Before even sitting down, he shouted: "Waiter, a cup of chocolate!" then rushed over to the mirror: the nose was there. Happy, he glanced around the room and twisted his face into a sarcastic expression by slightly screwing up his eyes, when he saw two army officers, one of whom had a nose about the size of a waistcoat button. Then he left for the department through which he was trying to get the vice-gubernatorial post or, failing that, a position in the administration. Walking through the reception room, he glanced in the mirror: the nose was in its place.

Then he drove to see another collegiate assessor, that is, a major like himself. This major was a biting wit, and, parrying his digs, Kovalev would often say to him:

"Oh, I see through you clearly, you needler!"

On his way there, Kovalev thought: "Now, if the major does not split his sides with laughter when he sees me, that will be a sure sign that whatever I may have is sitting in its proper place."

And when the other collegiate assessor showed no signs of hilarity, Kovalev thought:

"Fine! It feels good, it feels good, dammit!"

In the street he met Mrs. Podtochina and her daughter and was greeted with joyful exclamations which went to show that they did not find he was missing anything. He had a very long talk with them and, on purpose, took out his snuffbox and filled his nose with great deliberation, through both orifices, muttering under his breath:

"Here, look and admire, you hens! But still, I won't marry the daughter, just *par amour* as they say, but nothing more. . . ."

And from then on, Major Kovalev could be seen on Nevsky Avenue, in theaters, everywhere. And the nose was there, sitting on his face, as though nothing had happened. And after that, Major Kovalev was always in good spirits, smiling, pursuing absolutely every pretty lady without exception and even stopping one day in front of a small shop and purchasing some sort of ribbon for his lapel, although his reason for doing so remained a mystery because he had never been made a knight of any order.

So that's what happened in the northern capital of our vast country. Only now, on further thought, do we see that there is much that is improbable in it. Without even mentioning the strangeness of such a supernatural severance of the nose and its appearance in various places in the form of a state councilor, how could Kovalev have failed to understand that he could not go and advertise about a nose in the press? I don't mean that I think that an advertisement would have cost too much, that would be nonsense and I'm not stingy; but it's not decent, it's not clever, and it's not proper! And then too, how could the nose have got into the roll of bread, and how could Ivan Yakovlevich himself? . . . Now, that I cannot understand. It's absolutely beyond me. But strangest of all, the most incomprehensible thing, is that there are authors who can choose such subjects to write about. This, I confess, is completely inexplicable, it's like . . . no, no, I can't understand it at all. In the first place, there is absolutely no advantage in it for our mother country. Secondly . . . well, what advantage is there in it at all? I simply cannot understand what it is. . . .

However, when all is said and done, and although, of course, we conceive the possibility, one and the other, and maybe even . . . Well, but then what exists without inconsistencies? And still, if you give it a thought, there *is* something to it. Whatever you may say, such things *do* happen——seldom, but they do.

The Carriage

The little town had grown much livelier since the cavalry regiment had been quartered there. It had been incredibly dull before. When you drove through the town, the sour expression with which the dirty little houses stared out into the street depressed you in a way difficult to convey: you felt as though you'd been cleaned out at cards or had made a terrible fool of yourself. In a word, you did not feel good. Plaster had fallen off the houses, turning them from white to piebald. The roofs were thatched with reeds as in most of our southern towns. And, a long time ago, one of the town's mayors had ordered the front gardens done away with to make things look neater. You ran little risk of meeting anyone, except perhaps some rooster that happened to be crossing the street—a street as soft as a pillow with dust, the kind that turns to mud with the lightest rain. And with rain, the streets would become crowded with fat animals which the mayor liked to refer to as "Frenchmen." They sat in their mud baths, thrusting their great snouts out and grunting so loud that a traveler thought of nothing but whipping up his horses and getting away. But at that time only very few travelers passed through the town at all.

Occasionally, very occasionally, some landowner with about eleven serfs on his estate and wearing an alpaca coat would rattle over the cobblestones in something looking like a cross between a cart and a carriage, peering out from among flour bags and urging on his bay mare, beside which trotted a colt. Even the market place was gloomy. The tailor's shop, idiotically enough, is not parallel with the

56

street but sticks out into it at an angle. On the other side, some sort of stone building with two windows has been under construction for fifteen years. Further, there is a wooden stall standing by itself, painted gray to match the mud, which was originally intended as a model for others. It is the creation of the mayor when he was still young, before he had taken to afternoon naps and drinking a concoction with dried gooseberries in it in the evenings.

For the rest, in the market place, wattle fencing takes the place of stalls. In its center stand the smallest shops in which you were always sure to see a dozen pretzels on a string, a peasant woman in red kerchief, forty pounds of soap, a few pounds of bitter almonds, buckshot, lengths of cotton material, and two shop assistants who spent their time playing quoits in front of the door.

But after the arrival of the cavalry regiment, all this changed. The streets came to life, gained color, in a word, became unrecognizable. Now the low houses would often see some elegant officer with plumed headgear going to see a brother officer, to discuss promotion, good tobacco, and sometimes, in secret from the general, to play cards, staking the carriage which might as well be described as regimental since it was owned by all the officers in turn: one day it was the major who rolled off in it, the next it was to be found in the lieutenant's stable, and, the day after that the major's orderly was greasing its axles once more. The wooden fences between the houses were decorated with soldiers' caps hanging in the sun. A gray greatcoat would somehow be hanging on a gate. In the small streets, one came across soldiers with mustachios as stiff as boot brushes. These mustachios were to be seen in all sorts of places. No sooner did a few housewives of the town gather in the market place, than a mustachio was sure to be peeking over their shoulders.

The officers brought life to society, which, until then, had consisted only of the judge, who was living with some deacon's wife, and the mayor, who was a fairly reasonable man but who slept literally all day long—from lunch to supper and from supper to lunch.

And social life became still more active and interesting when the staff of the Brigadier General was quartered in the town. The landowners from all around, of whose existence no one would have guessed before, started coming into the little town. They wished to spend some time in the company of the officers, to play bank occasionally, a game which, until then, had been a mere blur in heads stuffed with crops, errands for wives, and the shooting of hare.

I am sorry I cannot remember the occasion which moved them to give a great dinner. The preparations were awe-inspiring. The clatter of the knives in the general's kitchen could be heard out beyond the edge of town. All the produce of the market was requisitioned for the dinner so that the judge and his deacon's wife were forced to eat flour-and-water pancakes with some fruit jelly. The courtyard of the house occupied by the general was crowded with all kinds of carriages. It was a strictly male affair, a dinner for the officers and the neighboring landowners.

Of the landowners, the most remarkable was Pythagoras Pythagorasovich Chertokutsky, a leading member of the local aristocracy. He made more noise than anyone else at the nobility's elections and drove a very elegant turnout. He had served in a cavalry regiment and had been one of its prominent and respected officers. At least, he was always to be seen at the regimental parties and gatherings, wherever the regiment happened to be quartered. But that can be verified with the ladies of the provinces of Tambov and Simbirsk. Possibly he would have extended his glory to other provinces had he not resigned because of a matter such as is usually referred to as an unpleasant business. Whether it was he who slapped someone or whether someone slapped him, I cannot say for sure, but he was asked to resign. This, however, did not affect his standing in the slightest.

Pythagoras Pythagorasovich always wore high-waisted, military-looking coats, spurs, and mustachios so that the local gentry should not be led to believe that he had served in the infantry, to which he referred scornfully as the foot-fantry, or sometimes the foottrottery. He never missed the many crowded fairs to which the heart of Russia, nannies, children, daughters and fat landowners, flocked to have a good time. They arrived in landaus, carriages, tarantasses, broughams, and vehicles such as no one has ever dreamt of. He would sort of smell out where the cavalry regiment was stationed and always came to see the officers. He would jump down very gracefully from his light calash or carriage and introduce himself with great ease of manner. During the last election he had given the gentry an excellent dinner and promised that if they elected him as their leader, he would set a tone of the utmost respectability. In a word, he behaved like a gentleman, as they put it in the provinces. He had married someone quite pretty and had acquired, along with her, an estate with two hundred serfs and a few thousand in capital.

The capital was immediately put to use in the acquisition of six really excellent horses, gilt locks for his doors, a tame monkey for the house, and a French butler. As to the two hundred serfs that had come with the dowry, they, like the two hundred he had had before, were mortgaged to finance a number of commercial ventures. In a word, a landowner.

Besides him, at the general's dinner, there were a few other landowners, but there is nothing to say about them. The rest were all officers of the regiment plus two officers from the general staff: a colonel and a very fat major. The general himself was there, a big, stout man who nevertheless had a reputation as a good commanding officer. He spoke in a rather thick, important bass voice.

The dinner was magnificent. The sturgeon, the whitefish, the asparagus, the quail, the partridges, and the mushrooms made it evident that the cook had not consumed any liquor since the day before. And the four soldiers assisting him had worked throughout the night, knives in hand, on the fricassee.

The myriads of bottles, the tall ones with claret, the short-necked ones with Madeira, the bright sunny day, the wide-open windows, the plates of ice chips in various spots on the table, the crumpled shirt fronts of the civilians, the brilliant conversation dominated by the general's voice and besprinkled with champagne—everything was in perfect harmony. The dinner over, they all rose from the table with a pleasant heavy feeling. The gentlemen lit their pipes and went out onto the terrace to drink their coffee.

"Now we can have a look at her," the general said. "Please, my dear fellow," he said, addressing his adjutant, a rather smart, pleasant-looking young man, "have the bay mare brought here." Then he turned back to the others. "You'll see for yourselves," he said.

At this point the general puffed at his pipe and let out a stream of smoke.

"She's not quite in shape yet. There's no decent stable in this damned backwater of a town. But she's—puff-puff—a very acceptable horse."

"How long have you had her, sir, puff-puff-puff?" Pythagoras Pythagorasovich asked.

"Puff-puff-puff, well . . . puff, not very long. I only got her from the stud farm a couple of years ago."

"Was she broken in when you got her, sir, or did you have her broken in here, sir?"

"Puff, puff, poo, poo . . . oo . . . ff . . . here," the general said, and disappeared in a cloud.

At that moment a soldier emerged from the stable, within which a trampling of hoofs could be heard. Then another soldier appeared who wore huge mustachios and a white smock and was leading by the bridle a quivering, nervous mare. Suddenly raising her head, she almost lifted the soldier, mustachios and all, off the ground, and he had to squat down to hold her.

"Come, quiet, Agrafena Ivanovna," the soldier said, leading the mare toward the porch.

The mare's name was Agrafena Ivanovna. She was strong and wild like a South-Russian beauty. Her hoofs drummed against the wooden porch and she suddenly stopped still.

The general took the pipe out of his mouth and started to look over Agrafena Ivanovna with obvious satisfaction. The colonel stepped down from the porch and personally took her by the muzzle. The major followed him out and patted the mare's leg. The rest of them clicked their tongues.

Pythagoras Pythagorasovich walked over toward her from behind. The soldier who was holding the horse by the bridle drew himself up, staring fixedly into the eyes of the guest as though he were about to jump on Pythagoras' back and gallop off.

"Very, very fine indeed," Pythagoras said, "a capital horse! And, sir, I suppose she's a wonderful trotter?"

"She goes well, to be sure . . . but . . . I'll be damned . . . that stupid vet gave her some kind of pill and since then she's been sneezing—for two days without letup."

"A very, very pretty beast. And may I ask, sir, do you have a carriage to go with her?"

"A carriage? But she's a riding horse."

"Of course, sir. I asked because I wondered whether you have carriages for your other horses?"

"Well, I must say I'm not too well fixed as far as carriages are concerned. . . . I must admit that for some time I've been hoping to get a modern calash. I wrote to my brother in St. Petersburg to that effect, but I don't know whether he'll send me one or not."

"I would think, sir," the colonel said, "that there are no better calashes than the Viennese ones."

"You're quite right, puff-puff-puff, to think so."

"I have, sir, a superlative calash of Viennese manufacture," Pythagoras Pythagorasovich said.

"Which one? The one you came in?"

"Oh no, sir. That one is just . . . to go places, that sort of thing. But the other . . . it is incredible how light it is. Like a feather. And, if you stepped into it, if you'll allow me to say so, sir, you'd feel as though your nanny were rocking you in your cradle."

"I suppose it's quite smooth then?"

"Very, very smooth. You know, pillows, springs, like a picture."

"Good, good."

"And it holds an incredible amount, sir. Personally, I've never seen anything like it. When I was an officer, sir, I managed to pack into its luggage space ten bottles of rum and twenty pounds of tobacco, six dress uniforms, underwear and two longest pipes imaginable. Moreover, sir, in the glove compartment, sir, there is room enough to stow a whole carcass of beef."

"Sounds good."

"I got it for four thousand, sir."

"Judging by the price, it must be a good one. You bought it yourself?"

"Oh no, sir, I got it by a stroke of luck. It was bought by a friend of mine, a childhood playmate, an exceptional man whom you'd have liked very much, sir, I'm sure. He and I, we were very close, sir. His or mine, it made no difference, you see, sir. I won the calash from him at cards. Won't you, sir, do me the honor of dining at my house tomorrow and at the same time having a look at the calash?"

"I don't know what to say. Alone . . . I feel rather, you know . . . Perhaps you would like me to come with the other officers. . . ."

"I beg them to come too. It would be a great honor for me, gentlemen, to see you in my house."

The colonel, the major and the other officers thanked Pythagoras with well-mannered bows.

"I myself, sir, am of the opinion that if one buys a thing

it should be good, and if it is not good it is not worth the trouble of getting it. And when you do me the honor of being my guest tomorrow, I will be bold enough to show you some items which I have introduced on my estate."

The general looked at him and puffed out some more smoke.

Pythagoras was very pleased at having invited the officers. He was already mentally working out the menu for the dinner—the meat pies, the sauces—while he looked gaily at his guests for the morrow. And they, on their part, became twice as amiable toward him, as could be gauged from their eyes and certain slight bodily movements such as little half bows, etc. Pythagoras, from then on, spoke with more familiarity and his voice acquired the languorous note of a man wallowing in satisfaction.

"And, sir, you will make the acquaintance of the mistress of the house."

"I'll be delighted," the general said, stroking his mustache.

At this point, Pythagoras would have liked to return home immediately to prepare everything for the next day's reception. He already had his hat in his hand, but somehow it happened that he stayed a little longer. In the meantime card tables were set out and the entire company broke up into groups of four and games of whist started in different parts of the room.

Candles were brought in. Pythagoras hesitated for a while over whether to sit down to a card table or not. But since the officers invited him to do so, he thought it would be unsociable to refuse. He sat down. Somehow a glass of punch appeared in front of him which, without thinking, he proceeded to empty. After a couple of rubbers, Pythagoras found another glass of punch at his elbow which, still absently, he downed, having said, "Really, gentlemen, I must be off." But he went on playing.

In the meantime, the conversations in various corners of the room became altogether individual. The players were quite silent. It was those who were not playing who talked among themselves.

In one corner a captain, sprawled on a sofa with a pillow under his ribs and a pipe between his teeth, was quite freely and smoothly relating his amorous adventures. He managed to hold the attention of the circle gathered around him. A remarkably fat landowner with very short arms, which looked rather like elongated potatoes, was listening to him with an understanding expression, only now and then attempting to pull his tobacco pouch out of the pocket of his coattail; his arm proved too short and his backside too wide. In another corner, a quite lively argument started on the subject of artillery drill, and Pythagoras, who had already played a knave for a queen twice, butted into this private discussion, shouting from his corner phrases like, "In what year was that?" or "In what regiment?" Frequently his questions had nothing to do with the subject under discussion.

Finally, a few minutes before supper, the actual game of whist stopped, although it continued in words. Pythagoras remembered distinctly that he had won quite a lot but somehow his hands had nothing to hold and when he got up from the table he stood like a man who has not even a handkerchief in his pocket. In the meantime, supper was served. Obviously, there was no shortage of wines and Pythagoras was forced by circumstances, almost involuntarily, to fill his own glass because there was always a bottle standing to the right and left of him.

The conversation was drawn out for a very, very long time. But it took a rather strange course. A landowner, who had been in the army during the 1812 campaign against Napoleon, told his listeners of a very hot engagement, so hot in fact that it had actually never taken place. And then, for completely unobvious reasons, he seized the stopper of the decanter and thrust it into a pie. In short, when the guests began to leave it was already close to three and the coachmen of certain personalities had to grab their masters as one grabs a package of groceries, and Pythagoras Pythagorasovich, for all his aristocratic background, bowed right and left with such zest as he was driven home that he arrived there with two thistles in his mustache.

At home, everything was asleep. The coachman had trouble finding the valet, who saw his master across the drawing room and handed him over to a chambermaid, with whose help Pythagoras managed to reach his bedroom, where he collapsed next to his pretty young wife, lying there in a delightful pose in a snow-white nightgown. The commotion created by the fall of her husband woke her up. She stretched herself, raised her eyelashes, three times squeezed her eyes closed, then opened them with a half-angry smile. But seeing that her husband definitely was not disposed toward any amiabilities at that time, she turned over on her other side, resting her fresh cheek on her hand, and went back to sleep.

It was already beyond the hour which is considered early in the country when the young wife woke up next to her snoring husband. Remembering that he had come home at four in the morning and not wishing to awaken him, she slipped her feet into the slippers Pythagoras had ordered for her by mail from St. Petersburg. Then, clad in a white dressing gown which draped her like the waters of a fountain, she went into her bathroom, washed in water as fresh as herself and glanced into the mirror. She had a couple of peeps at herself and saw that she did not look at all bad that morning. This fact, which may seem insignificant, caused her to sit in front of the mirror for a little over two hours. Finally she dressed herself, with very good taste at that, and went out into the garden to get some fresh air.

As if on purpose, the weather was as superb as can be imagined, even for a summer day. The sun had reached the meridian and was heating the air with the full power of its rays. But it was cool on the shady paths, and the flowers, warmed by the sun, trebled their fragrance. The pretty lady of the house completely forgot that it was past noon and that her husband was still asleep. She could hear the snores of two coachmen and one groom who were already taking their afternoon nap in the stable beyond the garden. But she continued to sit in the thick shade from which the road could be seen, gazing absent-mindedly at its emptiness.

Suddenly her attention was caught by a light cloud of dust rising in the distance. Soon she made out several carriages in single file coming toward her. The one in front was a light, two-seat calash and in it sat the general, his fat epaulets gleaming in the sun, with the colonel next to him. Behind was a four-seater with the major, the general's aide-de-camp, and two other officers facing. Behind it was the regimental chaise, mentioned earlier, now owned by the major. Behind that there was another four-seater of the type known as a *bon-voyage*. It contained five officers, one of them sitting on the knees of a comrade. Finally, behind it, there were three officers on three fine bays.

"Can they possibly be coming our way?" the young

mistress of the estate thought. "Good heavens, they're actually turning off the main road."

She let out a little cry, clasped her hands and flew straight over the flower beds, trampling the flowers, into her husband's bedroom. He was sleeping like a log.

"Get up, get up, quickly!" she shouted, pulling him by the arm.

"Ah-ah," Pythagoras said without opening his eyes.

"Get up, sugar angel, come on, do you hear me? We have guests."

"What . . . what guests?" Having said that, he let out a restrained mooing like that of a calf trying to find his mother's teat. "Mmmm . . . give me . . . give me your neck, lovey-dovey, I want to kiss it."

"Pussycat, get up, for heaven's sake. Quick. The general and his officers. Oh, goodness me, you have a thistle in your mustache."

"The general? He's already on his way? Why the hell wasn't I awakened? And the dinner . . . Now, is everything ready for the dinner?"

"What dinner?"

"The dinner I ordered."

"You ordered? But you came in at four in the morning and you didn't even answer when I spoke to you. And if I did not wake you up, lambkin, it was because I knew you hadn't slept all night, you poor dear. . . ."

These final words were uttered in a very languourous and beseeching tone.

Pythagoras Pythagorasovich lay in bed popeyed and motionless. Then he jumped up in just his nightshirt, forgetting that he was not even decent.

"I am nothing but a dumb horse," he exclaimed, slapping himself on the forehead with the palm of his hand. "I invited them to dinner. What are we going to do? How far are they?"

"I don't know . . . but they'll be here any minute."

"Hide yourself, love. Hey there, you, girl, come here, you fool! What are you afraid of? Some officers are about to arrive. You go and tell them that the master is not at home. Tell 'em he's not expected back, that he drove off early in the morning, you hear? And warn all the servants, understand?"

Having said this, he rushed to hide in the coach house.

He had thought he would be quite safe, but as he stood in a corner, he began to fear that he might be found there too. A better idea flashed through his head. He let down the steps of the calash that stood there next to him, jumped inside, closed the door, and as a further precaution covered himself with the leather apron. And there, doubled up in his dressing gown, he remained completely silent.

In the meantime the cavalcade had driven up to the front porch.

The general got out first and shook himself. The colonel followed him, smoothing the plumes of his hat. Then the fat major jumped out of the four-seater, gripping his sword under his armpit. Then the slim lieutenants and the sub-lieutenant who had been sitting on someone's knees skipped out of their carriage. And finally the riders who had been showing off their bays got down too.

"The master is not at home," said a servant appearing on the porch.

"What do you mean not at home? Still, he'll be in for dinner, I suppose."

"No, sir. He left for the day and I don't expect him back before, perhaps, this time tomorrow."

"Well, I'll be damned," the general said. "How is that possible?"

"I must say it's quite some joke," the colonel said, laughing.

"No, but I still don't understand," said the general with obvious displeasure. "Goddamm it! . . . If he can't receive us, why did he invite us?"

"I really don't understand, sir, how people can do such things," said one of the young officers.

"What?" said the general, who always used that interrogative when speaking to young subalterns.

"I was saying, sir, how is it possible to behave like that?"

"Naturally, naturally . . . Well, something may have happened. . . . Should have let us know at least—or then not invite us."

"Well then, sir, what can we do? Let's go back," the colonel said.

"Of course. There's nothing else left to do. But wait, we can still have a look at the calash. We don't need him for that. He can't have taken it with him. Hey, you there, come over here."

"Yes, sir?"

"You a stableman?"

"I am, sir."

"Then show us the new calash your master bought recently."

"If the gentlemen will be kind enough to follow me."

The general and his officers followed the stableman into the coach house.

"Here, sir. Shall I roll it out a bit? It's rather dark in here."

"All right, all right . . . that's good enough. Thank you."

The general and the officers walked all around the calash, carefully examining the wheels and the springs.

"Well, I don't see anything special about it," the general said. "Quite an ordinary calash, I'd say."

"Nothing much," the colonel said, "nothing remarkable in it."

"I wouldn't say it was worth four thousand, sir," one of the young officers said.

"What?"

"I was saying, sir, I don't think it could possibly be worth four thousand."

"Four thousand! It's not worth two. There's really nothing to it. Unless, of course, there's something special inside there. . . . Hey, fellow, unfasten this apron."

And before the eyes of the officers appeared Pythagoras Pythagorasovich, sitting, unbelievably contorted, in his dressing gown.

"Ah, there you are . . ." the general said, surprised.

Having said this, the general pushed the calash doors closed, put back the leather apron and rode off with his officers.

The Overcoat

Once, in a department . . . but better not mention which department. There is nothing touchier than departments, regiments, bureaus, in fact, any caste of officials. Things have reached the point where every individual takes an insult to himself as a slur on society as a whole. It seems that not long ago a complaint was lodged by the police inspector of I forget which town, in which he stated clearly that government institutions had been imperiled and his own sacred name taken in vain. In evidence he produced a huge volume, practically a novel, in which, every ten pages, a police inspector appears, and what's more, at times completely drunk. So, to stay out of trouble, let us refer to it just as *a department.*

And so, once, in *a department,* there worked a clerk. This clerk was nothing much to speak of: he was small, somewhat pockmarked, his hair was somewhat reddish and he even looked somewhat blind. Moreover, he was getting thin on top, had wrinkled cheeks and a complexion that might be aptly described as hemorrhoidal. But that's the Petersburg climate for you.

As to his civil-service category (for first a man's standing should be established), he was what is called an eternal pen-pusher, a lowly ninth-class clerk, the usual butt of the jeers and jokes of those writers who have the congenial habit of biting those who cannot bite back.

The clerk's name was Shoenik. There is no doubt that this name derives from shoe but we know nothing of how, why, or when. His father, his grandfather, and even his brother-in-law wore boots, having new soles put on them not more than three times a year.

His first name was Akaky, like his father's, which made him Akaky Akakievich. This may sound somewhat strange and contrived but it is not contrived at all, and, in view of the circumstances, any other name was unthinkable. If I am not mistaken, Akaky Akakievich was born on the night between the 22nd and the 23rd of March. His late mother, an excellent woman and the wife of a clerk, had made all the arrangements for the child's christening, and, while she was still confined to her bed, the godparents arrived: the worthy Ivan Yeroshkin, head clerk in the Senate, and Arina Whitetumkin, the wife of a police captain, a woman of rare virtue.

The new mother was given her pick of the following three names for her son: Mochius, Sossius, and that of the martyr, Hotzazat. "That won't do," Akaky's late mother thought. "Those names are . . . how shall I put it . . ." To please her, the godparents opened the calendar at another page and again three names came out: Strifilius, Dulius, and Varachasius.

"We're in a mess," the old woman said. "Who ever heard of such names? If it was something like Varadat or Varuch, I wouldn't object . . . but Strifilius and Varachasius . . ."

So they turned to yet another page and out came Pavsicachius and Vachtisius.

"Well, that's that," the mother said. "That settles it. He'll just have to be Akaky like his father."

So that's how Akaky Akekievich originated.

And when they christened the child it cried and twisted its features into a sour expression as though it had a foreboding that it would become a ninth-class clerk.

Well, that's how it all happened and it has been reported here just to show that the child couldn't have been called anything but Akaky.

No one remembers who helped him get his appointment to the department or when he started working there. Directors and all sorts of chiefs came and went but he was always to be found at the same place, in the same position, and in the same capacity, that of copying clerk. Until, after a while, people began to believe that he must have been born just as he was, shabby frock coat, bald patch, and all.

In the office, not the slightest respect was shown him. The porters didn't get up when he passed. In fact, they didn't even raise their eyes, as if nothing but an ordinary fly had passed through the reception room. His chiefs were cold and despotic with him. Some head clerks would just thrust a paper under his nose without even saying, "Copy this," or "Here's a nice interesting little job for you," or some such pleasant remark as is current in well-bred offices. And Akaky Akakievich would take the paper without glancing up to see who had put it under his nose or whether the person was entitled to do so. And right away he would set about copying it.

The young clerks laughed at him and played tricks on him to the limit of their clerkish wit. They made up stories about him and told them in front of him. They said that his seventy-year-old landlady beat him and asked him when the wedding would be. They scattered scraps of paper which they said was snow over his head. But with all this going on, Akaky Akakievich never said a word and even acted as though no one were there. It didn't even affect his work and in spite of their loud badgering he made no mistakes in his copying. Only when they tormented him unbearably, when they jogged his elbow and prevented him from getting on with his work, would he say:

"Let me be. Why do you do this to me? . . ."

And his words and the way he said them sounded strange. There was something touching about them. Once a young man who was new to the office started to tease him, following the crowd. Suddenly he stopped as if awakened from a trance and, after that, he couldn't stand the others, whom at first he had deemed decent people. And for a long time to come, during his gayest moments, he would suddenly see in his mind's eye the little, balding clerk and he would hear the words, "Let me be. Why do you do this to me?" and within those words rang the phrase, "I am your brother." And the young man would cover his face with his hands. Later in life, he often shuddered, musing about the wickedness of man toward man and all the cruelty and vulgarity which are concealed under refined manners. And this, he decided, was also true of men who were considered upright and honorable.

It would be hard to find a man who so lived for his job. It would not be enough to say that he worked conscientiously—he worked with love. There, in his copying, he found an interesting, pleasant world for himself and his delight was reflected in his face. He had his favorites among the letters of the alphabet and, when he came to them, he would chuckle, wink and help them along with his lips so that they could almost be read on his face as they were formed by his pen.

Had he been rewarded in proportion with his zeal, he would, perhaps to his own surprise, have been promoted to fifth-class clerk. But all he got out of it was, as his witty colleagues put it, a pin for his buttonhole and hemorrhoids to sit on.

Still, it would be unfair to say that no attention had ever been paid him. One of the successive directors, a kindly man, who thought Akaky Akakievich should be rewarded for his long service, suggested that he be given something more interesting than ordinary copying. So he was asked to prepare an already drawn-up document for referral to another department. Actually, all he had to do was to give it a new heading and change some of the verbs from the first to the third person. But Akaky Akakievich found this work so complicated that he broke into a sweat and finally, mopping his brow, he said:

"Oh no, I would rather have something to copy instead."

After that they left him to his copying forever. And aside from it, it seemed, nothing existed for him.

He never gave a thought to his clothes. His frock coat, which was supposed to be green, had turned a sort of mealy reddish. Its collar was very low and very narrow so that his neck, which was really quite ordinary, looked incredibly long—like the spring necks of the head-shaking plaster kittens which foreign peddlers carry around on their heads on trays. And, somehow, there was always something stuck to Akaky Akakievich's frock coat, a wisp of hay, a little thread. Then too, he had a knack of passing under windows just when refuse happened to be thrown out and as a result was forever carrying around on his hat melon rinds and other such rubbish.

Never did he pay any attention to what was going on

around him in the street. In this he was very different from the other members of the pen-pushing brotherhood, who are so keen-eyed and observant that they'll notice an undone strap on the bottom of someone's trousers, an observation that unfailingly molds their features into a sly sneer. But even when Akaky Akakievich's eyes were resting on something, he saw superimposed on it his own well-formed, neat handwriting. Perhaps it was only when, out of nowhere, a horse rested its head on his shoulder and sent a blast of wind down his cheek that he'd realize he was not in the middle of a line but in the middle of a street.

When he got home he would sit straight down to the table and quickly gulp his cabbage soup, followed by beef and onions. He never noticed the taste and ate it with flies and whatever else God happened to send along. When his stomach began to feel bloated, he would get up from the table, take out his inkwell, and copy papers he had brought with him from the office. And if there weren't any papers to copy for the office, he would make a copy for his own pleasure, especially if the document were unusual. Unusual, not for the beauty of its style, but because it was addressed to some new or important personage.

Even during those hours when light has completely disappeared from the gray Petersburg sky and the pen-pushing brotherhood have filled themselves with dinner of one sort or another, each as best he can according to his income and his preference; when everyone has rested from the scraping of pens in the office, from running around on their own and others' errands; when the restless human being has relaxed after the tasks, sometimes unnecessary, he sets himself; and the clerks hasten to give over the remaining hours to pleasure—the more enterprising among them rushes to the theater, another walks in the streets, allotting his time to the inspection of ladies' hats; another spends his evening paying compliments to some prettyish damsel, the queen of a small circle of clerks; another, the most frequent case, goes to visit a brother clerk, who lives somewhere on the third or fourth floor, in two small rooms with a hall of a kitchen and some little pretensions to fashion, a lamp or some other article bought at great sacrifice, such as going without dinner or outside pleasures

—in brief, at the time when all clerks have dispersed among the lodgings of their friends to play a little game of whist, sipping tea from glasses and nibbling biscuits, inhaling the smoke from their long pipes, relaying, while the cards are dealt, some bit of gossip that has trickled down from high society, a thing which a Russian cannot do without whatever his circumstances, and even, when there's nothing else to talk about, telling once again the ancient joke about the commandant to whom it was reported that someone had hacked the tail off the horse of the monument to Peter the First—in a word, when everyone else was trying to have a good time, Akaky Akakievich was not even thinking of diverting himself.

No one had ever seen him at a party in the evening. Having written to his heart's content, he would go to bed, smiling in anticipation of the morrow, of what God would send him to copy.

Thus flowed the life of a man who, on a yearly salary of four hundred rubles, was content with his lot. And perhaps it would have flowed on to old age if it hadn't been for the various disasters which are scattered along life's paths, not only for ninth-class clerks, but even for eighth-, seventh-, sixth-class clerks and all the way up to State Councilors, Privy Councilors, and even to those who counsel no one, not even themselves.

In Petersburg, there's a formidable enemy for all those who receive a salary in the neighborhood of four hundred rubles a year. The enemy is none other than our northern cold, although they say it's very healthy.

Between eight and nine in the morning, at just the time when the streets are filled with people walking to their offices, the cold starts to mete out indiscriminately such hard, stinging flicks on noses that the wretched clerks don't know where to put them. And when the cold pinches the brows and brings tears to the eyes of those in high positions, ninth-class clerks are completely defenseless. They can only wrap themselves in their threadbare overcoats and run as fast as they can the five or six blocks to the office. Once arrived, they have to stamp their feet in the vestibule until their abilities and talents, which have been frozen on the way, thaw out once again.

Akaky Akakievich had noticed that for some time the

cold had been attacking his back and shoulders quite vi-
ciously, try as he might to sprint the prescribed distance.
He finally began to wonder whether the fault did not lie
with his overcoat. When·he gave it a good looking-over in
his room, he discovered that in two or three places—the
shoulders and back—it had become very much like gauze.
The cloth was worn so thin that it let the draft in, and, to
make things worse, the lining had disintegrated.

It must be noted that Akaky Akakievich's overcoat had
also been a butt of the clerks' jokes. They had even deprived it of its respectable name, referring to it as the old
dressing gown. And, as far as that goes, it did have a
strange shape. Its collar shrank with every year, since
it was used to patch other areas. And the patching, which
did not flatter the tailor, made the overcoat baggy and ugly.

Having located the trouble, Akaky Akakievich decided
to take the cloak to Petrovich, a tailor who lived somewhere on the fourth floor, up a back stairs, and who, one-
eyed and pockmarked as he was, was still quite good at
repairing clerks' and other such people's trousers and
frock coats, provided he happened to be sober and hadn't
other things on his mind.

We shouldn't, of course, waste too many words on the
tailor, but since it has become the fashion to give a thorough
description of every character figuring in a story, there's
nothing to be done but to give you Petrovich.

At first he was called just Grigory and was the serf of
some gentleman or other. He began to call himself Petrovich when he received his freedom and took to drinking
rather heavily on all holidays, on the big ones at first and
then, without distinction, on all church holidays—on any
day marked by a little cross on the calendar. In this he
was true to the traditions of his forefathers, and, when his
wife nagged him about it, he called her impious and a German. Now that we've mentioned his wife, we'd better say a
word or two about her, too. But unfortunately very little
is known about her, except that Petrovich had a wife who
wore a bonnet instead of a kerchief, but was apparently no
beauty, since, on meeting her, it occurred to no one but
an occasional soldier to peek under that bonnet of hers,
twitching his mustache and making gurgling sounds.

Going up the stairs leading to Petrovich's place, which,

to be honest about it, were saturated with water and slops and exuded that ammonia smell which burns your eyes and which you'll always find on the back stairs of all Petersburg houses—going up those stairs, Akaky Akakievich was already conjecturing how much Petrovich would ask and making up his mind not to pay more than two rubles.

The door stood open because Petrovich's wife was cooking some fish or other and had made so much smoke in the kitchen that you couldn't even see the cockroaches. Akaky Akakievich went through the kitchen without even seeing Mrs. Petrovich and finally reached the other room, where he saw Petrovich sitting on a wide, unpainted wooden table, with his legs crossed under him like a Turkish pasha.

He was barefoot, as tailors at work usually are, and the first thing Akaky Akakievich saw was Petrovich's big toe, with its twisted nail, thick and hard like a tortoise shell. A skein of silk and cotton thread hung around Petrovich's neck. On his knees there was some old garment. For the past three minutes he had been trying to thread his needle, very irritated at the darkness of the room and even with the thread itself, muttering under his breath: "It won't go through, the pig, it's killing me, the bitch!" Akaky Akakievich was unhappy to find Petrovich so irritated. He preferred to negotiate when the tailor was a little under the weather, or, as his wife put it, "when the one-eyed buzzard had a load on." When caught in such a state, Petrovich usually gave way very readily on the price and would even thank Akaky Akakievich with respectful bows and all that. True, afterwards, his wife would come whining that her husband had charged too little because he was drunk; but all you had to do was to add ten kopeks and it was a deal.

This time, however, Petrovich seemed to be sober and therefore curt, intractable, and likely to charge an outrageous price. Akaky Akakievich realized this and would have liked to beat a hasty retreat, but the die was cast. Petrovich had fixed his one eye on him and Akaky Akakievich involuntarily came out with:

"Hello, Petrovich."

"Wish you good day, sir," said Petrovich and bent his

eye toward Akaky Akakievich's hands to see what kind of spoil he had brought him.

"Well, Petrovich, I've come . . . see . . . the thing is . . . to . . ."

It should be realized that Akaky Akakievich used all sorts of prepositions, adverbs and all those meaningless little parts of speech when he spoke. Moreover, if the matter were very involved, he generally didn't finish his sentences and opened them with the words: "This, really, is absolutely, I mean to say . . ." and then nothing more— he had forgotten that he hadn't said what he wanted to.

"What is it then?" Petrovich asked, looking over Akaky Akakievich's frock coat with his one eye, the collar, the sleeves, the back, the tails, the buttonholes, all of which he was already acquainted with, since, repairs and all, it was his own work. That's just what tailors do as soon as they see you.

"Well, it's like this, Petrovich . . . my cloak, well, the material . . . look, you can see, everywhere else it's very strong, well, it's a bit dusty and it looks rather shabby, but it's not really . . . look, it's just in one place it's a little . . . on the back here, and here too . . . it's a little worn . . . and here on this shoulder too, a little— and that's all. There's not much work . . ."

Petrovich took Akaky Akakievich's old dressing gown, as his colleagues called it, spread it out on the table and looked it over at length. Then he shook his head and, stretching out his hand, took from the window sill a snuffbox embellished with the portrait of a general, though just what general it was impossible to tell since right where his face used to be there was now a dent glued over with a piece of paper. Taking some snuff, Petrovich spread the overcoat out on his hands, held it up against the light and again shook his head. Then he turned the overcoat inside out, with the lining up, and shook his head again. Then, once more, he removed the snuffbox lid with its general under the piece of paper, and, stuffing snuff into his nose, closed the box, put it away, and finally said:

"No. It can't be mended. It's no use."

At these words, Akaky Akakievich's heart turned over.

"But why can't it be, Petrovich?" he said in the imploring voice of a child. "Look, the only trouble is that it's

worn around the shoulders. I'm sure you have some scraps
of cloth . . ."

"As for scraps, I suppose I could find them," Petrovich said, "but I couldn't sew them on. The whole thing is
rotten. It'd go to pieces the moment you touched it with a
needle."

"Well, if it starts to go, you'll catch it with a patch . . ."

"But there's nothing for patches to hold to. It's too far
gone. It's only cloth in name—a puff of wind and it'll dis-
integrate."

"Still, I'm sure you can make them hold just the same.
Otherwise, really, Petrovich, see what I mean . . ."

"No," Petrovich said with finality, "nothing can be done
with it. It's just no good. You'd better make yourself some
bands out of it to wrap round your legs when it's cold and
socks aren't enough to keep you warm. The Germans
thought up those things to make money for themselves."
—Petrovich liked to take a dig at the Germans whenever
there was a chance.—"As to the overcoat, it looks as if
you'll have to have a new one made."

At the word "new" Akaky Akakievich's vision became
foggy and the whole room began to sway. The only thing
he saw clearly was the general with the paper-covered face
on the lid of Petrovich's snuffbox.

"What do you mean a *new* one?" he said, talking as if
in a dream. "I haven't even got the money . . ."

"A new one," Petrovich repeated with savage calm.

"Well, but if I really had to have a new one, how would
it be that . . ."

"That is, what will it cost?"

"Yes."

"Well, it will be over one hundred and fifty rubles,"
Petrovich said, pursing his lips meaningfully. He liked
strong effects, he liked to perplex someone suddenly and
then observe the grimace that his words produced.

"A hundred and fifty rubles for an overcoat!" shrieked
the poor Akaky Akakievich, shrieked perhaps for the first
time in his life, since he was always noted for his quietness.

"Yes, sir," said Petrovich, "but what an overcoat! And
if it is to have marten on the collar and a silk-lined hood,
that'll bring it up to two hundred."

"Please, Petrovich, please," Akaky Akakievich said be-
seechingly, not taking in Petrovich's words or noticing his

dramatic effects, "mend it somehow, just enough to make it last a little longer."

"No sir, it won't work. It would be a waste of labor and money."

Akaky Akakievich left completely crushed. And when he left, Petrovich, instead of going back to his work, remained for a long time immobile, his lips pursed meaningfully. He was pleased with himself for having upheld his own honor as well as that of the entire tailoring profession.

Akaky Akakievich emerged into the street feeling as if he were in a dream. "So that's it," he repeated to himself. "I never suspected it would turn out this way . . ." and then, after a brief pause, he went on: "So that's it! Here's how it turns out in the end, and I, really, simply couldn't have foreseen it." After another, longer pause, he added: "And so here we are! Here's how things stand. I in no way expected . . . but this is impossible . . . what a business!" Muttering thus, instead of going home, he went in the opposite direction, without having the slightest idea of what was going on.

As he was walking, a chimney sweep brushed his dirty side against him and blackened his whole shoulder; a whole bucketful of lime was showered over him from the top of a house under construction. But he noticed nothing and only when he bumped into a watchman who, resting his halberd near him, was shaking some snuff out of a horn into his calloused palm, did he come to a little and that only because the watchman said:

"Ya hafta knock my head off? Ya got the whole sidewalk, ain'tcha?"

This caused him to look about him and turn back toward home. Only then did he start to collect his thoughts and to see his real position clearly. He began to talk to himself, not in bits of phrases now but sensibly, as to a wise friend in whom he could confide.

"Oh no," he said, "this wasn't the moment to speak to Petrovich. Right now he's sort of . . . his wife obviously has given him a beating . . . that sort of thing. It'd be better if I went and saw him Sunday morning. After Saturday night, his one eye will be wandering and he'll be tired and in need of another drink, and his wife won't give him the money. So I'll slip him a quarter and that will make him more reasonable and so, for the overcoat . . ." Thus

Akaky Akakievich tried to reassure himself, and persuaded himself to wait for Sunday.

When that day came, he waited at a distance until he saw Petrovich's wife leave the house and then went up. After his Saturday night libations, Petrovich's eye certainly was wandering. He hung his head and looked terribly sleepy. But, despite all that, as soon as he learned what Akaky Akakievich had come about, it was as if the devil had poked him.

"It can't be done," he said. "You must order a new one."

Here Akaky Akakievich pressed the quarter on him.

"Thank you," Petrovich said. "I'll drink a short one to you, sir. And as to the overcoat, you can stop worrying. It's worthless. But I'll make you a first-rate new one. That I'll see to."

Akaky Akakievich tried once more to bring the conversation around to mending, but Petrovich, instead of listening, said:

"I'll make you a new one, sir, and you can count on me to do my best. I may even make the collar fastened with silver-plated clasps for you."

At this point Akaky Akakievich saw that he'd have to have a new overcoat and he became utterly depressed. Where was he going to get the money? There was of course the next holiday bonus. But the sum involved had long ago been allotted to other needs. He had to order new trousers, to pay the cobbler for replacing the tops on his boots. He owed the seamstress for three shirts and simply had to have two items of underwear which one cannot refer to in print. In fact, all the money, to the last kopek, was owed, and even if the director made an unexpectedly generous gesture and allotted him, instead of forty rubles, a whole forty-five or even fifty, the difference would be a drop in the ocean in the overcoat outlay.

It is true Akaky Akakievich knew that, on occasions, Petrovich slapped on heaven knows what exorbitant price, so that even his wife couldn't refrain from exclaiming:

"Have you gone mad, you fool! One day he accepts work for nothing, and the next, something gets into him and makes him ask for more than he's worth himself."

But he also knew that Petrovich would agree to make him a new overcoat for eighty rubles. Even so, where was he to find the eighty? He could perhaps scrape together half that sum. Even a little more. But where would he get the other half? . . . Let us, however, start with the first half and see where it was to come from.

Akaky Akakievich had a rule: whenever he spent one ruble, he slipped a copper into a little box with a slot in its side. Every six months, he counted the coppers and changed them for silver. He'd been doing this for a long time and, after all these years, had accumulated more than forty rubles. So this came to one half. But what about the remaining forty rubles?

Akaky Akakievich thought and thought and decided that he would have to reduce his regular expenses for an entire year at least. It would mean going without his evening tea; not burning candles at night, and, if he absolutely had to have light, going to his landlady's room and working by her candle. It would mean, when walking in the street, stepping as carefully as possible over the cobbles and paving stones, almost tiptoeing, so as not to wear out the soles of his boots too rapidly, and giving out his laundry as seldom as possible, and, so that it shouldn't get too soiled, undressing as soon as he got home and staying in just his thin cotton dressing gown, which, if time hadn't taken pity on it, would itself have collapsed long ago.

It must be admitted that, at first, he suffered somewhat from these restrictions. But then he became accustomed to them somehow and things went smoothly again. He even got used to going hungry in the evenings, but then he was able to feed himself spiritually, carrying within him the eternal idea of his overcoat-to-be. It was as if his existence had become somehow fuller, as if he had married and another human being were there with him, as if he were no longer alone on life's road but walking by the side of a delightful companion. And that companion was none other than the overcoat itself, with its thick padding and strong lining that would last forever. In some way, he became more alive, even stronger-minded, like a man who has determined his ultimate goal in life.

From his face and actions all the marks of vacillation and indecision vanished.

At times, there was even a fire in his eyes and the boldest, wildest notions flashed through his head—perhaps he should really consider having marten put on the collar? The intensity of these thoughts almost distracted his attention from his work. Once he almost made a mistake, which caused him to exclaim—true, very softly—"Oof!" and to cross himself.

At least once each month he looked in on Petrovich to discuss the overcoat—the best place to buy the material, its color, its price . . . Then, on the way home, a little worried but always pleased, he mused about how, finally, all this buying would be over and the coat would be made.

Things went ahead faster than he had expected. Beyond all expectations, the director granted Akaky Akakievich not forty, nor forty-five, but a whole sixty rubles. Could he have had a premonition that Akaky Akakievich needed a new overcoat, or had it just happened by itself? Whatever it was, Akaky Akakievich wound up with an extra twenty rubles. This circumstance speeded matters up. Another two or three months of moderate hunger and he had almost all of the eighty rubles he needed. His heartbeat, generally very quiet, grew faster.

As soon as he could, he set out for the store with Petrovich. They bought excellent material, which is not surprising since they had been planning the move for all of six months, and a month had seldom gone by without Akaky Akakievich dropping into the shop to work out prices. Petrovich himself said that there was no better material to be had.

For the lining they chose calico, but so good and thick that, Petrovich said, it even looked better and glossier than silk. They did not buy marten because it was too expensive. Instead they got cat, the best available—cat which at a distance could always be taken for marten. Petrovich spent two full weeks on the overcoat because of all the quilting he had to do. He charged twelve rubles for his work—it was impossible to take less; it had been sewn with silk, with fine double seams, and Petrovich had gone over each seam again afterwards with his own teeth, squeezing out different patterns with them.

It was—well, it's hard to say exactly which day it was, but it was probably the most solemn day in Akaky Akakievich's life, the day Petrovich finally brought him the overcoat. He brought it in the morning, just before it was time to go to the office. There couldn't have been a better moment for the coat to arrive, because cold spells had been creeping in and threatened to become even more severe. Petrovich appeared with the coat, as befits a good tailor. He had an expression of importance on his face that Akaky Akakievich had never seen before. He looked very much aware of having performed an important act, an act that carries tailors over the chasm which separates those who merely put in linings and do repairs from those who create.

He took the overcoat out of the gigantic handkerchief—just fresh from the wash—in which he had wrapped it to deliver it. The handkerchief he folded neatly and put in his pocket, ready for use. Then he took the coat, looked at it with great pride and, holding it in both hands, threw it quite deftly around Akaky Akakievich's shoulders. He pulled and smoothed it down at the back, wrapped it around Akaky Akakievich, leaving it a little open at the front. Akaky Akakievich, a down-to-earth sort of man, wanted to try out the sleeves. Petrovich helped him to pull his arms through and it turned out that with the sleeves too it was good. In a word, it was clear that the coat fitted perfectly.

Petrovich didn't fail to take advantage of the occasion to remark that it was only because he did without a signboard, lived in a small side street, and had known Akaky Akakievich for a long time that he had charged him so little. On Nevsky Avenue, nowadays, he said, they'd have taken seventy-five rubles for the work alone. Akaky Akakievich had no desire to debate the point with Petrovich—he was always rather awed by the big sums which Petrovich liked to mention to impress people. He paid up, thanked Petrovich, and left for the office wearing his new overcoat.

Petrovich followed him and stood for a long time in the street, gazing at the overcoat from a distance. Then he plunged into a curving side street, took a short cut, and re-emerged on the street ahead of Akaky Akakievich, so that he could have another look at the coat from another angle.

Meanwhile, Akaky Akakievich walked on, bubbling with good spirits. Every second of every minute he felt the new overcoat on his shoulders and several times he even let out a little chuckle of inward pleasure. Indeed, the overcoat presented him with a double advantage: it was warm and it was good. He didn't notice his trip at all and suddenly found himself before the office building. In the porter's lodge, he slipped off the overcoat, inspected it, and entrusted it to the porter's special care.

No one knows how, but it suddenly became general knowledge in the office that Akaky Akakievich had a new overcoat and that the old dressing gown no longer existed. Elbowing one another, they all rushed to the cloakroom to see the new coat. Then they proceeded to congratulate him. He smiled at first, but then the congratulations became too exuberant, and he felt embarrassed. And when they surrounded him and started trying to persuade him that the very least he could do was to invite them over one evening to drink to the coat, Akaky Akakievich felt completely at a loss, didn't know what to do with himself, what to say or how to talk himself out of it. And a few minutes later, all red in the face, he was trying rather naively to convince them that it wasn't a new overcoat at all, that it wasn't much, that it was an old one.

In the end, a clerk, no lesser person than an assistant to the head clerk, probably wanting to show that he wasn't too proud to mingle with those beneath him, said:

"All right then, I'll do it instead of Akaky Akakievich. I invite you all over for a party. Come over to my place tonight. Incidentally, it happens to be my birthday today."

Naturally the clerks now congratulated the head clerk's assistant and happily accepted his invitation. Akaky Akakievich started to excuse himself, but he was told that it would be rude on his part, a disgrace, so he had to give way in the end. And later he was even rather pleased that he had accepted, since it would give him an opportunity to wear the new coat in the evening too.

Akaky Akakievich felt as if it were a holiday. He arrived home in the happiest frame of mind, took off the overcoat, hung it up very carefully on the wall, gave the material and the lining one more admiring inspection. Then he took out that ragged item known as the old dressing gown and put it next to the new overcoat, looked at it and began to laugh, so great was the difference between the two. And long after that, while eating his dinner, he snorted every time he thought of the dressing gown. He felt very gay during his dinner, and afterwards he did no copying whatsoever. Instead he wallowed in luxury for a while, lying on his bed until dark. Then, without further dallying, he dressed, pulled on his new overcoat and went out.

It is, alas, impossible to say just where the party-giving clerk lived. My memory is beginning to fail me badly and everything in Petersburg, streets and houses, has become so mixed up in my head that it's very difficult to extract anything from it and to present it in an orderly fashion. Be that as it may, it is a fact that the clerk in question lived in a better district of the city, which means not too close to Akaky Akakievich.

To start with, Akaky Akakievich had to pass through a maze of deserted, dimly lit streets, but, toward the clerk's house, the streets became lighter and livelier. More pedestrians began flashing by more often; there were some well-dressed ladies and men with beaver collars. And, instead of the drivers with their wooden, fretworked sledges studded with gilt nails, he came across smart coachmen in crimson velvet caps, in lacquered sledges, with bearskin lap rugs. He even saw some carriages darting past with decorated boxes, their wheels squeaking on the snow.

Akaky Akakievich gazed around him. For several years now he hadn't been out in the evening. He stopped before the small, lighted window of a shop, staring curiously at a picture of a pretty woman kicking off her shoe and thereby showing her whole leg, which was not bad at all; in the background, some man or other with side whiskers and a handsome Spanish goatee was sticking his head through a door leading to another room. Akaky Akakievich shook his head, snorted, smiled and walked on. Why did he snort? Was it because he had come across something that, although completely strange to him, still aroused in him, as it would in anyone, a certain instinct—or did he think, as many clerks do, along the following lines: "Well, really, the French! If they are after something . . . that sort of thing . . . then, really! . . ." Maybe he didn't even think that. After all, one can't just creep into a man's soul and find out everything he's thinking.

At last he reached the house in which the head clerk's assistant lived. And he lived in style, on the second floor, with the staircase lighted by a lantern. In the hall, Akaky Akakievich found several rows of galoshes. Amidst the galoshes, a samovar was hissing and puffing steam. All

around the walls hung overcoats and cloaks, some with
beaver collars and others with velvet lapels. The noise
and talk that could be heard through the partition became
suddenly clear and resounding when the door opened and
a servant came out with a tray of empty glasses, a cream
jug, and a basket of cookies. It was clear that the clerks
had arrived long before and had already drunk their first
round of tea.

Akaky Akakievich hung his coat up and went in. In a
flash, he took in the candles, the clerks, the pipes, the
card tables, while his ears were filled with the hubbub of
voices rising all around him and the banging of chairs
being moved. Awkwardly, he paused in the middle of the
room, trying to think what to do. But he had been noticed
and his arrival was greeted with a huge yell. Immediately
everybody rushed out into the hall to have another look
at his new overcoat. Akaky Akakievich felt a bit confused,
but, being an uncomplicated man, he was rather pleased
when everyone agreed that it was a good overcoat.

Soon, however, they abandoned him and his overcoat
and turned their attention, as was to be expected, to the
card tables.

The din, the voices, the presence of so many people
—all this was unreal to Akaky Akakievich. He had no
idea how to behave, where to put his hands, his feet, or,
for that matter, his whole body. He sat down near a card
table, stared at the cards and peeked in turn into the faces
of the players. In a little while he got bored and began to
yawn, feeling rather sleepy—it was long past his usual
bedtime. He wanted to take leave of the host, but they
wouldn't let him go. He really had to toast his new overcoat with champagne, they insisted. They made Akaky
Akakievich drink two glasses of champagne, after which
he felt that the party was becoming gayer, but nevertheless
he was quite unable to forget that it was now midnight and
that he should have gone home long ago.

In spite of everything his host could think up to keep
him, he went quietly out into the hall, found his overcoat,
which to his annoyance was lying on the floor, shook it,
carefully removed every speck he could find on it, put it
on and walked down the stairs and out into the street.

The street was still lighted. Some little stores, those
meeting places for servants and people of every sort, were

open, while others, although closed, still showed a long streak of light under their doors, which indicated that the company had not yet dispersed and that the menservants and maids were finishing up their gossip and their conversations, leaving their masters perplexed as to their whereabouts.

Akaky Akakievich walked along in such a gay mood that, who knows why, he almost darted after a lady who flashed by him like a streak of lightning, every part of her body astir with independent, fascinating motion. Still, he restrained himself immediately, went back to walking slowly and even wondered where that compulsion to gallop had come from.

Soon there stretched out before him those deserted streets which, even in the daytime, are not so gay, and, now that it was night, looked even more desolate. Fewer street lamps were lit—obviously a smaller oil allowance was given out in this district. Then came wooden houses and fences; not a soul around, nothing but glistening snow and the black silhouettes of the low, sleeping hovels with their shuttered windows. He came to the spot where the street cut through a square so immense that the houses opposite were hardly visible beyond its sinister emptiness.

God knows where, far away on the edge of the world, he could see the glow of a brazier by a watchman's hut.

Akaky Akakievich's gay mood definitely waned. He could not suppress a shiver as he stepped out into the square, a foreboding of evil in his heart. He glanced behind him and to either side—it was like being in the middle of the sea. "No, it's better not to look," he thought, and walked on with his eyes shut. And when he opened them again to see if the other side of the square was close, he saw instead, standing there, almost in front of his nose, people with mustaches, although he couldn't make out exactly who or what. Then his vision became foggy and there was a beating in his chest.

"Why, here's my overcoat," one of the people thundered, grabbing him by the collar.

Akaky Akakievich was just going to shout out "Help!" when another brought a fist about the size of a clerk's head up to his very mouth, and said:

"You just try and yell . . ."

Akaky Akakievich felt them pull off his coat, then he

received a knee in the groin. He went down on his back and after that he lay in the snow and felt nothing more.

When he came to a few minutes later and scrambled to his feet, there was no one around. He felt cold and, when he realized that the overcoat was gone, desperate. He let out a yell. But his voice didn't come close to reaching the other side of the square.

Frantic, he hollered all the way across the square as he scrambled straight toward the watchman's hut. The watchman was standing beside it, leaning on his halberd, and gazing out across the square, wondering who it could be running toward him and shouting. At last Akaky Akakievich reached him. Gasping for breath, he began shouting at him—what sort of a watchman did he think he was, hadn't he seen anything, and why the devil had he allowed them to rob a man? The watchman said he had seen no one except the two men who had stopped Akaky Akakievich in the middle of the square, who he had thought were friends of his, and that instead of hollering at the watchman, he'd better go and see the police inspector tomorrow and the inspector would find out who had taken the overcoat.

Akaky Akakievich hurried home; he was in a terrible state. The little hair he had left, on his temples and on the back of his head, was completely disheveled, there was snow all down one side of him and on his chest and all over his trousers. His old landlady, hearing his impatient banging on the door, jumped out of bed and, with only one shoe on, ran to open up, clutching her nightgown at the neck, probably out of modesty. When she saw the state Akaky Akakievich was in, she stepped back.

When he told her what had happened, she threw up her hands and said that he should go straight to the borough Police Commissioner, that the local police inspector could not be trusted, that he'd just make promises and give him the runaround. So it was best, she said, to go straight to the borough Commissioner. In fact, she even knew him because Anna, her former Finnish cook, had now got a job as a nanny at his house. And the landlady herself often saw him driving past their house. Moreover, she knew he went to church every Sunday and prayed and at the same time looked cheerful and was obviously a good man. Having heard her advice, Akaky Akakievich trudged off sadly to his room and somehow got through the night, though exactly how must be imagined by those who know how to put themselves in another man's place.

Early the next morning, he went to the borough Commissioner's. But it turned out that he was still asleep. He returned at ten and again was told he was asleep. He went back at eleven and was told that the Commissioner was not home. He tried again during the dinner hour but the secretaries in the reception room would not let him in and wanted to know what business had brought him. For once in his life Akaky Akakievich decided to show some character and told them curtly that he must see the Commissioner personally, that they'd better let him in since he was on official government business, that he would lodge a complaint against them and that then they would see.

The secretaries didn't dare say anything to that and one of them went to call the Commissioner. The Commissioner reacted very strangely to Akaky Akakievich's story of the robbery. Instead of concentrating on the main point, he asked Akaky Akakievich what he had been doing out so late, whether he had stopped off somewhere on his way, hadn't he been to a house of ill repute. Akaky Akakievich became very confused and when he left he wasn't sure whether something would be done about his overcoat or not.

That day he did not go to his office for the first time in his life. The next day he appeared, looking very pale and wearing his old dressing gown, which now seemed shabbier than ever. His account of the theft of his overcoat touched many of the clerks, although, even now, there were some who poked fun at him. They decided on the spot to take up a collection for him but they collected next to nothing because the department employees had already had to donate money for a portrait of the Director and to subscribe to some book or other, on the suggestion of the section chief, who was a friend of the author's. So the sum turned out to be the merest trifle.

Someone, moved by compassion, decided to help Akaky Akakievich by giving him good advice. He told him that he had better not go to his local inspector because, even supposing the inspector wanted to impress his superiors and managed to recover the coat, Akaky Akakievich would still find it difficult to obtain it at the police station unless he could present irrefutable proof of ownership. The best thing was to go through a certain important personage who, by writing and contacting the right people, would set things moving faster. So Akaky Akakievich decided to seek an audience with the important personage.

Even to this day, it is not known exactly what position the important personage held or what his duties consisted of. All we need to know is that this important personage had become important quite recently and that formerly he had been an unimportant person. And even his present position was unimportant compared with other, more important ones. But there is always a category of people for whom somebody who is unimportant to others is an important personage. And the personage in question used various devices to play up his importance: for instance, he made the civil servants of lower categories come out to meet him on the stairs before he'd even reached his office; and a subordinate could not approach him directly but had to go through proper channels. That's the way things are in Holy Russia—everyone tries to ape his superior.

They say that one ninth-class clerk, when he was named section chief in a small office, immediately had a partition put up to make a separate room, which he called the conference room. He stationed an usher at the door who had to open it for all those who came in, although the conference room had hardly enough space for a writing table, even without visitors. The audiences and the manner of our important personage were impressive and stately, but quite uncomplicated. The key to his system was severity. He liked to say: "Severity, severity, severity," and as he uttered the word for the third time, he usually looked very meaningfully into the face of the person he was talking to. True, it was not too clear what need there was for all this severity since the ten-odd employees who made up the whole administrative apparatus of his office were quite frightened enough as it was. Seeing him coming, they would leave their work and stand to attention until he had crossed the room. His usual communication with his inferiors was full of severity and consisted almost entirely of three phrases: "How dare you!" "Who do you think you're talking to?" and "Do you appreciate who I am?" Actually, he was a kindly man, a good friend and obliging,

but promotion to a high rank had gone to his head, knocked
him completely off balance, and he just didn't know how
to act. When he happened to be with equals, he was still a
decent fellow, and, in a way, by no means stupid. But whenever he found himself among those who were below him—
even a single rank—he became impossible. He fell silent
and was quite pitiable, because even he himself realized
that he could have been having a much better time. Sometimes he was obviously longing to join some group in a
lively conversation, but he would be stopped by the thought
that he would be going too far, putting himself on familiar
terms and thereby losing face. And so he remained eternally in silent, aloof isolation, only occasionally uttering
some monosyllabic sounds, and, as a result, he acquired a
reputation as a deadly bore.

It was to this important personage that Akaky Akakievich presented himself, and at a most unpropitious moment to boot. That is, very unpropitious for him, although
quite suitable for the important personage. The latter was
in his office talking gaily to a childhood friend who had
recently come to Petersburg and whom he hadn't seen for
many years. This was the moment when they announced
that there was a man named Shoenik to see him.

"Who's he?" the personage wanted to know.

"Some clerk," they told him.

"I see. Let him wait. I am not available now."

Here it should be noted that the important personage
was greatly exaggerating. He was available. He and his
friend had talked over everything imaginable. For some
time now the conversation had been interlaced with lengthy
silences, and they weren't doing much more than slapping
each other on the thigh and saying:

"So that's how it is, Ivan Abramovich."

"Yes, indeed, Stepan Varlamovich!"

Still Akaky Akakievich had to wait, so that his friend,
who had left the government service long ago and now lived
in the country, could see what a long time employees had
to wait in his reception room.

At last, when they had talked and had sat silent facing
each other for as long as they could stand it, when they
had smoked a cigar reclining in comfortable armchairs with
sloping backs, the important personage, as if he had just

recalled it, said to his secretary who was standing at the door with papers for a report:

"Wait a minute. Wasn't there a clerk waiting? Tell him to come in."

Seeing Akaky Akakievich's humble appearance and his wretched old frock coat, he turned abruptly to face him and said: "What do you want?"

He spoke in the hard, sharp voice which he had deliberately developed by practicing at home before a mirror an entire week before he had taken over his present exalted position.

Akaky Akakievich, who had felt properly subdued even before this, felt decidedly embarrassed. He did his best, as far as he could control his tongue, to explain what had happened. Of course, he added even more than his usual share of phrases like "that is to say" and "so to speak." The overcoat, he explained, was completely new and had been cruelly taken away from him and he had turned to the important personage, that is to say, come to him, in the hope that he would, so to speak, intercede for him somehow, that is to say, write to the Superintendent of Police or, so to speak, to someone, and find the overcoat.

For some unimaginable reason the important personage found his manner too familiar.

"My dear sir," he answered sharply, "don't you know the proper channels? Do you realize whom you're addressing and what the proper procedure should be? You should first have handed in a petition to the office. It would have gone to the head clerk. From him it would have reached the section head, who would have approached my secretary and only then would the secretary have presented it to me. . . ."

"But, Your Excellency," said Akaky Akakievich, trying to gather what little composure he had and feeling at the same time that he was sweating terribly, "I, Your Excellency, ventured to trouble you because secretaries, that is to say . . . are, so to speak, an unreliable lot. . . ."

"What, what, what?" demanded the important personage. "Where did you pick up such an attitude? Where did you get such ideas? What is this insubordination that is spreading among young people against their chiefs and superiors?"

The important personage, apparently, had not noticed

that Akaky Akakievich was well over fifty. Thus, surely, if he could be called young at all it would only be relatively, that is, to someone of seventy.

"Do you realize to whom you are talking? Do you appreciate who I am? Do you really realize, do you, I'm asking you?"

Here he stamped his foot and raised his voice to such a pitch that there was no need to be an Akaky Akakievich to be frightened.

And Akaky Akakievich froze completely. He staggered, his whole body shook, and he was quite unable to keep his feet. If a messenger hadn't rushed over and supported him, he would have collapsed onto the floor. They carried him out almost unconscious.

And the important personage, pleased to see that his dramatic effect had exceeded his expectations, and completely delighted with the idea that a word from him could knock a man unconscious, glanced at his friend to see what he thought of it all and was pleased to see that the friend looked somewhat at a loss and that fear had extended to him too.

Akaky Akakievich remembered nothing about getting downstairs and out into the street. He could feel neither hand nor foot. In all his life he had never been so severely reprimanded by a high official, and not a direct chief of his at that. He walked open-mouthed through a blizzard, again and again stumbling off the sidewalk. The wind, according to Petersburg custom, blew at him from all four sides at once, out of every side street. In no time it had blown him a sore throat and he got himself home at last quite unable to say a word. His throat was swollen and he went straight to bed. That's how severe the effects of an adequate reprimand can be.

The next day he was found to have a high fever. Thanks to the generous assistance of the Petersburg climate, the illness progressed beyond all expectations. A doctor came, felt his pulse, found there was nothing he could do and prescribed a poultice. That was done so that the patient would not be deprived of the beneficial aid of medicine. The doctor added, however, that, by the way, the patient had another day and a half to go, after which he would be what is called kaput. Then, turning to the landlady, the doctor said:

"And you, my good woman, I'd not waste my time if I were you. I'd order him the coffin right away. A pine one. The oak ones, I imagine, would be too expensive for him."

Whether Akaky Akakievich heard what for him were fateful words, and, if he heard, whether they had a shattering effect on him and whether he was sorry to lose his wretched life, are matters of conjecture. He was feverish and delirious the whole time. Apparitions, each stranger than the last, kept crowding before him. He saw Petrovich and ordered an overcoat containing some sort of concealed traps to catch the thieves who were hiding under his bed, so that every minute he kept calling his landlady to come and pull out the one who had even slipped under his blanket. Next, he would ask why his old dressing gown was hanging there in front of him when he had a new overcoat. Then he would find himself standing before the important personage, listening to the reprimand and repeating over and over: "I am sorry, Your Excellency, I am sorry."

Then he began to swear, using the most frightful words, which caused his old landlady to cross herself in horror; never in her life had she heard anything like it from him, and what made it even worse was that they came pouring out on the heels of the phrase, "Your Excellency." After that he talked complete nonsense and it was impossible to make out anything he was saying, except that his disconnected words kept groping for that lost overcoat of his. Then, at last, poor Akaky Akakievich gave up the ghost.

They did not bother to seal his room or his belongings because there were no heirs and, moreover, very little to inherit—namely, a bundle of goose quills, a quire of white government paper, three pairs of socks, a few buttons that had come off his trousers, and the old dressing-gown coat already mentioned. God knows whom they went to; even the reporter of this story did not care enough to find out.

They took Akaky Akakievich away and buried him. And Petersburg went on without him exactly as if he had never existed. A creature had vanished, disappeared. He had had no one to protect him. No one had ever paid him the slightest attention. Not even that which a naturalist pays to a common fly which he mounts on a pin and looks at through his microscope. True, this creature, who had meekly borne the office jokes and gone quietly to his grave, had had, toward the end of his life, a cherished visitor—the overcoat, which for a brief moment had brightened his wretched existence. Then a crushing blow had finished everything, a blow such as befalls the powerful of the earth. . . .

A few days after his death, a messenger from his office was sent to his lodgings with an order summoning him to report immediately; the chief was asking for him. But the messenger had to return alone and to report that Akaky Akakievich could not come.

"Why not?" he was asked.

"Because," the messenger said, "he died. They buried him four days ago."

That is how the department found out about Akaky Akakievich's death, and the next day a new clerk sat in his place: he was much taller and his handwriting was not as straight. In fact, his letters slanted considerably.

But who would have imagined that that was not the end of Akaky Akakievich, that he was fated to live on and make his presence felt for a few days after his death as if in compensation for having spent his life unnoticed by anyone? But that's the way it happened and our little story gains an unexpectedly fantastic ending. Rumors suddenly started to fly around Petersburg that a ghost was haunting the streets at night in the vicinity of the Kalinkin Bridge. The ghost, which looked like a little clerk, was purportedly searching for a stolen overcoat and used this pretext to pull the coats off the shoulders of everyone he met without regard for rank or title. And it made no difference what kind of coat it was—cat, beaver, fox, bearskin, in fact any of the furs and skins people have thought up to cover their own skins with.

One of the department employees saw the ghost with his own eyes and instantly recognized Akaky Akakievich. However, he was so terrified that he dashed off as fast as his legs would carry him and so didn't get a good look; he only saw from a distance that the ghost was shaking his finger at him. Complaints kept pouring in, and not only from petty employees, which would have been understandable. One and all, even Privy Councilors, were catching chills in their backs and shoulders from having their overcoats peeled off. The police were ordered to catch the ghost at any cost, dead or alive, and to punish him with due severity as a warning to others. And what's more, they nearly succeeded.

To be precise, a watchman caught the ghost red-handed, grabbed it by the collar, in Kiryushkin Alley, as it was trying to pull the coat off a retired musician who, in his day, used to tootle on the flute. Grabbing it, he called for help from two colleagues of his and asked them to hold on to it for just a minute. He had, he said, to get his snuff-box out of his boot so that he could bring some feeling back to his nose, which had been frostbitten six times in his life. But it was evidently snuff that even a ghost couldn't stand. The man, closing his right nostril with his finger, had hardly sniffed up half a fistful into the left when the ghost sneezed so violently that the three watchmen were blinded by the resulting shower. They all raised their fists to wipe their eyes and, when they could see again, the ghost had vanished. They even wondered whether they had really held him at all. After that, watchmen were so afraid of the ghost that they felt reluctant to interfere with live robbers and contented themselves with shouting from a distance: "Hey you! On your way!"

And the clerk's ghost began to haunt the streets well beyond the Kalinkin Bridge, spreading terror among the meek.

However, we have completely neglected the important personage, who really, in a sense, was the cause of the fantastic direction that this story—which, by the way, is completely true—has taken. First of all, it is only fair to say that, shortly after poor Akaky Akakievich, reduced to a pulp, had left his office, the important personage felt a twinge of regret. Compassion was not foreign to him—many good impulses stirred his heart, although his position usually prevented them from coming to the surface. As soon as his visiting friend had left the office, his thoughts returned to Akaky Akakievich. And after that, almost every day, he saw in his mind's eye the bloodless face of the little clerk who had been unable to take a proper reprimand. This thought was so disturbing that a week later he went so far as to send a clerk from his office to see how Akaky Akakievich was doing and to find out whether, in fact, there was any way to help him. And when he heard the news that Akaky Akakievich had died suddenly of a fever, it was almost a blow to him, even made him feel guilty and spoiled his mood for the whole day.

Trying to rid himself of these thoughts, to forget the whole unpleasant business, he went to a party at a friend's house. There he found himself in respectable company and, what's more, among people nearly all of whom were of the same standing so that there was absolutely nothing to oppress him. A great change came over him. He let himself go, chatted pleasantly, was amiable, in a word, spent a very pleasant evening. At supper, he drank a couple of glasses of champagne, a well-recommended prescription for inducing good spirits. The champagne gave him an inclination for something special and so he decided not to go home but instead to pay a little visit to a certain well-known lady named Karolina Ivanovna, a lady, it seems, of German extraction, toward whom he felt very friendly. It should be said that the important personage was no longer a young man, that he was a good husband, the respected father of a family. His two sons, one of whom already had a civil-service post, and his sweet-faced sixteen-year-old daughter, who had a slightly hooked but nevertheless pretty little nose, greeted him every day with a "Bon jour, Papa." His wife, a youngish woman and not unattractive at that, gave him her hand to kiss and then kissed his. But although the important personage was quite content with these displays of family affection, he considered it the proper thing to do to have, for friendship's sake, a lady friend in another part of the city. This lady friend was not a bit prettier or younger than his wife, but the world is full of such puzzling things and it is not our business to judge them.

So the important personage came down the steps, stepped into his sledge, and said to the coachman:

"To Karolina Ivanovna's."

Wrapping his warm luxurious fur coat around him, he sat back in his seat. He was in that state so cherished by Russians, in which, without your having to make any effort, thoughts, each one pleasanter than the last, slip into your head by themselves.

Perfectly content, he went over all the most pleasant moments at the party, over the clever retorts that had caused that select gathering to laugh. He even repeated many of them under his breath and, still finding them funny, laughed heartily at them all over again, which was natural enough. However, he kept being bothered by gusts of wind which would suddenly blow, God knows from where or for what reason, cutting his face, throwing lumps of snow into it, filling the cape of his coat like a sail and throwing it over his head, so that he had to extricate himself from it again and again.

Suddenly the important personage felt someone grab him violently from behind. He turned around and saw a small man in a worn-out frock coat. Terrified, he recognized Akaky Akakievich, his face as white as the snow and looking altogether very ghostly indeed. Fear took over completely when the important personage saw the ghost's mouth twist and, sending a whiff of the grave into his face, utter the following words:

"I've caught you at last. I've got you by the collar now! It's the coat I need. You did nothing about mine and hollered at me to boot. Now I'll take yours!"

The poor important personage almost died. He may have displayed force of character in the office and, in general, toward his inferiors, so that after one glance at his strong face and manly figure, people would say: "Quite a man", but now, like many other mighty-looking people, he was so frightened that he began to think, and not without reason, that he was about to have an attack of something or other. He was even very helpful in peeling off his coat, after which he shouted to the coachman in a ferocious tone:

"Home! As fast as you can!"

The coachman, hearing the ferocious tone which the important personage used in critical moments and which was sometimes accompanied with something even more drastic, instinctively ducked his head and cracked his whip, so that they tore away like a streak. In a little over six minutes the important personage was in front of his house. Instead of being at Karolina Ivanovna's, he was somehow staggering to his room, pale, terrified, and coatless. There he spent such a restless night that the next morning, at breakfast, his daughter said:

"You look terribly pale this morning, Papa."

But Papa was silent, and he didn't say a word to anyone about what had happened to him, or where he had been or where he had intended to go. This incident made a deep impression upon him. From then on his subordinates heard far less often: "How dare you!" and "Do you know whom you're talking to?" And even when he did use these expressions it was after listening to what others had to say.

But even more remarkable—after that night, Akaky Akakievich's ghost was never seen again. The important personage's overcoat must have fitted him snugly. At any rate, one no longer heard of coats being torn from people's shoulders. However, many busybodies wouldn't let the matter rest there and maintained that the ghost was still haunting certain distant parts of the city. And, sure enough, a watchman in the Kolomna district caught a glimpse of the ghost behind a house. But he was rather a frail watchman. (Once an ordinary, but mature, piglet, rushing out of a private house, knocked him off his feet to the huge delight of a bunch of cabbies, whom he fined two kopeks each for their lack of respect—then he spent the proceeds on tobacco.) So, being rather frail, the watchman didn't dare to arrest the ghost. Instead he followed it in the darkness until at last it stopped suddenly, turned to face him, and asked:

"You looking for trouble?"

And it shook a huge fist at him, much larger than any you'll find among the living.

"No," the watchman said, turning away.

This ghost, however, was a much taller one and wore an enormous mustache. It walked off, it seems, in the direction of the Obukhov Bridge and soon dissolved into the gloom of night.

Taras Bulba

Chapter 1

"Come on, boy, turn around. What a sight! What's that—a cassock or something? They all wear those in your seminary?"

This was old Bulba's welcome to his two sons, back home from the Kiev Seminary, where they had just completed their studies.

The sons dismounted. They were big and strong and they hung their heads and looked up from under their brows as befits seminary students. Their healthy faces were covered with down still untouched by a razor. Their father's reception took them aback and they stood staring at their feet.

"Fine, you just stand there. Let's have a good look at you," Bulba said, swinging the lads around, first one, then the other. "Well, your coats certainly aren't too short. Some coats! Never seen the like in my whole life. Come, I'd like to see one of you run in that garb. Come on, get going! I bet you get tangled up in your skirts and fall flat on your face."

"Stop it, Pa. Don't laugh at me, I tell you," the older of the two said finally.

"Look at that! Sensitive, eh? Why shouldn't I laugh?"

"Why? . . . because you may be my pa, but if you keep on baiting us, I'll take a poke at you, by God."

"What! At your father? Are you mad?" Bulba said, surprised, and retreated a few steps.

"Father or no father, I don't take that from anyone."

"So how shall we fight? Fists?"

"Anything'll do."

"So fists it is," Taras Bulba said, rolling up his sleeves. "Let's see what kind of a man you are with 'em."

And, instead of hugging one another after their long separation, father and son began to aim heavy blows at the other's ribs, belly and chest, side-stepping, moving back, attacking again, their eyes glued on each other.

"People should see it! The old man's gone right out of his head!" Taras's wife wailed. Thin, pale, and kindly looking, the boys' mother had come out onto the doorstep to kiss her precious sons. "The children come home after a whole year and he can think of nothing better than a fist fight!"

"Well, I swear, this one can fight," Bulba said, dropping his hands. "I'll say that for him." He was panting heavily. "Yes," he said, "I can tell right off he'll make a good Cossack. All right, son, let me kiss you."

And father and son embraced.

"Good boy! Just keep on swinging like you swung at me. Don't let anyone get away with anything! But I still say that's some getup you have on. What's this string? And you, you big lout, you still standing there with your arms hanging down?" Bulba said to his younger son. "Want to have a go at me too, you son of a dog?"

"Anything else?" the mother said, putting her arms around the boy. "What an idea! For a child to hit his own father! And what a time to pick, when he's traveled so far and is tired. . . ." The child in question was almost twenty and well over six feet tall. "He ought to rest and eat something and you want to make him fight!"

"Don't listen to your mother, boy," Bulba said. "She's a woman. She doesn't know a thing. You don't need her coddling. The only coddling you need is from the open steppe and a good horse. See this saber? That's your mother. All the rest is garbage, all the things they stuff your heads with at the seminary—all those books, dictionaries and philosophies. I wouldn't give a good goddamn for all that——" Here, Bulba uttered an unprintable word. "Tell you what I'll do for you. Next week, I'll send you to Zaporozhe. There you'll learn something. That's a school for you. They'll ram some sense into your heads there."

"So they'll only have a week at home?" the mother said, standing there, frail and pitiful, with tears in her eyes. "The poor dears won't have a proper rest or a chance to enjoy their home, and I'll never see enough of them."

"Come on, come on—stop whimpering! A Cossack's not made to spend his time with women. You'd like to hide them under your skirts and sit on 'em like a hen on her eggs. You'd better go and put everything we have in the house on the table. And that doesn't mean honey buns and poppy-seed cakes and puddings; give us a whole sheep, or maybe a goat, and our own old home-brew to go with it, and vodka, but not with raisins and stuff like that in it—real vodka to scorch our throats."

Bulba led his sons into the living room of the house. As they entered, two pretty servant girls wearing coin neck-laces darted out of the room. They had been tidying up and apparently the arrival of the two young masters had frightened them, or else they were simply bowing to the feminine custom, upon seeing a man, of letting out a little shriek, rushing away, and then, for a while, bashfully keep-ing the face covered with a sleeve.

The living room was furnished in the taste of the time. Only suggestions of that style have come down to us through the old songs, songs that used to be sung in the Ukraine by blind minstrels, to the strumming of the lute. In the style of those troubled times, of skirmishes and bat-tles for union of the Ukraine with Russia, the walls of the room were covered with smooth colored clay and hung with sabers, knouts, bird and fishing nets, guns, an elab-orately carved powder horn, gilded horse bits and tether ropes adorned with silver plates. The windows were small, with round, opaque panes, such as can only be seen today in old churches. Painted red bands ran around the windows and doors. On shelves in the corners there were jugs, bottles, and green and blue glass flasks, engraved silver mugs, and gilded drinking cups. They were of varied origin, the handiwork of Venetian, Circassian, and Turk-ish workmen that had reached Bulba's living room by roundabout ways, changing hands frequently, often vio-lently, as was usual in those restless times. Against the walls stood birch-bark benches. In the center, a large table. The icons hung in their special corner and on the other side of the room stood a huge, tiled stove which provided many comfortable nooks and cozy corners.

It was all familiar to the two lads. They had come home for their summer vacations each year—walking the whole way since, seminary students not being allowed to ride horseback, they couldn't keep mounts there. All that marked them as Cossacks was the tuft of hair left on their cropped heads, by which any arms-bearing Cossack had the right to pull them. It was only now that they'd completed their studies that Bulba had sent a couple of young stallions from his herd.

Bulba had invited all the local Cossack chiefs under him to celebrate the return of his sons. When his second-in-command, Dmitro Tovkach, an old friend, arrived with several others, he pointed to his sons and said:

"Look at 'em! Some lads, eh? Soon I'm going to send them to Camp Zaporozhe."

The guests congratulated father and sons, telling them it was the best thing they could do, that there was no better place to train young men than Camp Zaporozhe.

"Well, brothers, sit down anywhere you like. Sons— let's start with a good strong drink! God bless you! Your health, sons! To you, Ostap, and to you too, Andrei. God send you success in war. May you beat all comers—Turks, Tartars, and, if the Poles start scheming against the faith again, let 'em have it too. By the way, how do you say vodka in Latin? You see, boy, how stupid those Latins were? They didn't even know that there was such a thing as vodka. What was he called—the one who wrote those Latin verses—what's his name? I don't know, I'm not much of a scholar myself. Horace or something?"

"That's Pa for you," Ostap, the older son, thought, "the old dog knows it all and he still keeps playing the fool."

"I bet your Archimandrite wouldn't let you get even a sniff of this stuff," Taras went on. "And tell me the truth, boys, they gave you some good thrashings with those birch switches, on your backs and everything else a Cossack has? And when you got too smart, I'll bet they gave you the whip too. And I'll wager they not only beat you on Saturdays, but on Wednesdays and Thursdays too—right?"

"Forget it, Pa," Ostap said composedly, "all that's past."

"Let 'em try it now," Andrei said. "Let anybody try. Just let some Tartar turn up and I'll show him what a Cossack saber can do."

"Right, son, right! Come to think of it, I'll go to Zaporozhe with you. Why, yes, I'll come. What the devil have I got to gain by staying around here? Grow buckwheat, run the house, look after the pigs and sheep, get fussed over by the wife? The hell with it! I'm a Cossack! And what if there isn't a war just now? I'll come to Zaporozhe with you just for a change. By God, I will!"

And getting more and more excited, old Bulba rose from the table, thrust out his chest and stamped his foot.

"We'll ride out tomorrow! Why postpone it? What enemy can we stalk here? What do we need this house for? What can we do with all this? What are all these jars for?" And he started grabbing pots and jars and flasks, hurling them around and smashing them.

His poor wife was accustomed to this sort of thing and looked at him sadly without getting up from her seat. She did not dare object when she heard Taras's decision, but she could not suppress her tears. And when she glanced at her sons an indescribably deep, speechless sorrow fluttered in her eyes and over her convulsively compressed lips.

Taras Bulba was terribly stubborn. The cruel fifteenth century gave birth to such characters in that seminomadic corner of Europe. Russia, abandoned by her princes, had been devastated, burned to the ground, by the irresistible raids of the Mongolian predators. A man who lost his shelter became daring; he became used to facing fire, restless neighbors, and unending perils, and forgot the meaning of fear.

It was in that era, when the peaceful Slav was fired with a warlike flame, that the Cossacks made their appearance. They were like an explosion in which the free, exuberant Russian character found an outlet. Soon valleys, river crossings, sheltered spots, teemed with Cossacks. No one knew how many of them there were, and when the Sultan asked they answered in good faith:

"Who can tell? We are scattered over the entire steppe and wherever there's a hillock, there's a Cossack."

It was the ordeals they had gone through that had torn this strange manifestation of Russian vigor out of the breast of the Russian people. The erstwhile towns and princely domains, with their feuding and trading, had disappeared and their place had been taken by warlike settlements linked by the common danger and by hatred of the heathen predators. The unbreakable resistance of this people saved Europe from the merciless hordes from the East. The Polish kings had replaced the petty princes and become the official, although weak and distant, rulers of these vast lands. They had early realized the advantage of having the plains inhabited by a warlike, free-roving race and they tried to encourage and preserve the Cossacks' wild way of life. Under their remote guidance, the Cossacks elected headmen and divided the territory into military districts. They had no visible, regular army but, when a war or an uprising broke out, each man rode in, fully equipped, to report, and receive his gold piece from the King. Within a week's time a force assembled which could never have been recruited. And when the emergency was over, the trooper went back to his field or his river, traded, brewed beer—in a word, became once more a free Cossack.

There were few things, in fact, that a Cossack could not do. He knew the arts of blacksmithing and gunsmithing, how to distill vodka, build a wagon, prepare powder, and, above all, he knew how to drink and carouse as only a Russian can.

Moreover, besides the registered Cossacks, those who were paid to appear fully equipped in time of emergency, it was possible to recruit a whole army of volunteers. All that was needed was for Cossack chiefs to appear at various market places and village squares, mount a cart and call out:

"Hey, you beer brewers! Enough! You've lain around on your stoves too long, feeding the flies with your bacon! What about seeking a little glory! Hey, you plowmen, shepherds, skirt-lovers! Stop muddying your yellow boots and wasting your vigor on women! Time to act like Cossacks!"

And these words were like sparks on dried wood. The plowman broke his plow, the brewers threw away their casks and destroyed their barrels, the merchants let their stores go to ruin, broke pots and pans and everything else in their houses, mounted horses and were off. In a word, the Russian soul found its outlet in the Cossack and his powerful physique.

The Bulbas were an old Cossack family and Taras was one of their oldest and most respected colonels. He seemed to have been born especially for danger and war. He was blunt and straightforward. At that time, Polish influence was beginning to be felt among the Russian aristocracy. Many adopted Polish customs, wallowed in luxury, went in for large retinues, for falconry and for all sorts of amusements. Taras had never approved. He liked the simple Cossack life and quarreled with those of his friends who leaned toward Warsaw. He called them flunkies of the Polish gentry. Always on the alert, he regarded himself as a champion of the Russian Orthodox Church. He took justice into his own hands and rode into villages when people complained of being persecuted by landlords or of being forced to pay unbearable taxes. Bulba meted out his own justice. He had set himself a rule—he would always use his saber in the following three instances: when government officials failed to remove their caps before Cossack elders or to show them proper respect; when the Orthodox faith was slighted and ancestral customs were neglected: and finally when he had to deal with pagans or Turks, against whom he always considered it commendable to take up arms in the name of Christendom.

Now he was enjoying the thought of his arrival at the camp with his sons, when he would say:

"See what a pair of lads I've brought you."

He mused about how he was going to introduce them to his old, battle-tested brothers-in-arms; how he'd witness their first exploits in fighting and in drinking, which he also considered a major attribute for a warrior.

He had planned to send his sons by themselves. But when he saw how young and tall, how strong and handsome they were, the warlike spirit stirred in him and he decided to go along, although there was no reason for it outside of his own stubborn desire.

Right away, he began giving orders. He selected horses and their trappings for his sons, inspected the stables and the storehouses, designated the men who were to leave with him the next morning. He handed over his command to Dmitro Tovkach with firm instructions to rally immediately to the camp with the whole regiment if Bulba sent him a signal. And although he was feeling the effects of the drinks he had had, he forgot nothing. He even saw to it that the horses were watered and given the best grain. By the time he had completed these rounds, he was tired.

"All right, children," he said, "time to sleep now. Tomorrow we'll get off to an early start. No," he said to his wife, "don't bother to make our beds. We don't need 'em. We'll sleep outside."

Darkness had only just fallen but Bulba always liked to go to bed early. He sprawled out on a rug and covered himself with his sheepskin coat both because the night air was fresh and because he liked to cover himself warmly. Before long he began to snore and the rest of the household were soon following his example. They all snored and whistled; the watchman snored the loudest of all because he had drunk more than anyone else to celebrate the homecoming of the young masters.

Only the mother did not sleep. She sat by the heads of her two sons, who were sleeping side by side, combed their tousled locks and wet them with her tears. She gazed at them with all her being. All of her turned into vision and she could not get her fill of looking. She had breastfed both. She loved them, and now she was to be allowed to see them for a brief moment only.

"My sons, my dear sons, what will happen to you? What's in store for you?" she murmured, and her tears were caught in the wrinkles which had so changed her once-pretty face. She was indeed pathetic, as was any woman in that troubled time. She had had but a brief moment of love, during the first heat of passion, in the first flush of youth, and then her rough conqueror had deserted her for his saber, for his comrades, for revelry. She would see her husband for two or three days and then he would disappear for several years. And when she did see him, when he was home, what kind of a life was it? She put up with insults, even blows, and tenderness was hardly ever shown her at all. She was a strange being among all these wifeless warriors on whom Zaporozhe had left its grim imprint. Her youth flashed by without joy and her fresh cheeks withered unkissed before their time. All her love, all her feelings, all that is passionate in a woman, turned into a mother's tenderness. She wheeled above her children with anxiety and passion—like a gull over the steppe. And now they were taking her darlings away from her, this time possibly for good. Who knew—perhaps in the very first encounter their heads would fall, severed by the slash of a Tartar saber. And she wouldn't even know where their bodies lay, abandoned to be torn asunder by scavenging birds. She felt she would gladly have given all of herself for each drop of their blood. Crying, she had looked into their eyes until sleep had overcome them and thought:

"Perhaps after all Bulba will put off their departure for a couple of days, perhaps he decided to go off in such a hurry because he had a bit too much to drink."

The crescent moon, high in the sky, lighted the courtyard with its crowd of sleepers, the thick clump of pussy willows and the tall steppe grass which washed over the fence. The mother sat by her sons' heads, never taking her eyes off them, not thinking of sleep. Already the horses, sensing the approaching dawn, had stopped grazing and had lain down in the grass; the top leaves of the willow began to whisper and little by little the rustling current worked its way down to the lowest branches. And she sat there until daybreak, wishing that the night would last forever. The ringing whinny of a foal came from the steppe. Red stripes appeared clearly in the sky.

Bulba awakened suddenly and jumped to his feet. And he was well aware of what he had decided the evening before.

"All right, lads, you've slept enough—get up! Water your horses. And where's the old woman? Hey, old woman, fix us something to eat, we've a long way to go today."

The mother, sad and stooping, deprived of her last hope, went into the house. And while she was preparing their breakfast, Bulba tossed out orders, went to the stables and personally selected the best equipment for his sons.

The seminary students were suddenly transformed into quite different men. Soft red leather boots with silver studs replaced their old, muddy ones; their trousers were as wide as the Black Sea, had hundreds of pleats in them, and were belted with golden cords from which hung straps with tassels, tinkling charms, and pipes. Their scarlet cloth coats were girt with sashes in which Turkish pistols were stuck, and their sabers clanked at their heels. Their faces, not yet weatherbeaten, looked even handsomer, and their young black mustaches further emphasized the whiteness of their skin and their youthful freshness. They looked so good to their wretched mother, under their sheepskin hats with golden tops, that she simply stood speechless and even her tears stopped streaming.

"All right, children, we're all set. No use wasting time!" Bulba said finally. "And now, let's all sit down before leaving as is the Christian custom."

And everybody sat down, even the stableboys who had been standing respectfully by the door.

"Go on, Mother, bless your children," Bulba said. "Pray God that they may fight bravely, always stand up for their honor and for the true Church of Christ, and that, if they fail, they may disappear so that not one speck remains in God's world! Go to your mother, boys. A mother's prayer will help you on land and sea."

The mother embraced them, weak as she was and, tears pouring down her cheeks, put two small icons on cords around their necks.

"May the Mother of God preserve you . . . don't forget me, sons . . . send me news when you can . . ." She could not continue.

"All right, children, we're off," Bulba said.

Their saddle horses stood by the porch. Bulba jumped on his Devil, who reared crazily, feeling the three-hundred-pound load on his back. Bulba was heavy-set and fat besides.

The mother watched her sons mount their horses too, then she rushed toward the younger, in whose features there was somehow more gentleness. She grasped the stirrup and the back of his saddle and clung on to them with a desperate look in her eyes. Two big Cossacks pulled her gently away and carried her into the house. But when the cavalcade had already ridden out of the gates, she darted out behind them like a wild goat, with an agility quite unexpected in a brittle old woman. With surprising strength, she stopped the horse and, with a strange, uncontrolled violence, put her arms around her son's waist. They led her off again.

The two young Cossacks rode forward, confusedly fighting back their tears, afraid that their father might see them.

But he too was unsure and was also trying not to show it.

It was one of those gray days which lend a strange glitter to the green of the grass and cause the birds to twitter somehow discordantly. After a short while, they looked back. Their house seemed to have sunk into the earth. All they could see above the steppe were the two chimneys and the tops of the trees in whose branches they used to leap around like a couple of squirrels. Before them there still stretched the meadow with which the story of their lives was so closely intertwined, from the time they had rolled in the dewy grass to the time they had waited there for a dark-browed Cossack girl, timidly approaching on her quick, young legs. And now there was nothing to be seen on the horizon except the pole over the well with a cartwheel nailed to it, erect and lonely against the sky. And the terrain, which had seemed flat as they crossed it, loomed up behind as a hill, hiding everything that lay beyond.

And so it was the end of childhood, of games, of all such things.

Chapter 2

They rode in silence. Taras thought of the past, of his bygone youth, wishing sadly that he could have been always young. Then he thought of the old comrades he was going to meet in the camp. He tried to recollect which ones had died and which should still be around. A tear was slowly trying to find its way out of his eye, and his gray head was bowed.

The sons' thoughts were different. But first, more should be known about them. As each reached the age of twelve, he was sent to the Kiev Seminary. In that day, people of consequence considered it proper to give their children an education, although they expected them to forget everything they had learned soon after. Having been brought up in unrestrained freedom, such children arrived at the seminary quite wild. And they received a certain polish there which gave them all something in common.

Ostap, the elder, began his scholastic career by trying to run away. He was caught, given a terrible whipping and sent back to his books. Four times he tried to get rid of his primer by burying it and four times they gave him a sound thrashing and bought him a new one. There's no doubt that he would have buried it a fifth time had it not been for his father's solemn promise that he would put him in a monastery as a lay brother for twenty years and that he would never see Zaporozhe again unless he learned everything they had to teach him at the seminary. That threat must have sounded strange coming from Taras, who professed to despise all learning.

From that day on, Ostap began to work with extraordinary diligence. He would spend hours studying some

110

dull book and soon became one of the best pupils. At that time, there was little connection between actual life and what was taught. The scholastic, rhetorical, grammatical and logical refinements had no application in real life. Even men of learning were ignoramuses because they were completely lacking in experience. Moreover, the democratic organization of the seminary and the great number of healthy young lads attending it resulted in all sorts of extracurricular pursuits. The poor fare, the frequent deprivation of food as a punishment, the drive to satisfy the many urges of a vigorous youth—all this combined—produced in the students that spirit of adventure which would be further developed later in Zaporozhe. Hungry seminary students, roving the streets of Kiev, put everyone on his guard. At the sight of a passing student, stallkeepers covered pies and cakes with their hands like she-eagles spreading their wings over their young. The monitor, who was supposed to keep his fellow students in line, had such awesome pockets in his trousers that he could have stuffed them with all the goods displayed on the stall of a not-too-alert merchant. Even the military governor, Adam Kisel, although he was a patron of the seminary, kept the students out of Kiev society and insisted that an eye should be kept on them at all times. This recommendation was, of course, quite superfluous because neither the rector nor the monk-professors spared rod or whip, and, on their orders, the lictors often lashed the monitors so severely that they went around patting their trousers for weeks afterward. Many students took this quite nonchalantly; they considered it to have just a bit more bite than a good swig of vodka with pepper; others, tired of ceaseless whippings, escaped to Zaporozhe, if not caught and brought back. And Ostap Bulba, despite his zeal in studying logic and even theology, never managed to stay away from the merciless rod. Of course, all this went to harden him and develop in him the ruthlessness characteristic of many Cossacks. He was always considered the most reliable friend. Seldom did he initiate or lead a raid on an orchard or vegetable garden, but he was always one of the first to rally to an adventurous gang and, if caught, would never betray a comrade, despite incarceration, beatings, and all the rest. He seemed immune to all temptation except the temptation to fight and drink— at least he gave no thought to the others. He was straightforward with his equals. He was as kind as it was possible to be with his sort of character living at that particular time. And now, riding, he was deeply touched by his mother's tears; it was the only thing that disturbed him, causing him to lower his head thoughtfully.

His younger brother, Andrei, was experiencing feelings which were more vivid and somehow more complex. He had studied more willingly and his studies had not required so much effort that his will power was put to a test. He was more inventive than his brother and was often the leader of some risky venture. But he managed to avoid punishment by using his imagination at times when his brother would resignedly take off his coat and lie down on the floor without arguing or begging for mercy. Like his brother, he spoiled for adventure, but he had room for other feelings too. By the time he was eighteen, the need for love had flared up in him. The picture of a woman had begun to haunt his arid dreams. During the philosophical debates at the seminary, she was constantly before him, blooming, black-eyed, and tender. Her firm bosom, her wonderfully soft, bare arms, and even her dress, under which he could guess at her strong but feminine limbs, filled his dreams with a sort of unexpressed sensuousness. He saw to it that these stirrings of youthful passion remained secret from his comrades, because at that time it was considered shameful for a Cossack to think of women and love before he had seen battle. In his final years at the seminary, he had less often taken part in adventurous expeditions at the head of a band of students. Instead, he wandered alone through the quieter parts of Kiev, where the little cottages peeped out onto the streets from among the cherry orchards. Sometimes he would walk through the quarter where the Ukrainian and Polish gentry lived, where the houses had pretensions to elegance. Once, when he was meandering along absorbed in his dreams, he was almost run down by the carriage of some Polish gentleman and a terrifyingly mustached coachman slashed at him rather accurately with his whip. The young student was furious. Recklessly, he grabbed a spoke of the rear wheel of the carriage and brought it to a stop. But the coachman, fearing reprisals, whipped up the horses and they tore away. Andrei, lucky enough to get his hands away from the wheel, crashed to the ground, his face in the dirt. Ringing, musical laughter sounded above him. He looked up—the most beautiful girl he had ever seen was standing at a window. Her eyes were black and her complexion made him think of snow lit by the glow of the morning sun. She was laughing with abandon and her laughter added a sparkling power to her uncanny beauty. He was dumfounded. He stared at her, no longer knowing where he was, absent-mindedly rubbing dirt all over his face. Who was she? He tried to find out from the richly liveried servants who were gathered by the gates, listening to a strolling lute player. But they just laughed at his mud-caked face and wouldn't tell him. Still, in the end, he learned that she was the daughter of the Polish military governor of Kovno, who was in Kiev temporarily. The very next night, with schoolboyish brashness, he squeezed himself through the palings of the fence into the garden and climbed a tree whose branches spread over the very roof of the house. From the tree, he jumped onto the roof, hoisted himself up into the chimney and let himself down it, straight into the beautiful Polish girl's bedroom. She was sitting near a lighted candle taking off a pair of expensive earrings. The sudden appearance of a stranger so frightened her that she was unable to utter a sound. But when she saw him standing there with eyes downcast, too shy even to move an arm, she recognized the seminary student she had seen lying in the mud and burst out laughing again, her fright completely gone. Indeed, there was nothing frightening in Andrei's appearance —as a matter of fact, she thought he looked very handsome. She kept laughing and teasing him for quite a while. This beautiful girl, like many of her compatriots, was something of a scatterbrain, but her enchantingly clear, piercing eyes looked steadily at Andrei. And he could not stir a limb, as though he had been sewn up in a sack. The daughter of the Polish governor stepped up to him, put her sparkling diadem on his head, hung her earrings from his lips, threw her transparent muslin chemisette with its gold-embroidered frills round his shoulders. She adorned him thus and did a thousand other silly things, with the childish naughtiness so typical of pretty Polish girls. All this embarrassed the poor student more and more. He presented a laughable sight, standing there with his mouth open, gazing into her dazzling eyes. Then there was a knock at the door and she became frightened again. She bade him hide under the bed and as soon as the danger was past, called her maid, a Tartar prisoner, and told her to lead him cautiously out into the garden and from there to see him over the fence. But this time he was less lucky in getting over the fence. The awakened guard grabbed him by a foot and he had to take a beating from the servants, who kept hitting him even when he was out on the street, where only his speed of foot saved him. After that, it was dangerous even to walk past the house, because the governor had many servants. He met her once more in the Catholic church. She noticed him and smiled pleasantly, as if he were an old acquaintance. He saw her in passing yet once again. And soon after that the governor of Kovno left Kiev and, instead of the beautiful, black-eyed Polish girl, a fat face appeared in her window. That's what Andrei was thinking of, his eyes lowered to his horse's mane.

And meanwhile the steppe had taken them all into her green embrace, and the high grass, closing around them, hid them from view, so that only their black Cossack caps flashed among its green tips.

"Why so quiet, lads?" Bulba said finally, coming out of his own reverie. "You're like a lot of monks! Come on, all together, the hell with thinking! Take your pipes in your mouths and let's light up, let's spur on our horses, let's fly so fast that the birds won't be able to overtake us!"

And the Cossacks, bending over their horses' necks, disappeared completely into the grass. Now not even their black caps could be seen and only a ribbon of parted grass marked their swift passage.

The sun had long been up in the clear sky and was pouring its warm, life-giving light out over the steppe. Everything that was dim and gloomy in the Cossacks vanished and their hearts stirred like waking birds.

The farther they went the more beautiful grew the steppe. In those years, the entire southern part of Russia, all the way to the Black Sea, was a green, virgin wilderness. Never had a plow driven through the long waves of wild growth and only the horses, hidden in it as if among the trees of the forest, trampled the tall grass. There could be nothing more beautiful in the world: the visible surface of the earth looked like a golden green ocean, its waves topped by multicolored spume. Through the tall, slender stems of the grass showed sky-blue, marine, and purple star thistles;

yellow broom thrust up its pyramidal head; the white parasols of Queen Anne's lace gleamed near an ear of wheat that had appeared there God knows how and was now growing heavy. Partridges scurried among the thin stalks of the steppe plants, their necks outstretched, and in the sky hawks hung immobile on their outspread wings, eyes glued on the ground; and from the grass rose a steppe gull and bathed herself luxuriously in the blue waves of the air. Now she dissolved in the soaring heights; now she re-appeared like a little comma; now, as she turned, her wings reflected a ray of sunlight.

They stopped for only a few minutes to eat. The ten Cossacks who were accompanying them dismounted, got out the wooden casks of brandy and the pumpkin shells that they used as drinking vessels. They had nothing but bread and fat and dry biscuits to eat and had only one round of brandy—just enough to sustain themselves, because Taras Bulba allowed no one to get drunk while travel-ing. After that they kept riding until nightfall.

In the evening, the steppe was completely transformed: the whole multicolored area caught the last bright reflection of the sun and then began to darken. They could see the shadows invading it and turning it dark green. Fragrance from the plants increased—every flower, every blade of grass released its incense and the whole steppe was bathed in a wild, noble aroma. Right across the steadily darkening azure of the sky, bright pink and golden stripes appeared as if from under the brush of some Titan. Here and there whitish transparent cloudlets floated, pushed along a fresh little breeze that tenderly rippled the tops of the grass and almost imperceptibly tickled the cheeks of the riders. The daytime music was replaced by a different one: spotted marmots crept out of their holes, rose on their hindlegs and filled the steppe with their whistling. The whirr of grass-hoppers gradually dominated the other sounds. Sometimes, like a silver trumpet, the cry of a swan reached them from some distant lake.

They stopped in the middle of the steppe and selected a spot to spend the night. They lit a fire and hung a pot over it in which they cooked their supper. The steam rose into the air in a slanting column. When they had eaten, the Cossacks hobbled their horses and left them loose to graze, and then lay down themselves. They slept on their coats

with the stars staring into their eyes. Their ears took in an
infinity of little noises made by the insects teeming in the
grass: buzzing, whirring, chirping, clicking, humming—
they resounded, purified by the fresh air, and lulled them
to sleep. And when one of them got up in the night he had
in front of him a steppe sparkling with the gleaming dots of
fireflies. Here and there the night sky would be dimly lit
by the faraway glow of dry reeds burning in the fields and
along the riverbanks and then a dark flight of northbound
geese would suddenly appear in the reddish silver light
and they became pink handkerchiefs flying in a dark sky.

They continued their journey without incident. They
did not come across a single tree. All the way there was
the same boundless, free, beautiful steppe. Only from time
to time, could they make out the faraway roof of a forest
that framed the banks of the Dnieper. Only once did Taras
point out to his sons a black spot bobbing up and down in
the grass and say:

"Look, boys, see over there? That's a Tartar and he's
galloping."

The Tartar stopped at a good distance, turned his small
head so that they could see his drooping mustache, and
looked straight at them out of his slanting narrow eyes.
Then he sniffed the air like a greyhound, and, seeing that
there were thirteen of the Cossacks he had stumbled on,
disappeared in the grass.

"Try to catch him, boys! No, better not even try. You'll
never make it, his horse is even faster than my Devil."

After that Bulba took certain precautions, fearing a Tartar ambush. They changed direction and rode toward a
tributary of the Dnieper called the Tatarka. When they
reached it, they entered the water, horses and all, and swam
downstream for quite a while before climbing out onto the
bank again and turning directly toward their destination.

And three days later, they were almost there. The air
suddenly became cooler and they felt the proximity of the
Dnieper. Soon the big river appeared in the distance, a
black ribbon against the horizon. It breathed on them its
cold, damp, watery breath, and, as they drew still nearer, it
suddenly filled half the earth's surface. This was the part
of the river's course where it finally escapes the narrow-
banked confines of the rapids and broadens out freely like
a sea, the spot where the islands scattered in it push its

waters far over the low banks, which have neither rocks nor steep places to contain them. The Cossacks dismounted, embarked on the ferry and three hours later reached the shores of the island of Khortitsy, where at that time the constantly shifting Camp Zaporozhe was situated.

A group of people on shore were arguing with the ferryman. The Cossacks tightened their saddle girths and straightened their horses' bridles. Taras stood straight, hitched his belt, and swaggeringly smoothed his long mustache. His sons also gave their appearance a once-over, feeling a strange sort of joy mixed with fear. Then they all rode off toward the camp.

Within about half a mile of it, they came to a settlement. They were deafened by the clang of fifty blacksmiths' hammers banging against twenty-five anvils sunk into the earth. Strong tanners sat under awnings softening oxhides with their big hands; merchants sat in booths with piles of flint and powder before them; an Armenian displayed expensive kerchiefs; a Tartar turned pieces of mutton on spits around a fire; a Jew, his head thrust forward, slowly poured liquor out of a cask. Then they came across the first Zaporozhe Cossack. He was sleeping in the middle of the road, his arms and legs outstretched. Taras stopped to admire him.

"Just look at him lying there! A stout lad, by God!"

The sight was quite impressive. The man lay there like a lion, the long tuft of hair above his forehead was thrown back like a lion's mane, his trousers, of expensive, blood-red cloth, were bespattered with tar, a mark of their wearer's utter disdain for them. Having admired the Cossack to their hearts' content, the Bulba party passed on through the narrow streets filled with craftsmen practicing their trades on the spot, people of all nationalities who lived on the fairlike outskirts of the camp, outskirts which dressed, fed, and equipped the camp-dwellers who knew only how to carouse and to shoot.

At last they left this behind and came upon a few scattered barracks covered with turf or, in Tartar fashion, with felt. Some of these were surrounded by cannon. Here there were none of the small houses with awnings in front of them, like those they had seen in the outskirts. A low wall and a ditch without sentries attested to an incredible recklessness. A few Zaporozhe Cossacks, lying in the very middle of the street with their pipes between their teeth, looked at them indifferently without budging. The Bulba party carefully made their way among the reclining bodies and Taras kept saying, "Greetings, gentlemen," and they replied, "Greetings to you, too."

They found groups of brightly clad men scattered all over the central square. By their sunburned faces it could be seen that these were battle-hardened veterans who had been exposed to all sorts of weather during raids and campaigns. This was Camp Zaporozhe, the nest from which the strong, bold Cossacks took off and rode all over the Ukraine.

On the square where the Council of the Camp usually assembled, a Cossack, stripped to the waist, sat on a barrel sewing up holes in his shirt. Further, their path was barred by a group of musicians in the middle of which a young fellow, his hat clinging somehow to the very back of his head, was doing a wild Cossack dance and shouting:

"Faster! Faster! Go on, Thomas, give more vodka to these Orthodox Christians! Faster!"

And Thomas, a Cossack with a blackened eye, complied, pouring out a huge tot of vodka for everyone upon request. Around the young dancer four older Cossacks who had been jigging their feet in short, brisk steps suddenly leaped into the air, landing almost on the heads of the musicians and making the firm soil ring resoundingly under their silver-shod heels.

But the young Cossack shouted the loudest and jumped the highest. His tuft streamed through the air, his bare muscular chest, covered with sweat, was completely exposed, his thick jacket flung wide open.

"At least take your jacket off," Taras said finally, "it's fairly steaming."

"I can't," the Cossack shouted without stopping. "What I take off, I drink!"

The lad had already lost his hat. His belt was gone too and so was his neckerchief. All had gone the way of vodka.

The crowd was growing around him. More and more people joined in the dance and it was fascinating to see how these men succumbed to the beat of this free, wild Cossack dance which bears the name of its inventors.

"If it weren't for these damned horses, I'd have joined them," Taras exclaimed.

Meanwhile, he had begun to recognize in the gathering

venerable gray heads who had been prominent chiefs and were respected by one and all. Ostap and Andrei heard nothing but greetings:

"How're you making out, Pesherits? Hello, Kozolup!"

"God! Where've you been, Taras?"

"And you, what are you doing here, Doloto?"

And these adventurers, gathered from all the corners of the free Cossack world, embraced one another fondly and Taras kept firing questions about common friends:

"Heard anything of Pidsishok? What about Borodavka? What happened to Koloper?"

And the answers Taras obtained were to the effect that Borodavka had been hanged in Tolopan, that they had torn Koloper's hide off him at Kizkir, that Pidsishok's head had been sent to Constantinople in a barrel of brine. And the old Bulba lowered his own mournfully and kept repeating sadly:

"A great Cossack, what a great Cossack he was. . . ."

Chapter 3

Taras Bulba and his sons had been at the camp for almost a week. Ostap and Andrei spent little time on military exercises. The Cossacks of that era did not bother with them much, believing that experience in action was sufficient training for a young man. And, indeed, the fighting was almost uninterrupted. It bored the Cossacks to exercise their warlike skills during the quiet intervals. They did some target shooting, perhaps, or held horse races, or pursued some animal across the steppe. And the rest of their time was devoted to revelry, which was considered a mark of manliness and generosity. The camp presented an incredible sight: an endless noisy party. A few Cossacks ran small shops, some others practiced certain crafts, but the overwhelming majority caroused from morning to night, as long as there was an opportunity and as long as the wealth they had acquired had not passed into other hands. This permanent party had something bewitching about it. This was no gathering of people drinking to forget their misery—it was the simple release of an exuberant gaiety. Everyone entering the camp shed all his erstwhile preoccupations. In fact, one might say, he spat on his past and gave himself unstintingly to the brotherhood of reckless revelers who, like himself, were quite unconcerned about home, family, relatives, in fact about anything except the open sky and eternal gaiety. This was what produced the insane exhilaration that otherwise would have been impossible. The stories which circulated among the gathering, lazily sprawled out on the ground, were often so comical and told so vividly that it required a great deal of self-control to maintain the expressionless composure, without

so much a twitching the mustache, that has become
characteristic of the southern Russian, distinguishing him
from his northern brethren. And with all this, it was not
the gloomy drinking of a man trying to forget himself
among gloomy companions; it was rather like a bunch of
schoolboys having a wildly good time. The only difference
was that instead of sitting with a textbook and listening to
some teacher's boring explanations, they went out on five
thousand horses to raid the outside world, and, instead of
playing ball in a closed field, they had playing fields with
unguarded boundaries near which they might catch sight
of a rapidly vanishing Tartar head and from which the
Turk frowned grimly at them from under his green turban. Another difference was that while they had been
forced to share the community of school, to come here they
had left their fathers and mothers of their own free will,
sometimes had even fled their homes. Some of these men
had already felt the rope round their necks and then, instead of pale death, they had found life here in its full flow.
Some of them, following a noble tradition, could never
keep a kopek in their pockets; to some, before coming
here, a ruble had seemed a fortune and you could have
turned their pockets inside out without ever hearing anything fall. In the camp were to be found former seminary
students who had been unable to stand the academic switch
and had never learned one letter of the alphabet and others
who knew Horace and Cicero and what the Roman republic was all about. There were many officers here who were
later to distinguish themselves in the army of the King,
many who felt that it made no difference whom and where
they fought as long as they had a chance to fight. Some had
come to the camp just so that later they would be able to
say that they had been there and were therefore hardened
warriors. But, as a matter of fact, who wasn't there? The
strange republic was a product of the century, a place
where those who sought gold coins, rich brocades, golden
cups, and precious jewels could always find employment.
Only worshipers of women found nothing there for them
—no woman was allowed even in the vicinity of the camp.

Ostap and Andrei found it strange that people kept
pouring into the camp without anyone ever asking where
they had come from or even what they were called. It was
as though they were returning to a home they'd left an

hour before. The newcomer simply reported to the headman, who usually said:

"Welcome. Do you believe in Christ?"

"I do."

"And in the Holy Trinity?"

"I do."

"And you attend church, don't you?"

"I do."

"Cross yourself then!"

And when the newcomer had crossed himself, the headman would tell him:

"Fine. Go and pick yourself a unit, whichever you prefer."

And that was that.

The whole camp attended the same church and was ready to defend it to the last breath, although none of them wanted to hear anything about fasting or abstinence.

Typical of the Zaporożhe Cossacks was their refusal to bargain. They would thrust a hand into a pocket and whatever it happened to grab was paid to the merchant. That is why, prompted by the prospect of gain, Jews, Armenians, and Tartars accepted the risks involved in living on the fringe of the camp. And the life of these merchants was quite precarious. They were like people living at the foot of Vesuvius, because whenever the Cossacks were short of cash they tore the shops apart and took the goods for nothing.

The camp consisted of more than sixty military units —troops—each with its own barracks, which were somewhat like independent republics and even more like boarding schools where the children could find a bed ready and meals. No one acquired or kept anything for his personal use; everything was handed over to the troop chief. He was entrusted with everyone's money, clothes, provisions, and even firewood. Often there were quarrels between troops which usually turned into free-for-alls. The inhabitants of two barracks would pour out into the square, belabor one another with their fists until one side gained the upper hand. Then the drinking bouts took over. This was the life the camp had to offer young men.

Ostap and Andrei flung themselves into it headlong, with all the enthusiasm of youth, and soon forgot their home, the seminary, and all that had touched them before. Everything fascinated them: the revelry that went on around them and the uncomplicated traditions of self-government which at times seemed to them rather severe for such a free republic. When, for instance, a Cossack stole something, even a thing of little value, it was considered a disgrace to the whole Cossack community. The culprit was tied to the pillar of shame and a club was placed at his feet. Each passerby was obliged to strike him one blow until he was beaten to death. A debtor who did not pay up was shackled to a cannon and had to sit there until one of his comrades decided to buy him out by settling his debt. But what produced the grimmest impression upon Andrei was the horrible execution of a man for murder. They dug a pit in front of the condemned man, then lowered him into it and on top of him placed the coffin containing the body of his victim. Then both were covered with earth. For a long time afterward, the youth relived the grim ceremony and saw the face of the man buried alive with the terrible coffin.

Soon the two brothers gained good standing among the Cossacks. They rode out into the steppe with their troops to shoot deer, wild goats, and the infinite variety of steppe birds. At other times they went to the lakes, rivers, and streams to lay nets and to pull in a rich catch on which the whole troop would feast. And although there was no way to test the value of a Cossack directly, they soon stood out among the young men because of their reckless daring as well as their all-round achievements. They could shoot fast and straight and swim across the Dnieper in a strong current—the sort of things that made a newcomer acceptable in Cossack society.

But the old Taras had other plans for them. This idleness was not to his taste. He was spoiling for action and kept thinking up ways to draw the camp into the sort of daring venture in which a man could really show his mettle. Finally, one day, he went to the headman and said:

"Say, headman, isn't it time for our Cossacks to set out and enjoy a bit of fighting?"

"Nowhere to set out for," the headman said, taking his short pipe out of his mouth and spitting sideways.

"What d'you mean nowhere? We could go for the Turks or have a poke at the Tartars."

"Turks, Tartars—can't be done," the headman said coldly, and pushed his short pipe back into his mouth.

"Why can't be done?"

"Just so. We've promised the Sultan peace."

"But he's an infidel, isn't he? Remember, God Himself, in His Holy Scriptures, ordered us to fight the infidels. You know that."

"We've no right. Perhaps we could've if we hadn't sworn by our faith. But now it's impossible. Can't be done."

"How can you say impossible? I've got two sons, two young men, see. Neither of them has seen war yet, and you try to tell me that we've no right. Then there's no need for Cossacks, is that it?"

"Well, we mustn't attack."

"Does that mean that our young Cossack manpower is to be wasted? That a man should die like a dog without having done his duty to his motherland and to Christendom, and, in general, without having been of any use? What are we on this earth for? What do we live for?"

The headman did not answer. He was a stubborn Cossack. For a short while he remained silent altogether, then he said:

"And I still say—no war."

"No war?" Taras insisted.

"Right."

"Not even a hope?"

"Not even a hope."

Taras thought, "I'll show you yet, you scrawny old cockerel," and decided to teach the headman a lesson.

He took a few men into his confidence and organized a drinking bout, after which several drunken Cossacks rushed to the square where the kettledrums stood that were used to beat out the general assembly. Not finding the drumsticks, which were in the custody of the official drummer, they grabbed pieces of wood and started banging on the kettledrums. The first to arrive was the tall, one-eyed drummer. He came running, rubbing his single eye, which looked very sleepy.

"Who the hell dared to beat the kettledrums?" he wanted to know.

"Shut up. Go get your goddamn drumsticks and start beating when you're told!" the drunks told him.

The drummer produced the sticks from his pocket, knowing only too well where this sort of thing was likely to lead him. The drums sounded and soon black groups of Cossacks were pouring into the square like bumblebees. A circle was formed and, after the third roll of the drums, the elders made their appearance. The headman, his mace, the symbol of his office, in his hand, the judge with the seal, the scribe with an inkpot, and the senior troop chief with his staff. The headman and the elders removed their fur hats and bowed in all four directions to the assembled Cossacks, who stood proudly, their arms akimbo.

'What does this assembly mean? What do you want, gentlemen?" the headman said. Shouts and curses drowned him out.

"Put down your mace! Put it down, you son of a toad, put it down immediately! We don't want you any longer!" some voices shouted from the crowd. Some of the Cossacks from troops that happened to be sober objected and soon everything was a fist fight between drunk and sober troops.

The headman was on the point of saying something, but, knowing that the crazed mob might beat him to death, as almost always happened if resistance was shown, bowed low, put down his mace and disappeared in the crowd.

"And do you wish, gentlemen, that we too should give up our symbols of office?" the judge asked, and he, the scribe, and the senior troop chief made as if to lay down seal, inkpot, and staff.

"No, no, you stay. We only wanted to get rid of the headman—he's an old woman and we need a man for the job."

"Who, then, is to be the new headman?" one of the elders inquired.

"We want Kukubenko!" some shouted.

"No, no! Not Kukubenko! It's too early for him yet! His mother's milk is still dribbling from his mouth."

"Shilo! Let Shilo be headman!"

"Take your Shilo and get out of here! What kind of a Cossack is he? Remember, he was caught red-handed, stealing like a Tartar!"

"Stuff that no-good Shilo in a bag and drown him!"

"Borodaty, what about Borodaty?"

"No Borodaty for me! Off with him to the accursed mother of hell!"

Taras Bulba was elbowing his way through the crowd whispering into many ears: "Kirdiaga, Kirdiaga, demand Kirdiaga . . ." and the crowd shouted:

"Kirdiaga! Kirdiaga! Borodaty-Borodaty-Borodaty! Kirdiaga! Shilo! To hell with Shilo! Kirdiaga. . . ."

When they heard their names shouted, the candidates immediately left the crowd lest people should suspect that they were taking a direct part in promoting their own election.

"Kirdiaga—Kirdiaga!" The name seemed to resound the loudest.

"Borodaty!"

The fist fight that ensued brought Kirdiaga the headmanship.

"Go and fetch Kirdiaga!"

A dozen men detached themselves from the crowd. They could hardly stand on their feet, having managed to take on an enormous load. They went to announce his election to Kirdiaga.

Kirdiaga, an elderly man who still nevertheless had a firm grip on things, was sitting in his barracks as though completely unaware of what had happened.

"What, gentlemen, can I do for you?"

"Come. You've been elected headman."

"Oh no, no! I don't deserve the honor. I lack the wisdom for such a post. Is it possible that, in the whole camp, they couldn't find anyone better qualified?"

"Go on. Do as you're told," the Cossacks shouted, grabbing him under the arms. He tried to backpedal with his feet but was finally dragged to the assembly square to the accompaniment of curses, pushes, and kicks.

"Don't try to get out of it, son of a toad; accept the honor when it's offered, you dog."

When he was in the middle of the circle, those who had brought him addressed the crowd:

"What do you say, gentlemen, are you wiliing to accept Kirdiaga as your headman?"

"We are willing! We are willing, all of us!" the crowd howled ar.d their shouts thundered for a long time over the square.

One of the elders picked up the mace and handed it to the newly elected headman. According to custom, Kirdiaga refused it. Offered it a second time, he again refused, only accepting it at the third offering. A roar of approval came from the crowd and again their shouts resounded all over the square. Then four of the oldest Cossacks in the camp, the four men with the whitest mustaches and the whitest tufts, stepped out of the crowd. They weren't really all that old but there were none older in the camp—the Zaporozhe Cossacks never died of old age and these four were the oldest available. Each of them bent down, took a handful of earth, which, since it had rained that day, had turned to mud, and placed it on Kirdiaga's head. The wet earth ran off his head, down his cheeks and his mustache and muddied his whole face. But Kirdiaga stood there without budging and thanked the Cossacks for the honor shown him.

Thus the rowdy election was completed, and if anyone was pleased with the result it was Taras Bulba. To start with he had taught a lesson to the former headman. Then, Kirdiaga was an old friend. They had shared many land and sea campaigns, and had past dangers and hardships in common. The crowd scattered and proceeded forthwith to celebrate the election of the new headman. This celebration exceeded anything that Ostap and Andrei had witnessed thus far. Liquor stores were taken to pieces and vodka, beer, and mead were seized without payment, the owners considering themselves lucky if they got away with their hides intact. The whole night was spent in shouting, singing and rejoicing, and the crescent moon looked down for a long time on bands of musicians parading in the streets with balalaikas, guitars, flutes, and tambourines, along with the church choir kept in the camp to sing songs glorifying the exploits of the Cossacks, in addition to their church singing.

In the end, alcohol and fatigue began to overcome their stubborn heads. Now here, now there, a Cossack would collapse on the ground, and a friend, deeply touched and with tears in his eyes, would embrace him as a brother and fall beside him. Here, a whole group would lie down in a heap; there, a provident man would carefully pick out a log to put under his head. The last of them, the one who had the strongest head, still went on giving a disconnected speech. But in the end the spirits got him too. He fell and moved no more. The entire camp was now asleep.

Chapter 4

The very next day, Taras Bulba conferred with the new headman about stirring up the Cossacks for some venture or other. The headman was shrewd and knew Cossacks through and through. At first he said:

"An oath cannot be violated. It's out of the question."

Then, after a pause, he added:

"Never mind. We'll manage something without violating our oath. Assemble the people . . . I mean, not on my order, just by themselves, you understand. . . . You can arrange it, I'm sure. Then the elders and I, we'll happen to come along, as if we knew nothing about it."

And within an hour the kettledrums rolled. All at once, hundreds upon hundreds of Cossack caps poured out onto the square. Some of the Cossacks were drunk, of course, and others unreasonable. A murmur arose:

"Who sounded the assembly? Who ordered it?"

There was no reply. But from various corners, voices were raised:

"Cossack energy is wasted without war! The elders have grown sluggish lying around! Their eyes are buried in fat! There's no justice in the world!"

At first the other Cossacks listened. Then they began to repeat:

"True enough—no justice in the world!"

The elders appeared to be thunderstruck at such remarks. Finally the headman came forward and said:

"Cossacks! Allow me to speak."

"Speak!"

"Probably, gentlemen, you know better than anyone else that many of our Cossacks have got into debt to the tavernkeepers, to the Jews, as well as to their brother Cossacks, so that now not even the devil will give them credit. Then, we have among us many lads who have never seen war. And you know, gentlemen, a young man cannot be brought up without war. How can he become a Cossack if he has never fought the heathen?"

"He puts it just right," Bulba thought.

"Don't imagine for a moment, gentlemen, that I am saying this because I intend to break the truce. God forbid! I'm just stating facts. Now, let's take our church. It's in a disgraceful state. Look how many years, by the Grace of God, the camp has stood here, and, to this day, not only the church but even the icons themselves have been left undecorated. If at least someone had wrought a silver frame for them. But all the church receives is what Cossacks leave it in their wills. And you know yourselves that that's not much, because they mostly drink up just about everything they have while they're still alive. So I'm not saying this because I want to make war on the infidels. We have sworn by our faith that we won't start a fight against the Sultan, and it'd be a great sin on our part to break our oath."

"What's he getting it all mixed up for?" Bulba muttered under his breath.

"So you see, gentlemen, while our code of honor prevents us from starting a new war, in my humble opinion our young men could still go out in the boats and pay a little visit to the coast of Asia Minor. Now what would you think of that, gentlemen?"

"Lead us, lead us all!" they shouted from all over the square. "We're ready to lay down our lives for the Faith!"

The headman was alarmed. He did not at all want to arouse the whole of Camp Zaporozhe. To break the peace in that way seemed wrong to him.

"Gentlemen! Allow me to speak once more!" he cried.

"We've heard enough," shouted the Cossacks, "you couldn't put it any better."

"Well, if that's it—so be it. You're giving the orders. And it says in the Scriptures that the voice of the people is the voice of God. No one is wiser than the people. I must only warn you, gentlemen, that the Sultan won't let the pleasures our young lads will indulge in go unanswered. But by then we would be prepared, our forces would be fresh and afraid of no one. But if we all went, the Tartars might attack in our absence. They're just the Turks' dogs and they wouldn't attack openly; they won't dare come when the master is home, but they'll bite at his heels from behind, and painfully too. And if it comes to that, to tell the truth we haven't enough boats or powder for everyone to go. But I'll gladly go, nevertheless—I'm at your service."

The shrewd headman fell silent. The Cossacks split into little groups and began to talk the matter over. The troop chiefs conferred. Fortunately, not too many of them were drunk and so they decided to abide by the headman's sensible advice.

Right away, several men crossed to the opposite bank of the Dnieper, where the army's stores were kept in inaccessible hiding places, under the water and in the reeds. This was where the treasury chest and a part of the captured arms were secreted. The others all rushed to inspect the boats and fit them out for the trip. In no time, a crowd of people thronged the bank. Carpenters appeared carrying axes. Weather-beaten, broad-shouldered, sturdy old Cossacks, some with black mustaches, others already turning gray, stood in the water with their trousers rolled up to their knees and pulled the boats down from the bank into the water. Others collected lumber and all sorts of wood. They planked the boats, and, turning them bottom up, calked and tarred them. They lashed long-stemmed reeds to them, Cossack fashion, so that they would not be sunk by sea waves. Farther along the shore they built fires and boiled pitch in copper caldrons to pour over the boats. The old and the experienced guided the young. Banging, hammering, and shouting filled the air and the whole bank seemed to sway and move, as though it had come alive.

At that moment, a large ferryboat came alongside. The knot of people standing on it had been waving at the shore even while quite a distance away. Now one could make out that they were Cossacks. Their coats were torn and their disheveled appearance—many of them had nothing but their shirts and the short pipes between their teeth—indicated that they had just escaped from some disaster or that they had been on a real binge and had squandered even the clothes on their backs. A broad-shouldered, stocky Cossack of about fifty stepped forward and started shouting and waving his hands, but his words could not be heard over the din ashore.

"What happened to you?" the headman asked when the ferry pulled in. All the workers, stopping and raising their axes and chisels, looked up expectantly.

"Disaster!" the stocky Cossack shouted from the ferry.

"What disaster?"

"Cossacks—gentlemen—may I speak?"

"Speak!"

"But perhaps you'd rather call your assembly."

"Speak! We're all here."

They all crowded closely together.

"Have you really heard nothing of what's going on around us?"

"What do you mean?"

"What do I mean? The Tartars must have stuffed your ears with mud."

"Go on, speak, man. What's been happening?"

"Things are going on the like of which no living Christian has ever seen before."

"Tell us what's happening, you dog!" shouted someone in the crowd, fast losing patience.

"The time has come upon us when our churches are no longer our own."

"What do you mean by that?"

"They've been mortgaged to the Jews. Nowadays, if you don't pay up, you just can't say mass in 'em."

"What are you babbling about?"

"And if some dog of a Jew doesn't first make his sign with his dirty hand on the holy Easter cake, then it can't be blessed."

"He's lying, brothers—it can't be that an unclean Jew could be allowed to put his sign on the holy Easter cake."

"Listen! That's not the half of it. The Catholic priests are riding all over the Ukraine in carriages. And it's not the fact that they travel in carriages that's so terrible but that they're drawn not by horses but by Orthodox Christians! And even that's not all. They say that Jewish women are making themselves skirts out of our priests' vestments. That's what's going on in the Ukraine, gentlemen! And you sit here in Camp Zaporozhe and have yourselves a good time. It looks like the Tartars have scared you so much that you've neither eyes nor ears—nothing—and you just don't know what's going on in the world!"

"Stop, stop!" the headman interrupted him. Up till then, he had been standing with his eyes lowered to the ground, as indeed had all the Cossacks. In important matters, they never gave way to their first impulses, but kept silent. But their anger was growing.

"And now, tell me, what—may the devil boil you alive —what have you been doing yourselves over there? Surely you must have had your sabers? How did you allow such lawlessness?"

"How did we allow it? I'd like to see you try to take care of fifty thousand Poles alone. And then, let's face it, there were treacherous dogs among our own people who switched to the Roman faith."

"And what about your headman and your chiefs—what about them?"

"What about them? Well, God preserve us from such a fate!"

"What do you mean by that?"

"I mean that by now our headman, roasted in a copper pot, lies in Warsaw, while the hands and the heads of our chiefs are being exhibited in all the fairs. That's what about our chiefs!"

The crowd froze. Over all its length the bank became dead-quiet. Then suddenly it came violently alive. It seemed as if the whole bank had burst out talking.

"What! Jews renting our own churches to us!"

"Whoever heard of papist priests harnessing Orthodox Christians!"

"Incredible! How can such things be tolerated from filthy unbelievers!"

"You realize what they did to the headman and the chiefs?"

"No, no, no! We won't stand for it! And on Russian soil! We won't, we won't, we won't!"

The words flew over the heads of the Cossacks and they were not an expression of superficial agitation. Their tempers were becoming heated now, slowly and thoroughly, and they were going to retain their heat for a long time.

"String up the Jews!" a shout came from the crowd. "That'll teach 'em to sew skirts from the cassocks of our priests! That'll stop 'em from tracing signs on the Easter cakes! Let's drown the whole bunch of unbelievers in the Dnieper!"

This little harangue made by somebody in the crowd had the effect of lightning striking dry wood. The throng stirred, then rushed toward the outskirts of the camp with the intent of slaughtering all Jews.

The wretched sons of Israel tried to hide in empty vodka barrels, under stoves, and some even crawled under the skirts of their women, but the Cossacks always found them.

"Gentlemen, gentlemen!" shouted a tall, thin, sticklike Jew whose fear-distorted features stuck up above the heads of his comrades. "Give us a chance to speak and you'll learn something important, something you don't even suspect. . . ."

"Let him have his say," Bulba said. He always liked to hear out the accused.

"Thank you, gentlemen," the Jew said, "you are extremely fair and generous—how could we possibly have a bad word to say about Zaporozhe Cossacks? Those who are renting churches in the Ukraine have nothing to do with us. They are no Jews, I assure you. God knows what they are. Here, ask them. I'm telling the truth, am I not, Isaac? You tell him, Shmul."

"He's telling the truth—he's right," Isaac and Shmul confirmed with bloodless lips.

"We've never had any contact whatsoever with your enemies, and as for the Catholics—we don't want anything to do with them, may they see the devil in their dreams! And the Zaporozhe Cossacks—we treat them like our own brothers——"

"What? What's he saying? Brothers, did you say? . . . Damn you, Jew! Into the Dnieper with the lot of 'em, let's drown the unbelieving dogs!"

These words, shouted by someone in the crowd, were like a signal and Jews were seized and hurled into the choppy river. Frightened wails came from the water, but the grim Cossacks just laughed at the sight of legs encased in shoes and stockings kicking in the air.

The tall thin Jew who had spoken tore free from those holding him by slipping out of his coat, and rushed up to Taras Bulba.

"Sir," he said imploringly, "I used to know your brother,

the late Dorosh. There was a warrior for you! I gave eight hundred sequins to pay his ransom when he was captured by the Turks. . . ."

"You knew my brother? What's your name?"

"Yankel."

"All right," Taras said. "Listen," he said to the Cossacks, "you'll have plenty of time to hang him. Let me have him for the moment."

Taras led Yankel to his wagons, by which his Cossacks were standing.

"All right, climb under that cart and stay there, and you, brothers, see that he stays there."

After which Taras went to the assembly square into which the crowd was now flowing.

The preparation and equipping of the boats were abandoned because the Cossacks were now faced with a land campaign rather than a sea venture and what they needed was not boats but horses and wagons.

Now there was unanimity. Everyone wanted to go, old and young. The headman, the council of the elders, and the barrack chiefs—all agreed, and with popular approval, that they would drive straight for Poland to avenge the insults to the faith and to Cossack honor, to capture a lot of booty, to set fire to Polish cities, villages and wheat fields, to spread the renown of the Cossack army far and wide.

Everyone began to prepare arms and equipment. The headman grew by a whole foot. He was no longer the subtle interpreter of the unreasonable whims of an exuberant bunch of people—he had become an absolute, despotic ruler who only gave orders. When he spoke even the hottest-tempered Cossacks stood quietly with lowered heads, not daring to lift their eyes, and the headman spoke unhurriedly, as an experienced Cossack who knew how to carry out his own well-devised plans.

"Inspect your gear thoroughly," he said. "See that your wagons are in good order, the axles properly greased. Do not take too many clothes with you: one extra shirt, two pairs of trousers. Bring two cooking pots of cereal. No more. We'll carry the necessary provisions in the wagons. Each man is to have two horses. We'll also take with us two hundred oxen—we'll need them at the fords and in the marshes. And, above all, gentlemen, I want you to maintain discipline. I know that some of you are greedy enough to stuff silk or velvet into your boots rather than leave such things behind. Well, you're not going to. You'll throw away all those skirts and things and take only good weapons and gold and silver coins as well, because they occupy little space in proportion to their usefulness. And now I warn you—if one of you gets drunk, there'll be no trial; he'll have his head put in a noose and be dragged like a dog behind a baggage wagon no matter if his past record is the most glorious imaginable. Then he'll get a bullet through his head and be left without burial to be eaten by scavengers, because a man who drinks on the march doesn't deserve a Christian burial. Young men, you'll obey your seniors. Now, if a ball grazes you, if you get nicked by a saber slash, in the head or anywhere else, don't let it stop you. Mix a little gunpowder in a cup of brandy, swallow it down, and you'll be all right—you won't even have a fever. As to the wound, if it's not too deep, just pick up a handful of earth, mix it with some spit and then the bandage won't stick to it. All right, get to work, lads. Don't rush though—do things thoroughly. Get moving."

And when the headman had finished, the Cossacks immediately became busy. The whole camp grew sober. It seemed impossible to believe that drunkards had ever been found among its inhabitants. Some repaired the hoops on wagon wheels, others changed axles, still others carried bags with food supplies. From every side could be heard horses' hoofbeats, shots fired in practice, swords clanging, oxen mooing, wagons creaking as they were turned over, the businesslike exchange of words, and sharp cries urging on the beasts.

And soon the Cossack caravan was spread out over the plain; anyone wishing to race all the way from its head to its tail would have been out of breath before he reached his goal.

In the small wooden church the priest conducted the services, and, as each in turn kissed the cross, he sprinkled holy water on him. As the caravan moved out, Cossacks turned to look back at the camp and many muttered:

"Good-bye, Mother, may God keep you from all harm."

Passing through the outskirts, Taras saw that his protégé Yankel had already managed to erect a stall with an awning for himself and was selling flints, handfuls of gunpowder in paper cones, and other military items—even bread rolls and dumplings.

"What the hell's he waiting here for?" Taras thought, and riding up to him, he said:

"Fool, do you want to be shot?"

Yankel made him a sign with his hands that he wanted to tell him some secret, and, coming very close, said:

"Please keep it to yourself, sir, but among the wagons there's one of mine with all sorts of supplies that'll be needed during the campaign, and I'll supply you at lower prices than you'll be able to find anywhere else. I swear it, sir."

Taras shrugged, marveling at this sample of Jewish enterprise, and rode on toward his wagons.

Chapter 5

Soon all southwest Poland was a prey to fear. Everywhere the alarm went out: "Cossacks! The Cossacks are coming!" Everyone who could fled. In those unsettled years, people just picked themselves up and scattered. At that time, men built neither fortresses nor castles. Each man set up a flimsy hut for himself, figuring to use it for a short time only, thinking to himself:

"Why should I waste time and money building myself a real house? The Tartars'll raze it in their next raid anyway."

Everyone took fright at the news of the Cossack advance. Some swapped oxen and plows for a horse and a gun and set out to join the armies; others fled, driving off their cattle and taking along everything that could be carried. There were some who resisted the invaders, weapons in hand, but mostly people fled even before they arrived. They all knew that it was almost impossible to get along with the violent crowd known as the Zaporozhe Band, a force which for all its apparent wild disorderliness was actually very thoughtfully organized and well disciplined in time of war. The mounted Cossacks rode without burdening or straining their horses; those afoot calmly followed the wagons. They moved only at night, resting during the daytime in a concealed spot or in the forest. The main body was preceded by reconnaissance patrols sent out to find out what was what and who was where.

Often the army would appear in places where it was least expected. They would appear from nowhere and then everything around was doomed. Fire devoured whole villages, the cattle and the horses that were not driven off with the

army were slaughtered on the spot. They seemed to be at
a wild party rather than on a military expedition. Today
one's hair would stand on end at the horrible marks of
bestiality that the Zaporozhe Cossacks of that wild century
left in their wake. Babes with broken skulls, women with
breasts cut off, the skin from the soles of the feet to the
knees flayed from the legs of those who were left alive. In
brief, the Cossacks paid back with interest the horrors they
had suffered themselves. The abbot of a monastery sent a
couple of monks to them with a reminder that there was
an agreement between the Zaporozhe Cossacks and the
King of Poland and that they were breaking it and at the
same time violating the rights of innocent people.

"Assure your abbot," the headman told these messen-
gers, "that he's seen nothing yet. We're just lighting our
pipes."

And soon afterward the imposing Gothic abbey was
blazing wildly, its huge carved windows looking grimly out
at the world through the fiery flames.

Monks, Jews, and women crowded into towns where
some hope could be placed in the garrison and the city
ramparts. The belated rescue forces dispatched by the
Polish government either never found the Cossack troops
or, when they did, beat hasty retreats after brief encounters,
fleeing on their swift horses. But sometimes it happened
that officers of the King who had previous triumphs over
the Zaporozhe Cossacks to their credit joined forces and
made a firm stand against the invaders. And it was in such
battles that the young Cossacks were eager to try out their
skill. They were not interested in looting and were reluctant
to massacre those who were in no position to fight back.
They wanted to pit their strength against the boastful Poles
on their prancing horses, with plumes on their helmets and
their wide sleeves thrown back and floating in the wind.

They acquired experience in these battles and, along
with it, expensive trappings and valuable weapons. Within
a month, the young cubs became men, and their faces,
which until then had retained some of the softness of youth,
now became strong and stern. Old Taras saw with joy that
his two sons were among the very best of this young brood.

It seemed as though Ostap had been especially picked by
fate to perform the most difficult warlike exploits. Never at
a loss whatever the contingency, with a cold calculation

uncanny in a twenty-two-year-old, he could appraise a situation at a glance, find a way to avoid a blow in order to place his own final counterblow. In no time his movements became self-assured and it was obvious that he was of the stuff of which leaders are made. His physical strength was exceptional and he had the noble comportment of a lion.

"By God, he'll be a terrific colonel, that boy," Taras mused, "a colonel who'll make his pa look like nothing."

Andrei was completely immersed in the music of bullets and sabers, and it enchanted him. He never stopped to weigh their own or the enemy's strength, to calculate their chances. He found a mad delight in battle. He was filled with a sort of holiday feeling, when his face felt as if afire, when everything flashed brightly before his eyes, when slashed-off heads rolled around him, when horses collapsed with thunderous thuds, while he flew through it all as if drunk, to the whistle of the bullets and the lightning of the saber blades, hitting out right and left, not believing in the blows of the enemy. Often Taras wondered at Andrei, watching him perform feats, guided by sheer ardor and by instinct, that would never have been tried by a cold-blooded, thinking warrior. At times the sheer madness of his attack performed miracles that left the old Cossacks gaping. And Taras would murmur:

"And this one, too, is a good one. I just hope he won't get killed with the things he's doing. A good fighter. Not the same as Ostap, but a good one."

It was decided that the army should push directly on to Dubno, where, it was rumored, there was a considerable quantity of stored gold and there were also many rich citizens. The inhabitants decided to fight to the last, preferring to die on their streets, squares, and doorsteps rather than allow the enemy to break into their homes. A high earth rampart surrounded the city and, in places where it was low, a stone barrier, the wall of a house, or an oak fence jutted out above it. The garrison was strong and fully aware of the terrible stakes.

First the Cossacks tried a frontal assault against the rampart, but the garrison met them with grapeshot. And the townsmen apparently did not intend to stand idly by; they crowded onto the rampart. Desperate determination could be read in their eyes. Even the women joined the defenders. Stones, barrels, pots, and boiling water flew down onto the Cossacks' heads and their eyes were blinded by bagfuls of sand. The Cossacks did not like to deal with fortresses. Siege warfare was not their forte. The headman ordered them to draw back.

"Never mind, brothers," he told them, "we'll withdraw. But I'm a heathen Tartar and no Christian if we let a single one of these dogs out of the city! They'll all die of hunger!"

The Cossack force drew up in a vast ring around the city. And, having nothing better to do while they were waiting, they laid waste the surrounding countryside, setting fire to villages and to the stacks of grain standing in the fields and letting their horses loose to feed on unharvested grain, of which, as luck would have it, the crop was exceptionally good that year. From the city walls people watched horrified as their very means of existence was destroyed. In the meantime, the Cossacks had taken up their positions, divided, as in the camp, into troops, with a sector assigned to each. And they smoked their pipes, swapped loot and weapons, played games, gambled, and watched the town with murderous calm. At night they lit fires. The cooks boiled supper for each troop in huge copper soup kettles; by each fire, a sentinel was posted. But the Cossacks soon grew bored with having nothing to do while sober. Although the headman had doubled the wine ration, as was usual when not on a forced march or in continuous action, this was not enough. The young men, the Bulba brothers in particular, didn't care for this kind of life and Andrei in particular chafed.

"You young goat," Taras said to him, "patience is the mother of virtue. To be a good soldier takes more than bravery in battle; a soldier must endure inactivity and whatever else may come. Only then will he achieve what he's after."

But youth and old age see things differently and cannot communicate.

In the meantime, Taras's troop, led by Tovkach, had managed to join them before the city. There were more than four thousand in the troop, including the volunteers who had joined as soon as they heard the news. The boys' mother had sent them her blessings with a captain and a medallion for each from the Mezhigorsky Monastery in Kiev. Being reminded of their mother somehow made them sad. Perhaps they felt that their mother's blessing carried an omen. Would it bring victory over the enemy and a happy homecoming with spoils and glory to be sung of forever by the lute players? Or was it . . . ? But the future is unknown and it stands before a man like the autumn mist rising from a marsh. The birds fly frantically up and down in it, flapping their wings, unable to make one another out, the dove not seeing the hawk and the hawk not seeing the dove, and neither knows how far he is from his own death. . . .

Ostap returned to his daily preoccupations first, but Andrei remained where he was, strangely depressed for a long time. The Cossacks had already finished their supper. The evening light had long disappeared from the sky and the gorgeous July night saturated the air. But instead of rejoining his troop, instead of trying to sleep, he stood gazing at the scene around him. In the sky numberless stars shone with a sharp, fine glitter. Scattered far over the field were wagons with their grease pots hanging beneath them and carts piled high with provisions and loot taken from the enemy. And under, on top, and around the vehicles, the Cossacks lay sleeping. They lay in picturesque poses, one with a sack beneath his head, another, with his cap, another simply using his comrade's side. Beside each Cossack lay his saber, his gun, his short pipe with its copper-mounted stem, his tinderbox. The heavy oxen lay with their feet doubled under them, looming huge and whitish-looking from a distance, like pale rocks scattered across the sloping plain. From every side snores rose from the grass, intertwined with the indignant neighing of the horses protesting at their hobbled feet. But something awesome and threatening had also crept into the warm July night. The reflections of remote fires shivered in various parts of the sky. Somewhere on the outskirts of the town, buildings were aflame. In one section, the fire was outlined against the summer sky in calm, subdued tones; in another, the flames, having reached something highly combustible, suddenly burst into a whirling flash and soared hissing upward toward the stars. Then incandescent, shapeless fragments, dying, fell down from the heights. Here a burned-out monastery, grim as a black Catholic monk, displayed its bleak magnificence at every flash. Next to it burned the monastery orchard. It seemed as though one could hear each tree hiss

as it disappeared in its wreath of smoke. Succumbing to
the fire, the ripe plums stepped out of the darkness and
appeared in a lilac-colored phosphorescence, while the
pears gleamed like yellow gold. Not far off, the blackened
bodies of several monks and Jews dangled from the building's wall and from the branch of a tree. And above it all
hovered a flock of birds looking like little black crosses
against the reddish, fiery background.

One would have thought that the besieged city was quietly breathing in its sleep. Its spires, its towers, the roofs
and the walls of its tallest buildings quietly reflected the
flashes of the distant conflagrations.

Andrei walked along the Cossack lines. The campfires,
beside which sat the men on watch, were nearly out. As to
the watchmen, they were asleep, digesting the good meals
they had devoured with carefree appetites. He was somewhat surprised at such dereliction of duty and thought
how lucky it was that the enemy they were facing here
was not really dangerous. Finally, he went over to one of
the wagons, climbed on top of it and lay down on his
back, his hands clasped under his head. But he could not
fall asleep and stayed there staring upward. The sky was
completely open above him, the air was transparent and
the stars of the Milky Way, which crossed the firmament at
a slant, were all immersed in its whitish light. After a
while little waves of sleep started to wash over Andrei
and the light mist of his dreams would veil the stars for a
brief moment, but then it would clear and the outlines of
things stood out sharp and precise again.

During one of these veiled moments he had the impression that a strange human face had flashed close by him.
Deciding that it was a shadow in his dream that would
vanish with it, he forced his eyes open completely and saw
that a real, strange, exhausted-looking face was bent over
him looking straight at him. Long, coal-black, tangled hair
escaped from under a dark shawl thrown over the head
and the sharp-featured, deathly sallow face, with its eerily
gleaming eyes, made him think that he was facing a ghost.
His hand instinctively grasped his pistol and he said, gasping a little:

"Who are you? If you are an evil spirit, vanish! If you
are a live man, I don't like such jokes and I'll blow your
head off with the first bullet!"

The apparition answered by placing a finger to its lips, apparently imploring him to be quiet. He looked closer at it, lowering his hand. By the long hair, by the shape of the neck, and by the crescents formed by the top of breasts over a dress, he saw that it was a woman. And he saw too that she was not a native of that land. Her exhausted face was dark, the prominent cheekbones stood out above her sunken cheeks, the narrow eyes arched upward. The longer he looked at her face, the more it seemed familiar. Finally he said:

"Who are you? It seems to me I used to know you or that I've seen you somewhere."

"You did. Two years ago in Kiev."

"Two years ago in Kiev," Andrei repeated slowly, trying to muster what was left in his memory of student life at the seminary. He looked at her intently again and suddenly exclaimed aloud:

"Yes—yes, you're the Tartar maid of the young Polish lady, the daughter of the military governor of Kovno! . . ."

"Sh-sh-sh!" the Tartar said, folding her hands in an imploring gesture. She was trembling terribly and turned her head to see whether Andrei's exclamation had awakened anyone near them.

"Tell me, tell me, how did you come here . . ." Andrei whispered, almost breathless from the wave of emotion that had passed over him. "Where is she, where is the Polish girl? She's alive, is she? . . ."

"She's here, in the city."

"In the city?" he exclaimed, again almost shouting, feeling the blood rush to his heart. "Why is she in the city?"

"Because her father is here. . . . He was transferred here. . . . He's been the military governor of Dubno for eighteen months now."

"Is she married? Come on, speak up, why are you so strange? . . . What is she now . . ."

"She hasn't eaten all day."

"What?"

"None of the inhabitants of the city have had any bread for days, some have been eating earth. . . ."

Andrei was like one paralyzed.

"My lady recognized you among the Cossacks from the city wall. She told me, 'Go and tell him that if he remembers me, he should come to me and, if he won't come, to send me a piece of bread for my old mother because I do not wish to see her die, I'd rather die myself first. Beg if you have to, because he too must have an old mother. Let him give you some bread for her sake.' "

Myriads of diverse feelings awoke and began burning in the young Cossack's chest.

"But how did you manage to get here? How did you come over?"

"Through an underground passage."

"Is there one?"

"Yes."

"Where?"

"You won't give me away?"

"I swear by the holy cross I won't."

"You reach it through the creek over there, you cross the brook and go through the reeds. . . ."

"And it takes you inside the city?"

"Straight into the chapel of the monastery."

"Let's go then! Let's go right now!"

"But in the name of Jesus Christ and the Virgin Mary, a piece of bread. . . ."

"Yes, yes, of course. Wait here, by the wagon . . . no, better lie down. No one will find you here, they are all asleep, anyway. I'll be back in no time."

And he walked over to the wagons where his troop's stores were kept. His heart was beating wildly. The past, superseded by the absorbing dangers and excitements of war, came violently back to the surface, in its turn blotting out the present. Again, as if emerging from the dark depths of the sea, he saw in front of him the proud, laughing girl; his memory brought back in a flash the shape of her arms, the curve of her laughing lips, the thick, hazelnut waves of her hair, streaming down her neck and shoulders as she bent forward. He remembered her firm young breasts, the feminine curves of her beautifully proportioned limbs. . . . No, these visions had never been completely extinguished, they had simply been pushed under to make room for other powerful impressions and emotions. And often they had haunted the deep, deep dreams of the young Cossack who, when he was torn awake, would lie sleepless and restless without understanding why.

As he walked, his heart beat faster at the thought that he would see her again. His knees shook. When he reached the provision wagon, he had forgotten what he had come for. He put his hand to his brow and rubbed it, trying to remember what he had to do. Then he suddenly shuddered, filled with fear at the thought that she might die of starvation. He jumped up on the wagon, grabbed several loaves of black bread and was about to rush off with them under his arm when he stopped short. It had occurred to him that, while black bread was all right for a crude Zaporozhe Cossack, it must be quite unsuitable for a graceful, delicate girl. He remembered that the previous evening the headman had reproached the cooks for using up all the buckwheat at once when there was enough of it for three meals. He inspected all the kettles of his father's troop. They were empty—even the huge caldron that held at least ten bucketfuls and under which ashes were still glowing. He was vaguely astounded at the voracity of the Cossacks and was not too hopeful of finding anything left in the kettles of the other troops, since they all received an equal amount of food and Bulba's troop had somewhat fewer men than the others. Automatically the Cossack saying flashed into his mind: "If offered too little—we'll eat it; if offered too much—we'll eat it." Then he decided that there must be a bag of white bread somewhere in their wagon. The bag was not there. Then he saw it: it was under Ostap's head. His brother lay stretched out on the ground, breathing loudly. Andrei seized the bag and gave it a jerk so that Ostap's head banged against the ground. He sat up and, his eyes still closed, shouted so that his voice seemed to fill the whole night:

"Hold him, hold him, the damn Polish bastard! Hold his horse! His horse!"

"Shut up or I'll kill you," Andrei hissed in a panic, swinging at his brother with the sack.

But he did not have to worry—Ostap did not pursue his appeal. Instead, letting out a tremendous snore, he sank down again, breathing so hard that the grass around his nose swayed in rhythm.

Andrei looked gingerly around to see whether Ostap's ravings had awakened anybody. He saw a tufted head rise at some distance, stare for a moment and then fall down again. He waited a couple of minutes, then grabbed the sack of white bread and went back to the Tartar girl, who lay on the wagon scarcely breathing.

"Come," he said, "let's get going. They're all asleep, you've really nothing to fear. Do you think," he asked her, "that you could carry these loaves? I'd like to take some more. . . ."

He put his bag on his shoulder, grabbed another one with millet in it, and at the last second himself took the loaves he had asked the Tartar girl to carry. Then, bending somewhat under his load, he walked boldly among the outstretched Cossacks.

"Andrei!" he heard his father's voice ring out suddenly, as he was passing near the emplacement of their troop. His heart died. He halted, shivering, and asked softly:

"What?"

"There's a woman with you. Wait until I get up, I'll show you! Women will lead you to no good." As he said this, he raised himself, leaning on an elbow, and, resting his cheek on his hand, scrutinized the draped silhouette of the Tartar girl intently.

Andrei stood half-alive, half-dead, unable to look into his father's face. But when finally he did, he realized that the old Bulba had gone back to sleep in the same position, his cheek on his hand.

Andrei crossed himself. Suddenly fear left him completely. He turned back and looked at the Tartar girl. She appeared to him like a granite statue wrapped in her shawl, and when her figure was lighted up by the remote flaring of a fire he could make out only the flash of her eyes in her face, a wooden brilliance, like the eyes of someone dead. He pulled her by the sleeve and they moved on, constantly looking back. Finally they came to the creek and went down its bank. Andrei saw that the slope rising behind him was higher than a man and he could make out some tall blades of grass and behind them the sky with the moon in an oblique crescent—they were completely out of sight of the Cossack camp.

The stir of a small steppe breeze announced the approach of dawn. But not a single cock crowed. For a long time now all the chickens in the entire district had been exterminated. They went across the stream on a plank. The bank on the city side was higher. At this point the city's defenses were apparently considered quite safe and the earth wall was not even manned, because immediately beyond it rose the thick wall of a monastery.

The steep bank was covered with coarse grass and between it and the creek bed grew reeds as tall as a man. Along the top of the bank ran a broken wattle fence which must formerly have surrounded a garden. In front of it grew burdock with blackthorn and sunflowers lifting their heads from among its leaves. Here, the Tartar threw off her slippers and pulled up her skirts because the soil was marshy and full of water. They worked their way among the reeds and stopped before a pile of dry wood. She pushed some logs aside and uncovered an opening like the mouth of a large oven. The girl bent her head and went in. Andrei squeezed himself in behind her, pulling the bags along. They found themselves in total darkness.

Chapter 6

Andrei, loaded down as he was, had difficulty following the Tartar girl along the dark, narrow earthen tunnel.

"We'll soon be able to see," she said. "We're nearly at the spot where I left a lamp."

Soon the dark walls grew lighter. The passage widened and they came to what might have been an underground chapel: there was a sort of altar by one wall with a very faded Catholic Madonna hanging above it, dimly lit by a small silver lamp. There was also a larger brass lamp on a long thin stand with snuffers, a pin for adjusting the flame, and an extinguisher dangling on little chains. The Tartar girl picked it up from the floor and lit it from the altar lamp. They moved on. And now the swaying lamp made their coal-black silhouettes jump on the walls, which were almost dazzling in the light. It was like a painting by a Spanish master come alive. The handsome, strong features of the young warrior, overflowing with exuberant health, presented a sharp contrast to the thin, exhausted face of his companion. Gradually there was more headroom and Andrei could straighten his shoulders. He examined the underground passage curiously. It reminded him of the Kiev catacombs. As in Kiev, there were recesses in the walls, holding coffins. And here and there he stumbled on loose human bones which had turned soft and crumbled into powder. Apparently here, too, pious people had taken refuge from the world's storms, griefs and temptations. The tunnel was quite damp and from time to time they found themselves walking in water. Again and again Andrei had to stop to let his companion rest, but, even so, her tiredness returned almost immediately. A small piece of bread she had swallowed caused sharp cramps in a stomach unaccustomed to food and forced her to remain motionless for several minutes at a time.

At last, they saw a small iron door ahead of them.

"Well, thank heaven—we've arrived," the Tartar girl said in a weak voice, trying to lift her hand and knock on the door but finding that she lacked the strength. Andrei banged on it for her. His knock reverberated, indicating that there was a space on the other side of the door. Then the sound of the reverberation changed as if it were now ringing in a high vault. A few moments later there was a clinking of keys; someone, it seemed, was coming down some steps. Finally the door was unlocked and opened by a monk. He stood at the bottom of a narrow staircase holding the keys and a candle. Instinctively Andrei drew back. The sight of a Catholic monk aroused in the Cossacks even greater hatred and disdain than the sight of a Jew. The monk too stepped back when he saw the Zaporozhe Cossack, but a whispered word from the Tartar girl reassured him. He held up the light for them, locked the door behind them, and led them up the staircase. They came out under the high, somber arches of the monastery church. Near one of the altars, on which candles burned in tall candlesticks, a kneeling priest was quietly praying. On either side of him, also kneeling, were two altar boys in lilac cassocks under white lace stoles, with censers in their hands. He was praying for a miracle to save the town, to lift up their fallen spirits; he was praying that the people might be given the strength to endure their hardships, praying for the banishment of the Tempter who brought self-pity and tearful moaning over the ordeals of the flesh.

People were kneeling all around—women, as pale as ghosts, allowed their heads to rest on the backs of chairs and dark wooden benches in front of them, and men leaned against the pillars and columns. The stained-glass window above the altar was lighted up by the pink glow of the dawn, and circles of blue, yellow and other colors fell from it to the floor. Suddenly, deep in its recess, the altar appeared in a halo of light and the smoke from the censers hung in the air in an iridescent cloud. As Andrei gazed in wonder at the extraordinary effect of the light, a majestic chord from the organ filled the whole church. It swelled and swelled, spread out, changed to heavy peals of thunder, and then, without warning, it turned into heavenly music and floated high up under the arches in sounds reminiscent of girlish voices; then once again it became a mighty roar of thunder and fell silent. For a long time the peals of thunder shook under the arches and, his mouth half-open, Andrei marveled at the majestic music. Then he felt someone pulling at his coat.

"We must go," the Tartar girl said.

They crossed the church without anyone noticing them and came out onto the square in front of it. Now the dawn sky was reddish. The sun was about to rise. The square was completely deserted. In its center stood wooden tables, suggesting that perhaps not more than a week ago this had been a market where food could be bought. The square, which was unpaved (they did not pave streets in those days), was simply a mass of dried mud and was surrounded by one-story stone and mud houses with wooden posts running the whole height of their walls and joined by carved cross-beams, in the style of houses of those days, some of which can still be found in Lithuania and Poland today. They all had very high roofs, with many dormer windows and ventilating holes. On one side of the square, not far from the church, a tall house stood apart from the others. It looked like a town hall or other government building. It had two stories and was topped by an arched belvedere where a soldier stood on watch. Under the roof there was a big clock face.

Although the square seemed dead, Andrei thought he heard a weak moan. He looked all around and saw several bodies lying almost motionless on the ground in a corner. He was trying to make out whether they were dying or just waking up, when he stumbled against something. It was a dead body, a woman, probably Jewish. Something about her suggested that she was still young, although this could not have been told from her distorted, emaciated face. On her head she wore a red silk kerchief and, where it covered her ears, it was decorated with two rows of some sort of pearls or beads. Two or three long, curly locks had escaped from her kerchief and lay on her shriveled neck with its distended veins. Beside her lay an infant, its hand grasping spasmodically at her gaunt breast and twisting at it with an innocent ferocity because it yielded no milk. Now the infant no longer cried nor yelled and only the slight rise and fall of its stomach showed that it was not yet dead, or at least that it still had a few more breaths to draw.

They turned into a side street and were abruptly brought to a stop by a madman who, seeing Andrei's precious load, threw himself on him like a tiger, clinging to him and yelling: "Bread!" But his strength was not equal to his madness and, when Andrei pushed him off, he collapsed on the ground. Moved by pity, Andrei tossed him a loaf. The man threw himself on it like a mad dog, sinking his teeth into it and tearing at it, and died then and there in the street in terrible agony, having become completely unaccustomed to food. At almost every step, they came upon the horrible victims of starvation. It seemed as if many of them had run out onto the street because they were unable to bear their sufferings indoors, almost as if they hoped to find some nourishment in the air. They passed an old woman sitting at her door and it was impossible to tell whether she had fallen asleep, was dead, or was simply deep in thought. In any case, she no longer heard or saw anything and only sat immobile, her head drooping. From the roof of another house hung a rope from which dangled the limp, wasted body of a man. The wretch had been unable to endure the sufferings of hunger and had decided it was better to hasten his end by suicide.

At the sight of this awful starvation, Andrei could no longer restrain himself and asked the Tartar girl:

"Is it possible that these people couldn't find anything —just to stay alive? In dire circumstances, men eat things that would disgust them normally, that are forbidden by religion, everything is made use of. . . ."

"We've eaten everything, every animal; you won't find a horse, a dog, a cat, or even a mouse alive in this city. Besides, we never kept any supplies here, everything was brought in from the countryside."

"But if you're going through this terrible death agony, how can you hope to save the city?"

"Well," the Tartar girl said, "perhaps the military governor might even have surrendered if he hadn't received word yesterday, flown in by a hawk. The colonel, the one in Budzany, asks him to hold out a little longer. He is coming to our rescue. He's only waiting for another colonel to join forces with him . . . but here we are."

Andrei had noticed the house quite a while before. It

was not like the others. It was two stories high, built of fine brick, probably by an Italian architect. The windows of the ground floor had very prominent high granite cornices; the upper story looked like a gallery with its arches and lattices covered with coats of arms. Coats of arms could also be seen on the corners of the house. An outside staircase led onto the square itself and at its foot two sentries stood, picturesquely symmetrical, each holding a halberd in one hand while the other supported a bowed head. They were not asleep, not even dozing, but seemed somehow insensitive to the outside world and they paid no attention to anyone passing on the stairs. At the top of the staircase, Andrei saw a warrior, richly attired and equipped, holding a missal in his hand. He lifted his eyes to them, but the Tartar whispered something in his ear and he lowered them again to the pages of his book. They went through into a vast hall that may have been a reception room. It was filled with a throng of people sitting along the walls in every imaginable position: soldiers, maids, valets, kennelmen, cellarmen—all the domestics a Polish nobleman needs to maintain his title or his military rank. There was the smell of a just-extinguished lamp, and two other lamps on stands as tall as a man were still burning, although daylight was already evident beyond the latticed window. Andrei was on the point of going straight through to a heavy oak door adorned with coats of arms and other carvings, but the Tartar caught his sleeve and pointed to a small side door to one side. Through it they entered a corridor and from there a room which Andrei could not make out too well. Light through a crack in the blind allowed him to see only a raspberry-colored curtain, a gilded cornice and an oil painting on the wall.

The Tartar signaled to him to remain where he was and opened another door through which he saw the gleam of a fire. He heard a whisper and a low voice which made him forget everything else. He saw through the open door the flash of a supple feminine form with a luxurious braid caught on a raised arm. The Tartar girl returned and asked him to come in. He was unaware of following her and of the door shutting behind them. Two candles burned in the room. A lamp smoked under a statue of the Virgin. Before it stood a tall *prie-dieu* such as Catholics use to pray. But he took all this in only vaguely and turned around. He saw a woman who seemed frozen in the middle of some quick movement. It looked as if her whole body had been about to throw itself toward him when it had suddenly become petrified. And looking at her, he felt turned to stone.

He had never expected to find her like this. She was not the one he remembered. She was completely altered, more marvelous, more extraordinary. Before, there had been something unfinished about her. Now she was a work of art to which the artist had put the very last stroke of the brush. The other, the one of the past, had been an enchanting, lighthearted girl; this was a finished woman. Her wide-open eyes radiated full-blooded emotion—not a little emotion, nor a hint of emotion, but a full, total emotion — and the bright traces of tears still stood in her eyes. Her breasts, her neck and her shoulders fell exactly within the narrow boundaries assigned to perfect beauty, her hazelnut hair, which once scattered in soft waves over her face, was gathered in a magnificent heavy braid. It seemed to him that every one of her features had changed. In vain he tried to recognize at least one from his memory of her.

She was terribly pale but this did not mar her incredible beauty. On the contrary, it seemed to add something irresistible, something supernatural, to it. Awe filled Andrei's soul as he stood immobile, staring at her.

And she too was impressed by the looks of the young Cossack. He was strikingly handsome and manly and even in his immobility one could guess at the freedom and grace of his movements. His eyes sparkled under velvety, firmly arched eyebrows, the youthful freshness of his cheeks showed through his deep tan, his thin black mustache looked soft and silky.

"No, I cannot—it is beyond my power to thank you, generous knight," she said finally and the silvery sound of her voice vibrated tenderly. "God alone can reward you, not a weak woman like me. . . ." She dropped her eyes, lowering the hemispheres of her heavy lids with their arrowlike, silky black lashes. As her head bent forward, a delicate blush, rising from her neck, colored her face.

Andrei could find nothing to say. He would have liked to tell her all that he felt but he could not. Something locked his mouth. He knew he would not be able to find the right words. How could he, educated in the seminary, raised in the steppe, leading a nomadic, restless life, answer her? At that moment, he deeply despised his Cossack nature.

The Tartar girl returned to the room. She had already sliced some of the bread which Andrei had brought and carried the slices on a golden dish which she placed before her mistress, who glanced at the bread and then looked up at Andrei. There were many things in that long look—tenderness, exhaustion and also her feeling that she could not convey to him what she felt, and it touched him directly, even more than her words, and suddenly he felt free and easy. His heavy shackles were broken and an inexhaustible flow of words was about to pour out of him.

At that moment, she suddenly turned toward the Tartar girl and asked:

"And what about Mother? Have you taken some to her?"

"She's asleep, ma'am."

"And Father?"

"Yes, ma'am. The master said he would come and thank the knight personally."

The beauty then took a slice of bread and brought it to her mouth. Andrei, hardly breathing, watched her slender white fingers break off small pieces of bread and put them into her mouth. Suddenly he remembered the man who had died in front of his eyes after swallowing a piece of bread. He turned pale and grasped her hand.

"Enough," he shouted, "no more! You haven't eaten for so long. . . . It can be like poison."

She immediately dropped her hand and replaced the slice in the golden dish with a childlike obedience, looking into his eyes with . . .

But neither chisel nor brush nor the mighty word can express what may be found sometimes in the eyes of a woman, any more than they can convey the storm of tenderness which sweeps over the one those eyes are looking upon.

"My tsarina, my empress!" Andrei muttered, overwhelmed. "Tell me what you want me to do. Order me to accomplish the most impossible things and I'll obey you. If you want me to do what no man alive can do, I'll do it or die trying. And I swear to you by the holy cross that dying thus would be sweet for me, I cannot tell you how sweet. . . . I have three farms, and half of my father's herds of horses belong to me; also, all that my mother had when she married my father, much of which she has concealed from him . . . all that must go to me, to me alone. None of our Cossacks owns weapons such as I do: for the hilt of my saber alone they would give me their best drove of horses and three hundred sheep. And all this I would gladly give up, discard, flood, scorch, lay waste, if you were to say one word, if you simply made a sign with your curved black eyebrow. . . . But I know I must seem stupid and uncouth—I've spent my life in the seminary and in the Zaporozhe steppes and I'm not fit to speak in a house where kings, princes, and the flower of knighthood are received. I see that you are a creature altogether different from us— the wives and daughters of our boyars are unworthy of you. We, we are unworthy even to serve you—only the heavenly angels are good enough for that."

The young woman listened to him with growing amazement, without uttering a word. She felt that his speech reflected his young, violent spirit like a mirror. And each simple sound, coming straight from the depths of his heart, had in it a singular force. Her beautiful face was turned toward him, her unruly hair was pushed impatiently back, her lips parted and for a long time remained parted while her eyes were fixed on his. She began to say something, but stopped. . . .

It had struck her suddenly that the Cossack was destined for different things. His father, his brothers, his entire country, loomed behind him as grim avengers. She remembered that the terror-instilling Zaporozhe Cossacks were besieging the city, that they had doomed everybody in the city to a horrible death. . . . Her eyes suddenly filled with tears. She seized a silk kerchief and covered her face with it. He saw the damp marks of her tears darkening it. For a long time she remained in that position, biting her lip with her white, even teeth, feeling as though she had been bitten by a viper. Her head was pushed back and she kept her face covered to conceal her heartbreaking grief from him.

"Say just one word," Andrei said, taking her satin-smooth hand.

A sparkling flame shot through his entire body as he squeezed her inert hand in his.

But she did not speak, did not uncover her face and remained immobile.

"Why are you so sad? Tell me, why are you so sad?"

She tore the kerchief from her face, threw back the long tresses of hair that fell over her eyes and spoke in a very quiet, sad tone reminiscent of the breeze that rises suddenly on a calm evening and whispers through a thicket of reeds on a riverbank with a mournfully tender sound—that brings the traveler to a halt, filled with an unaccountable nostalgia, and makes him forget the approach of night, the songs of the laborers returning from the fields and the rattling of the wheels of a passing cart.

"Am I not to be eternally pitied, just like the mother who brought me into this world? Is not fate crueler than a hangman or a torturer? Oh, life threw at my feet the scions of the nobility, the wealthiest lords and counts, foreign barons and the very flower of our Polish knighthood. Many of them loved me and I had only to wave my hand and any one of them, the handsomest and the noblest, would have considered it a supreme happiness, and an honor too, to become my husband. But, as cruel fate would have it, none of them ever touched my heart—it had to let pass the finest knights in my own world and go out to a stranger, to the enemy. Why, Holy Mother, why do you torture me so cruelly? What horrible sins have I committed? My days once flowed by in luxury and abundance; the most delicate foods and the oldest wines were my fare. And what was it all for? Was it all so that I might end up dying a death more miserable than that of any beggar in the kingdom? And, as if it were not enough to be doomed to such a cruel end, as if it were not enough to have to watch my mother and father, for whom I would have given my life twenty times, die in unbearable agony, before I die myself; as if all this were not enough, I have been sentenced before this end to meet, to hear and to feel the words and the love I have never known. He had to come now, to tear my heart to shreds, to make my destiny even more bitter, to make me cry even more despairingly over my young life, to make my impending death even more terrifying and force me to curse you even more angrily, you, my fate, and you, too, Mother of God, may I be forgiven for it. . . ."

Her voice died and an infinite hopelessness covered her face. Every one of her features, the pale lowered brow, the downcast eyes, her cheeks with the traces of her tears on them, seemed to cry out that this beautiful girl was not destined for happiness.

"That's unheard of, impossible—it won't happen," Andrei said. "The most beautiful of all women could only be born to be worshiped by all that is best in the world. No, you shall not die. Dying is not for you, I swear to it by my birth, by everything that is dear to me in life. But, should it happen that neither strength, nor prayer, nor daring, nor anything, can change that bitter fate, then we shall die together and I will be the first. And only when I am dead, if then, will they be able to take you away from me."

"Don't deceive yourself, Cossack, and do not deceive me," she said, slowly shaking her finely shaped head. "I realize—oh, I realize it to my great sorrow—but, alas only too well, that you *must* not love me. I know your place and your duty: your father, your comrades, and your native land call out to you—and we, we are your enemies."

"And what's my father to me, what are my comrades and my native land?" Andrei said. He threw his head back, straightened himself up, standing there strong as an oak. "Well, if it comes to that, I have no one in the world. No one, no one, no one!" he repeated and stressed his words with a happen-what-may gesture of his hand. "And who says that the Ukraine is my country? Who made her my country? A man's country is something sought by the heart, the thing that is dearest to him. . . . My country . . . you are my country! And I shall carry that country in my heart as long as I live. Let any Cossack try to tear it out! Everything I have, I'll sell, give away, destroy, for that country!"

For one second she was again a magnificent stone statue gazing into his eyes. Then suddenly she burst into a torrent of tears, and as only a great-hearted, noble woman could do, she threw herself toward him, put her arms around his neck, sobbing. And, although at that very moment shouts and the sound of drums and trumpets came from the street, Andrei heard nothing. He felt only her warm, pure breath, her tears wetting his face, and her perfumed silky tresses.

Suddenly the Tartar maid rushed into the room shouting:

"We're saved, we're saved! Our troops have broken

through and entered the city, bringing bound Cossacks with them."

But neither he nor she understood who were these "our" troops who had brought in the captured Cossacks. Andrei turned his face and, feeling something unlike anything he could imagine existed on earth, he kissed her soft lips. She responded and they were united in a way people can be but once in their lives.

And that was the end of the Cossack. He was lost to the great Cossack brotherhood! Never again would he see his native Zaporozhe, his father's farms, his Orthodox churches. And never again would the Ukraine see one of her boldest children, pledged to defend her. And old Taras would tear a handful of hair from his gray Cossack tuft and curse the hour when, to his disgrace, he had conceived this son.

Chapter 7

The Cossack camp was in an uproar. At first, no one could explain how the Polish force had managed to make its way into the city. Only later did it turn out that every last man of the Pereyaslav troop, which had been stationed before the side gate of the city, had been dead drunk and that it was no wonder that half of them had been killed and the other half captured before they knew what had hit them. And by the time the nearest detachments, awakened by the noise, had grabbed their arms, the Polish relief force was already entering the gates with the rear guard firing at the sleepy and only half-sober Cossacks pursuing them.

The headman ordered a general assembly and when they all stood around him with heads uncovered, he spoke:

"So you know what happened last night, my very dear friends. You see now what drunkenness can do. That's quite a slap we got from the enemy. Apparently a few too many glasses of vodka make you so blind that the enemy of Christ's army can not only pull the trousers off you but can sneeze in your faces without your knowing it!"

The Cossacks stood with lowered heads, abashed. Only Kukubenko, the chief of the Nezamaikovsky troop, protested:

"Wait, headman," he said, "I know it's not usual to object when the headman speaks to the assembled force, but I must tell you it didn't happen that way. It's not fair to blame the entire Christian force. The Cossacks would be guilty, they would deserve death, if they had drunk themselves into such a state while on the march or in action or doing strenuous work. But we've been sitting around with nothing to do in front of this city. And there's been no fast day or any other Christian reason for abstinence. Now, how can a man not get drunk when he's idle? There's nothing wrong with that. What we'd better do is to teach the Poles a lesson for their cowardly attack. We've walloped them before and now we'll give them such a walloping that they won't get home standing up."

The Cossacks liked Kukubenko's speech. Many raised their lowered heads and nodded their approval. They began to shout:

"Well said, Kukubenko! Well put!"

And Taras Bulba, who was standing near the headman, said:

"Well, headman, looks like Kukubenko has a point there —what d'you say to that?"

"What do I say? Well, I say lucky is the father who begot a son who'll say a word which, instead of knocking a man down when he is in trouble, will spur him on and give him courage. That takes more wisdom than is needed to reproach him. I was going to say a word of comfort myself, after my reproaches, but Kukubenko beat me to it."

"Well said, headman!" voices were heard from the crowd. "The headman speaks well!"

And the elders, who stood there puffed up like gray-headed pigeons, nodded, and, stroking their mustaches, agreed:

"He certainly knows how to put it, this headman."

"Now listen, friends," the headman said, "I don't believe in taking a fortress by climbing and digging as the Germans do. I leave that to the enemy. It's not a fitting occupation for a man and a Cossack. Well, the way things look, the enemy have entered the city without many supplies. They brought only a few carts along. Now, the people in there must be hungry, so the chances are they'll gulp everything down. Then, horses must have hay . . . unless, of course, one of their saints tosses some down from the sky— although these Catholics are better at words than at miracles. So for one reason or another, they'll come out of the gates. Therefore, we'll break up into three detachments, one stationed on each of the roads facing the three city gates. The detachment before the main gate will consist of five troops, the two others of three each. The Diadkiv and the

Korsun troops will wait in ambush. The Bulba troop also in ambush. The Tytarev and Tymashov troops will be held in reserve on the right flank, behind the wagons, Sherbinov and Stablikiv—on the left flank. Now I want those of you who have the sharpest tongues to step forward: you'll taunt and tease the enemy. The Poles are empty-headed, they can't stand abuse and possibly we'll be able to lure the lot of them out no later than today. I want every troop chief to inspect his troop thoroughly. If you are short of men, fill up your ranks from what is left of the Pereyaslav troop. Check everything carefully. And to keep the men going, have them each issued a loaf of bread and a glass of vodka, although they should still be full from yesterday —they put away so much that it's a sheer miracle they haven't burst. And now, one more thing: if any Jewish merchant sells a Cossack even one single jug of vodka, I'll have a sow's ear nailed to the bastard's forehead and then I'll have him hung by his feet. Now, get on with it— get going!"

The Cossacks bowed to him and dispersed toward their troops and wagons, only putting their hats back on when they were quite a distance away. Then they proceeded to prepare for action, testing their sabers and broadswords, filling their powder flasks, rolling their wagons into position and choosing themselves horses.

Walking toward his troop's emplacement, Taras was worrying about Andrei. Could he have been bound up in his sleep and taken prisoner with the others? "No," he thought, "that's unlikely, he'd never let them capture him alive." But then, Andrei's body had not been found among the Cossacks killed. Taras was deep in thought and for quite a while did not hear his name being called.

"Who wants me?" flashed through his mind when awareness of the world returned to him. It was Yankel, the Jew.

"Colonel Bulba, sir," he was saying in a hurried, gasping voice, sounding as though he had something urgent to tell, "I have come straight from inside the city, sir . . ."

"How the hell did you manage to get in there?" Taras asked, bewildered.

"You see, Colonel Bulba, sir, when I heard the shooting at dawn, I grabbed my coat and rushed off without even bothering to put my arms through the sleeves, for I had to find out what the uproar was all about and why the

Cossacks were firing so early in the morning. So I found myself by the gates at the very moment when the last Polish troops were pouring through them. And whom do you think I recognized among them but Pan Galiandovich, an old acquaintance of mine, who happens to have owed me a hundred gold pieces for about three years. So I decided to claim the debt and followed him into the city."

"You mean you entered the city and started claiming the debt? What was there to stop him from having you strung up like a dog?"

"Well, he almost did have me hanged. His servants had already got hold of me and put a noose round my neck but I begged the Polish gentleman to let me loose. I said he didn't have to pay me until he felt like it, on the contrary, I'd lend him more money if he'd help me to collect some other debts from the other Polish gentlemen . . . for it must be said that Galiandovich doesn't have a gold coin in his pocket, although he has estates and farms and four castles and grazing land right near Shklov. Still, for pocket money he's no better off than a Cossack—his pockets are just as empty. . . . And had it not been for the Breslau Jews, he couldn't have bought his arms and then he wouldn't have been able to fight in this war. And that's why he doesn't attend the Sejm any more——"

"So what did you do in the city? See any of our people?"

"Our people, sir? Of course, sir, Isaac, Haim, the Jewish contractor——"

"Goddam you, I'm asking about Cossacks—did you see any Cossacks?"

"No, sir, I didn't see any Cossacks, but I saw the young gentleman, Andrei Bulba, your son, Colonel, sir."

"You saw Andrei? Well, tell me, tell me, where? Where did you see him? In a dungeon? Tied up in a pit? Beaten up? Bound?"

"Oh no, sir, there's no one who could lay a hand on Knight Andrei Bulba. He is a very important knight, sir. I hardly recognized him myself: his shoulderpieces are gold, his arm guards are gold, his breastplate is gold, his helmet is gold, and there's plenty of gold on his belt. In fact there's gold all over him. He's like the sun in spring when all the little birds twitter and sing and every blade of grass is fragrant and radiates light—he's all radiant too, all flooded with golden glitter! And the military governor gave him the best horse. . . . I'd say the horse by itself would fetch a couple of hundred . . ."

Bulba was dumfounded. He muttered woodenly:

"Why . . . why did he put on . . . their attire? . . ."

"He put it on because it's more costly. And now he's riding all over the place with them and he instructs them and they instruct him and he's like one of the wealthiest Polish noblemen."

"But how did they make him do it?"

"But I didn't say that anybody forced him. Don't you know, sir, he went over to the other side of his own free will?"

"Who did?"

"Knight Andrei."

"Went over where?"

"To the other side, sir. Now he is completely one of them."

"You're lying, you swine!"

"How could I lie? Do you think I'm mad or something? Do you think I'm asking to be hanged? I know that it'd cost me my life if I lied. . . ."

"So you're trying to tell me that he's sold his country and his faith, is that it?"

"But I never said he'd sold anything. I simply said he'd gone over to them."

"You're lying, you damned Jew. Such a thing couldn't happen to an Orthodox Christian. Unless you're mixing something up, you muddleheaded fool. . . ."

"Let the grass grow over the doorstep of my home if I'm lying. Let every passer-by spit on the grave of my father, my mother, and my mother's father if I have it all confused. And if you want to know, sir, I can even tell you why he's gone over to them."

"Why?"

"The military governor has a beautiful daughter. By the God of my fathers, an incredibly beautiful daughter, sir."

At this point, Yankel tried to convey the beauty of the Polish lady. He spread out his arms, screwed up his eyes, twisted his mouth to one side as though he had tasted something delicious.

"Well, what's that got to do with it?"

"So he did it all for her. When a man falls in love, he

becomes like a boot sole soaked in water, it can be bent anyway you like."

Bulba was plunged deep in thought. He remembered how powerful a weak woman can be, how many strong men she has sent to perdition. He also thought of Andrei's vulnerability to women and he remained standing there for a long time like a post.

"Listen, sir, and I'll tell you everything," Yankel said. "As soon as I heard the uproar and saw the Poles pouring through the gates, I grabbed a string of pearls, reckoning that there were beauties in the town and noblewomen and as long as there are beauties and noblewomen around, even if they have nothing to eat, they'll still buy pearls. And as soon as the servants of Galiandovich let me go, I dashed to the military governor's place to sell my pearls. I found out everything from a Tartar maid. She told me: 'The wedding will be celebrated as soon as the siege is lifted. Sir Andrei has promised to chase the Cossacks away.' "

"And you didn't kill the son-of-a-bitch on the spot?"

"Why should I kill him? He acted of his own free will. What wrong has he done? He was happier over there, so he went over."

"And . . . and did you see his face?"

"Of course I did, sir. What a glorious figure of a warrior! The handsomest of them all! May God preserve him! He recognized me at once and when I came up to him, he said——"

"Go on, go on, what did he say?"

"First he made me a sign with his hand and then he said: 'Hello, Yankel.' 'Pan Andrei,' I said to him. 'Yankel,' he says, 'tell my father, tell my brother, tell the Cossacks, the lot of them, that my father is my father no longer, my brother, no brother, my comrades, no comrades to me. That I'll fight them all, I'll fight the lot of them.' "

"You're lying, you damn Judas," Taras howled, losing all control of himself. "You're lying, you swine! You crucified Christ, you God-accursed bastard! I'd like to kill you, Satan! Go on, run, run as fast as you can, if you don't want to die on the spot!"

Taras unsheathed his saber and Yankel took to his heels and ran as fast as his puny calves would carry him. And he kept running for a long time without looking back, between the Cossack wagons and then further, clear across the field, although Taras did not even try to pursue him— he had realized that it was unreasonable to take out his rage on the first person who happened to be at hand.

Now it came back to him that he had seen Andrei walking past their wagons with a woman, and his gray head sank onto his chest. But he still refused to believe that such ignominy could have befallen him, that his own son could have sold his faith and his soul.

Finally he snapped out of it and deployed his troop in ambush behind a wood, the only one that hadn't been scorched by the Cossacks. In the meantime, the Cossacks, on foot and on horseback, advanced along the three roads toward the gates. One after the other, the troops advanced: the Uman, the Popovich, the Kanev, the Steblikiv, the Nezamaikovsky, the Guguziv, the Tytarev, and the Timashev. Only the Pereyaslav was missing. The men of the troop had drunk well and they had drunk away their lives. Some had awakened bound and in enemy hands, others had never awakened at all and had passed in their sleep into the damp earth; Khlib, their chief, had found himself a Polish prisoner with neither weapons nor trousers.

The city became aware of the Cossacks' movements. They all hastened to the ramparts and the Cossacks saw a painting come alive: Polish knights, each more magnificent than the next, profiled against the skyline. Their copper helmets shone like suns and were topped by feathers as white as swans. Some wore light blue and pink caps cocked on the sides of their heads, their doublets had wide, loose sleeves and were embroidered with gold or adorned with several rows of braid. Their swords and other weapons had sumptuous settings which must have cost a great deal. There was a great variety of dazzling apparel. At their head was the colonel from Budzany wearing a red, gold-spangled headgear. The colonel was heavy, taller and bigger than the others, and his expensive doublet was tight on him. On the opposite side, almost above a side gate, stood another colonel, a smallish, dried-up man with sharp little eyes looking brightly out from under his thick eyebrows. He kept turning from one side to the other and pointing with his thin, dry hand, giving orders, and it was obvious that despite his small stature, he knew much about the art of war. Not far from him stood Galiandovich, extremely tall and thin, with a thick mustache and a face that was certainly not lacking in color. It was obvious that this Polish knight liked good food and strong liquor. Behind them stood many of the nobility, some equipped by their own gold, some by courtesy of the king's treasurer, others on funds obtained from the Jews, by pledging everything that they could lay hands on in their grandfathers' castles. Among them also were plenty of parasites who buzzed around the senate, whom the senators invited to feasts because of their illustrious names, and who stole silver cups from the table and from the cupboards and then, after the day's glory, were to be found on a coachbox, employed as coachman by some gentleman. There were all sorts of men up there and some of them could not even have afforded a drink. But to go to war, all had managed to turn out elegantly.

Before the walls, the Cossacks stood in silence. There was no gold on them—only here and there precious metal flashed on the hilt of a saber or the inlaid stock of a gun. The Cossacks did not dress up for battle. They wore dark clothes and plain coats of mail and their uniform red-topped, black sheepskin hats dotted the plain in a black and red crescent.

Two Cossacks rode out from the ranks. One of them still very young, the other older, but both known for their sharp tongues and both quite good in action too. They were Okhrim Nash and Mykyta Golokopytenko and behind them rode Demid Popovich, a thickset man who had seen much. He had taken part in the siege of Adrianople, was nearly burned alive, and had returned to the camp with his head all blackened and singed and his mustache scorched. But Popovich grew himself a new tuft long enough to reach his ear, and a new mustache as thick and black as tar. This Popovich was no amateur at the taunting, acid word.

"Beautiful those red coats you people have. But I'd like to know if there's any red blood under them?"

"I'll show you!" the big colonel shouted. "I'll have the lot of you bound up! You'd better hand over your guns and your horses, you bunch of peasants! You serfs! You see how I bound up your men? Hey!" he shouted, turning back, "bring the prisoners out onto the rampart!"

And they brought the bound Cossacks out onto the rampart. At their head was Troop Chief Khlib, with neither trousers nor coat, just as he had been when they had captured him drunk. The Cossack chief hung his head, ashamed before his comrades because of his nakedness and because he had let himself be captured, like a pig, while asleep. His hair had turned gray overnight.

"Cheer up, Khlib! We'll rescue you!" the Cossacks shouted from below.

"Cheer up, friend," Troop Chief Borodaty called out, "it's not your fault they took you naked, anyone can have bad luck. The shame is theirs for bringing you out here without decently covering your nakedness."

"I can see you're all very brave men when it comes to fighting sleeping men!" said Golokopytenko, looking up at the ramparts.

"Just wait, we'll be cutting off your tufts!" the Poles shouted from above.

"I'd like to see that! I'd like to see 'em cut off our tufts!" Popovich said, twisting and turning in front of them on his horse. Then turning to look at his own men, he shouted:

"Who knows? Maybe the Poles are right, especially if big-belly there leads them out. That'll give 'em good cover."

"How will it give 'em cover?" asked the Cossacks, knowing that Popovich had the answer all prepared.

"You blind? The whole army can hide behind him and you won't get to more'n a couple of the dogs with your spears."

The Cossacks burst out laughing, and, for a long time, many of them continued to shake their heads, saying:

"That Popovich! If you need someone to turn a phrase, well just . . ."

But well just what, they did not say.

"Back! Get out from under the wall!" the headman shouted suddenly. It looked as if the Poles could not stand even this much taunting. The colonel made a signal with his hand.

The Cossacks got out of the way just in time. A hail of grapeshot rattled from the rampart. There was a commotion and the old military governor in person appeared on horseback. The gates flew open and out marched the Poles.

First came the embroidered hussars, riding in even columns. They were followed by the mailed foot soldiers. Behind these came the lancers in armor, then a column of men, all of them in brass helmets. And finally the noblemen appeared, separately, each outfitted to his own taste. The proud noblemen did not like to mix with the others and those without a command rode surrounded by personal retinues. Then several columns marched out with the mounted standard-bearer, Galiandovich, between them and more infantry columns, followed by the stout colonel. And, finally, after all the rest, the short little colonel.

"Don't wait! Don't give them a chance to deploy themselves!" the headman shouted. "Everybody at 'em! Every troop! Forget the other gates! Tytarev troop, get onto their left flank! Diadkiv, on the right! Press on the rear, Kukubenko and Palyvoda! Harass them, harass them. Stop them from forming ranks!"

And the Cossacks fell on them from all sides, toppled them, and, breaking their own ranks, wrought havoc in the Polish formation. They didn't even give them a chance to fire but closed in and fought at close quarters with sabers and spears. They fought in a tight mass and each man had only himself to rely on.

Demid Popovich ran his spear through three foot soldiers and then unhorsed two of the noblemen.

"Those are good horses!" he said. "I've been after something like them for a long time!"

And he drove the horses far out into the field, calling out to the Cossacks standing there to catch them. Then he fought his way back into the knot of fighters again and once more fell upon the noblemen he had unhorsed. He killed one and flung a noose around the neck of the other, tying it to his saddle and dragging him right across the field, having first taken his saber, which had a valuable hilt, and untied a bag of gold coins from his belt.

Kobita, a young Cossack but already a good one, also picked out one of the finest-looking Poles, and they battled a long time. They fought hand to hand. The Cossack won: he stabbed his foe in the chest with a sharp Turkish dagger. But he did not escape himself—as he struck, a scorching bullet hit him in the temple. He had been slain by an illustrious and handsome Polish knight who came from an ancient princely family. He sat astride his dun-colored horse like a shapely poplar. And he had already displayed his daring by cleaving two Cossacks from shoulder to hip. Then he'd toppled over Fedor Korzha, horse and all, shot the horse and dug the good Cossack from under with his lance. He'd slashed off many more Cossack heads and arms and now he slew Kobita with a bullet through the temple.

"There's one I'd like to tangle with!" Kukubenko, the chief of the Nezamaikovsky troop, said. He spurred his horse and hit the Pole from behind with his horse's chest, letting out such an inhuman cry that those standing near shuddered. The Pole tried desperately to turn his horse and face Kukubenko, but his mount did not answer to the rein. Frightened by the terrible cry, it shied to one side and Kukubenko's bullet struck the rider between the shoulder blades, knocking him from his horse. The Pole still managed to get his blade out of its sheath and lift it to strike, but his strength was leaving him fast and his saber hand fell limply to his side. Then Kukubenko took his heavy broadsword in both hands and smote him right across his bloodless lips. The sword knocked out a couple of the Pole's teeth, split his tongue in two, broke his spinal cord and bit deep into the ground. And so he remained nailed to the damp earth forever. His bright red blood gushed upward in a jet, staining the yellow gold-embroidered coat. Kukubenko left him there, and, followed by his Nezamaikovsky troop, pushed his way into another knot of fighters.

"Well, well! He left him without taking his things!" Borodaty, the chief of the Uman troop, exclaimed.

He left his men and rushed toward Kukubenko's dead nobleman.

"I've killed seven noblemen myself but none of them had trappings nearly this rich."

Borodaty's greed overcame him. He bent to strip the Pole of his expensive armor—he took his Turkish dagger, set with precious stones, unfastened from his belt a purse full of gold, and took from his breast a pouch containing fine linen, valuable silver and a lock of a girl's hair. And he was so absorbed in what he was doing that he failed to hear the red-nosed Galiandovich bearing down on him

—Galiandovich whom he had knocked from his saddle once earlier and given a good slash to remember him by. The red-nosed Pole swung his saber from the shoulder and struck Borodaty's bent neck. The Cossack's greed had brought him no good. His fearsome head flew off and the headless body fell, drenching the ground far around it. His stern Cossack soul rose, puzzled and angry, surprised to be parted so early from the strong, young body. Galiandovich did not have time to grab the troop chief's head by its tuft to tie it to his saddle before a stern avenger appeared. As a hovering hawk, after describing many circles on smooth-flying wings, suddenly stretches out and hurls himself like an arrow upon a calling quail cock, Ostap Bulba, Taras' son, came down upon Galiandovich. He swung his rope and threw it around the Pole's neck and his already red face grew crimson as the cruel noose tightened. He tried to use his pistol, but his twitching hand could not aim and the bullet flew far afield. Ostap unwound from Galiandovich's saddle the silk cord the Poles carry to tie up their prisoners, bound him with his own cord, and dragged him across the field, calling loudly for all Cossacks of the Uman troop to have a look at the one who had slain Borodaty and to come and pay their last respects to their troop chief.

When the Uman troop heard that their chief was no longer alive, they left the battle and ran to pick up his body and then went into a huddle to discuss whom they should choose to be their new chief. They quickly agreed.

"What's there to discuss?" one of them said. "Where would we find a better chief than Bulba's Ostap? Although he's younger than any of us, he's as smart as an older man."

Ostap Bulba, removing his cap, thanked all his Cossack comrades for the honor and without stopping to plead either his youth or his inexperience, knowing that in an emergency there is no time for such things, he led them all straight back into the fray and proceeded to show them that they hadn't picked him as chief for nothing. The Poles began to feel that things were getting too hot. They disengaged, withdrew, and tried to re-form their lines. The little colonel waved toward the gate, where a reserve of four hundred men was waiting. These men opened up with grapeshot. The shot hit only very few men; most of it landed instead among the Cossacks' oxen, who were staring at the battle. The oxen bellowed in fright, turned, and were about to stampede the Cossack wagons. But, at that moment, Taras Bulba and his men tore out of their ambush and with frightful shrieks rushed to intercept the beasts. The crazed herd, frightened by the shrieks, turned back again, and, in a wild stampede, cut into the Polish regiments, creating havoc among the cavalry and toppling and scattering the lot of them.

"Well done, oxen, thank you, brothers! Thank you!" the Cossacks cheered all around. "You've been auxiliaries for a long time and now you've seen real combat duty!"

And they followed up by attacking the Poles with redoubled fury. Many of the enemy were slaughtered that day. Many Cossacks distinguished themselves. Finally, the Poles saw that things didn't look too good for them. So they lowered their standards and shouted for the gates to be opened. The iron-studded gates drew back with a screech and received the exhausted, dust-covered riders like sheep into the fold. Many Cossacks wanted to rush after them but Ostap stopped his Uman troop, admonishing them:

"Keep back from those walls, brothers—it could be dangerous to get too close."

And he was right, because all sorts of things came flying from the walls and many who were underneath were hit. At that moment, the headman rode up to Ostap. He was full of praise and said:

"Here's a new chief and he leads his troops like a veteran!"

Old Taras Bulba heard this and turned his head to find out what new chief the headman was talking about and saw his Ostap at the head of the Uman troop, his sheepskin hat pushed jauntily to one side and a commander's staff in his hand. And Taras muttered to himself, "Well, I'll be damned," and rode over to thank all the men of the Uman troop for the honor they had shown his son.

The Cossacks withdrew again toward their encampment and the Poles reappeared on the city rampart, but now their bright garments were torn, there was dried blood on their expensive coats, and their beautiful copper helmets were covered with dust.

"Well, why didn't you tie us up?" the Cossacks taunted them from below.

"We'll show you yet!" the big fat colonel shouted from the wall, brandishing a rope at them. And the exhausted, dusty men kept exchanging threats and some even managed to find biting words to hurl at one another.

Finally, however, they all dispersed. Some lay down to recuperate from the battle, others poured loose earth on their wounds and bandaged them with scarves and expensive linens taken from the enemy, and those who were less tired went to attend to the dead. They used swords and spears to dig graves and scooped out the earth in their hats and the skirts of their coats. Then they laid the Cossack bodies neatly in the graves and covered them with fresh earth, to save their eyes from being pecked out by ravens and eagles. As to the Polish bodies, they tied them by the dozen to horses' tails. Then they set the horses loose and pursued them for a long time, whipping them across their flanks. The frenzied animals galloped over ridges and hills, over ditches and streams, and the blood-covered, dusty bodies of the Poles were battered against the ground.

Then they sat in circles and discussed at length the exploits and deeds performed that day, which would be retold many a time to their descendants and to strangers. It was a long time before they began to lie down to sleep.

And, as he sat up, old Taras kept wondering why he hadn't seen Andrei among the enemy force. Had the Judas been conscience-stricken at the idea of coming out against his own people? Or had Yankel lied—had he simply been taken prisoner? But then he remembered how vulnerable was Andrei's heart to a woman's ardent word, and anguish swept over him. He cursed the beautiful young Pole who had bewitched his son. And he swore that without even a glance at her beautiful face, he would grab her by her thick, luxuriant braid and drag her behind his horse across the field in full sight of all the Cossacks. He imagined her splendid, magnificent body torn asunder, limb from limb. But Bulba could not know what God was preparing for the morrow. He began dozing, off and on, and finally fell asleep. And some Cossacks still talked among themselves and, all night long, the guards stood by the fires, gazing fixedly all around without once closing their eyes.

Chapter 8

Before the sun had run even half its course, the Cossacks had gathered in groups. News had arrived from the camp: during their absence, Tartars had stormed it, looted everything they had found there, dug up the buried treasure, murdered half of those who had been left behind and driven the rest into captivity along with the herds of cattle and horses. And from there, it seemed, the Tartars had ridden directly to Perekop. Only one of the captured Cossacks, one Maxim Golodukha, had managed to escape. He had stabbed a Tartar chieftain, untied the bag of gold coins from his saddle, stolen his Tartar garments, and, disguised in them, had galloped for thirty-six hours without stopping, riding one horse to death, finding another, riding him to death too—only on the third horse had he reached a Cossack village where they had told him that the Zaporozhe army was besieging Dubno. This was all the Golodukha had said; he did not have time to explain how the disaster had happened, whether those left behind to guard the camp had been drunk and had been captured in that state, or how the Tartars had managed to find out where the treasure was buried. None of this did Golodukha mention. He was completely exhausted, his face swollen from exposure to sun and wind. He collapsed into a deep sleep.

Usually, in such circumstances, the Cossacks would have set out immediately after the raiders and tried to overtake them on their way, because otherwise the prisoners would find themselves in the market places of Asia Minor, Smyrna, Crete—and God knows where else their tufted Cossack heads would pop up. And that was why the Cossacks had assembled. All kept their hats on because they had not gathered to hear orders from their headman but to discuss the matter as equals.

"Let's hear what the elders have to say," one suggested.

"Let the headman have his say first," another said.

And the headman, taking off his hat, and, not as chief but just as one of them, thanked the Cossacks for the honor and said:

"There are many among us who are senior to me in years and in wisdom, but since you have honored me by asking my advice, here it is. Let us waste no time. Let's go after the Tartars. For you know yourselves what kind of man a Tartar is: he won't wait to squander the goods he has plundered from us. We won't find so much as a trace of our treasure. So, I say, let's go. We've had enough of a good time here. We have shown these Poles what Cossacks are. We have vindicated our faith as far as possible under the circumstances. And then, there's not much to take in this starved city. So my advice is—go after the Tartars."

"Let's go! Let's go!" loud voices rose from various troops.

But Taras Bulba did not like it. And he knitted tighter than ever his iron-and-coal brows which were like bushes growing on the slope of a hill, their tops covered with white frost. And he spoke next:

"No, headman, I don't agree. You seem to be forgetting our people imprisoned by those damn Poles. Do you suggest that we break the sacred vow of brotherhood, that we leave our brothers behind to be flayed alive, to have their Cossack bodies quartered and their limbs exhibited in Polish towns and villages, as they did with our headman and the best Russian warriors of the Ukraine? Don't you think they have already insulted enough the things we hold sacred? No, I ask you, friends, what sort of people are we, to abandon our comrades in their misfortune, to leave them behind like dogs to die on alien soil? If that's the way you feel, if your honor is nothing to you, if some of you wish to allow people to spit into your gray mustaches, then let no one blame me if I don't go along. I'll stay here alone if necessary."

There was hesitation in the ranks, then the headman spoke again:

"You've perhaps forgotten, gallant colonel, that the Tartars have some of our comrades too. If we do not save them now, they'll be doomed for the rest of their lives to be the slaves of all sorts of pagans—and that's worse than the cruelest death. And perhaps you've forgotten too that they have our treasure, paid for with Christian blood?"

The Cossacks did not know what to think. None of them wanted shamefully to abandon their comrades. Then from their ranks stepped Kasia Bovdug, the oldest man in the entire army. He was much respected by all the Cossacks; he had twice been elected headman and had been a great fighting Cossack in his day. But for some time now he had been too old for such things and he did not even like to give advice any more. All the old warrior liked now was to lie on his side in a group of Cossacks and listen to them talking about all sorts of things that had happened in past and present campaigns. He never interfered in their conversation. Pressing the ashes into a very short pipe which was never out of his mouth, he would lie in the same position for a long time with eyes half-closed so that those around him could never tell for certain whether he was asleep or still listening. For some time now he had stayed behind during campaigns, but on this last expedition something had roused the old man. He'd made a gesture with his hand as though pushing everything around him out of his way and decided to come along. Maybe, he thought, I can somehow still be of some service to the Cossack brotherhood.

The Cossacks fell silent now when he came forward, for they hadn't heard a word from him for a long time. One and all wanted to know what Bovdug had to say.

"I guess my turn has come to say a word, gentlemen and brothers," he began. "Listen to an old man, children. What the headman has said is wise. Being our headman, his duty is to look out for our interests and to worry about our treasure. No one could give you wiser advice. Well, let that be my first speech! And now, listen to my second. Colonel Bulba told a great truth too, may God grant him long life and may there be more such colonels in the Ukraine! The first duty of a Cossack is to respect the laws of comradeship. I have lived a long time, gentlemen, and I have yet to hear of a Cossack abandoning or selling a comrade. Now, both those in the hands of the Tartars and those in the hands of the Poles are our comrades and it does not matter whether there are more of them here or there: all our comrades are dear to us. So here's what I propose: let those whose closest comrades have been captured by the Tartars go, and those whose dearest ones are in the city stay. Let the headman lead those who go after the Tartars and let those who stay here, if they want to listen to a white head, elect as their acting headman Taras Bulba and no one else, because no one is superior to him in bravery."

Bovdug had said what he had to say and the Cossacks seemed relieved. They threw their hats into the air and shouted:

"Thank you, Father Bovdug! You've kept silent so long and now that you have spoken at last, you've been of great service to all the Cossacks, as you felt you'd be when you decided to come with us this time!"

"You all agree to this?" the headman asked.

"Yes, yes, yes!"

"Can we end the discussion?"

"End it, end it!"

"Now, listen to instructions," the headman said, putting on his hat while all the Cossacks took theirs off and bowed their heads, looking down as they were supposed to do when their headman spoke in his official capacity. "Those," he said, "of you gentlemen who wish to go after the Tartars, step to the right, those who elect to stay here, to the left. Each troop chief must follow the majority of his troop, while the minority will join another troop."

And they all started moving, some to the right, others to the left, and finally there were about an equal number of men on each side. Among those who elected to continue the siege were the entire Nezamaikovsky troop, most of the Popovich and Uman troops, the whole of the Kanev troop, and more than half of the Stablikiv and Tymashev troops. All the rest wanted to go after the Tartars.

Among those who decided to go were many bold Cossacks, including Demid Popovich, who was temperamental and never liked to stay in the same place for long. He had had his fun with the Poles, now he wanted to have some with the Tartars for a change. Among the troop chiefs, Nostugan, Pokrysha, Nevylychy, and many valiant Cossacks wanted to try out their swords and their strong shoulders fighting the Tartars.

There were also many of the best among those who were

staying: there were Troop Chiefs Demetrovich, Kukubenko, Vertykhvist, Balaban, and the young Bulba, Ostap,
and many, many Cossacks who had been all over—had
raided the shores of Asia Minor, had ridden over the Crimean salt marshes and steppes, knew well all the rivers,
large and small, that flow into the Dnieper, knew all the
fords and all the islands, had raided Moldavian, Wallach-
ian, and Turkish territories, had sailed all over the Black
Sea in their double-ruddered Cossack boats, had attacked
with fifty boats the tallest and richest ships, sunk many a
Turkish galley and used up a lot of gunpowder in their
time. They had often made foot bands of the finest linens
and velvets and many of them had belt buckles made of
gold sequins. As to the amount of goods each of them
had drunk and squandered during those years, it would
have supported another man all his life. The Cossacks
spent everything, treating every comer, hiring musicians, so
that everyone in the world should have a good time. Even
now most of them had some precious cup or casket or
bracelet buried somewhere or concealed under the reeds in
case the Tartars managed to raid the camp. And it is unlikely that a Tartar would have discovered any of these
private treasures because even their owners often forgot
where they had hidden them.

Such were the Cossacks who decided to remain behind
to avenge their faithful comrades and the Christian
faith insulted by the Poles! And old Bovdug also decided
to stay among them, saying:

"I'm too old nowadays to run after Tartars. And why
should I, since there's plenty of room here for me to die
a decent Cossack death? I have been praying God for
some time now that, if my life has to end, it may be in a
war for a holy Christian cause. And this seems to be it.
There can be no better end for an old Cossack."

When they had all divided up and were aligned in two
parallel rows, troop by troop, the headman walked between
them and said:

"Well, brothers, is everyone satisfied?"

"We are, headman, we are!"

"Fine! Then kiss one another farewell, for God knows
whether we'll meet again in this life. Obey your chiefs and
do as your Cossack consciences dictate."

And all the Cossacks, every last one of them, embraced

one another. First the two headmen, holding their mustaches out of the way, kissed each other crosswise and then squeezed each other's hands hard, as though wondering whether they would meet again. They did not utter a word and they lowered their old gray heads. And the other Cossacks were taking leave of one another knowing that they all had many things to do. They did not part immediately but waited for night to fall so as not to attract the enemy's attention to the reduction in their numbers. In the meantime, they dispersed by troops and sat down to dinner.

After dinner they lay down and fell into a deep sleep as though they felt this might be the last they would enjoy in safety. They slept until the sun was completely down, and, as it grew dark, they began to grease the wagons. When this was finished, they sent the wagons on ahead, and, with a last wave of their fur hats to comrades staying behind, they quietly followed. Then those on horseback, without shouting or whistling at the horses, trotted behind with muffled hoofbeats. And soon they had all dissolved in the darkness. And only the dull echo of a hoofbeat and the occasional screech of a wheel that was still stiff or had not been properly greased in the dark flew back out of the night.

For a long time after they had lost sight of the last rider, the remaining comrades waved their hats into the darkness. And when they returned to their places and saw under the starlight that half the wagons were gone, that many friends were no longer with them, sad thoughts possessed them, buzzing in their downcast heads.

Taras saw how troubled his troops were, and, although he knew that it was not good to allow fighting men to be gloomy, he said nothing for a while, giving them time to overcome the sadness of parting with friends and comrades. In a little while he planned to snap them out of it with a Cossack reveling cry, which would bring their gaiety back and, with it, an even stronger determination. He was relying on that resilience of which only the Slav soul is capable, a soul compared to which others are what shallow rivers are to the sea. When it is stormy, the sea roars and thunders and lifts its waves into the air, as the weak rivers cannot do, but when it is calm, it is brighter and shinier than any river, stretching out its brilliant surface in a limitless delight to the eye.

And Taras ordered his men to unpack one of his wagons that stood apart by itself, the sturdiest and the biggest in the entire train. Its strong wheels were rimmed with double bands of iron, it was heavily laden and covered with oxhides and horse blankets tied with taut, tarred ropes. It contained all the kegs and barrels of the best wine from Bulba's cellars. He had brought it along for some great occasion, for the important moment preceding an action destined to be remembered by their descendants —at that time the Cossacks would drink this precious wine and be equal to the occasion. On their colonel's command, the men ran to the wagon, slashed the ropes with their sabers, removed the covers and the oxhides, and unloaded the kegs and barrels.

"Take all you want," Bulba said, "help yourselves. Grab whatever you can lay your hands on, a jug, your horse's bucket, or what have you, a gauntlet, a hat, and, if you have nothing, just cup your hands!"

Every Cossack did as he was told and Taras's men walked among them and poured wine out of the kegs and barrels. But they had to wait to down it until Taras gave the signal because he wanted them to drink it all at the same time. And, first, he intended to say something to them. He knew well that even the very strongest and noblest wine, that strengthens and cheers a man's spirit, becomes stronger, even twice as strong, when it is accompanied with the appropriate words.

"I am treating you, brothers and gentlemen," Bulba said, "not to thank you for the honor you showed me by making me your commander. Nor is it on the occasion of our parting with our comrades. No, at other times both these occasions would be worth a drink, but things are different now. We are faced with the utmost exertion and the greatest glory! And so, let us drink, friends, first of all to the holy Orthodox Church, to the time when it will have spread all over the world and be the only faith, the time when every single pagan and Moslem on earth will have become a Christian! And while we are at it, let us drink to Camp Zaporozhe too, may it stand firm against the undoing of the infidels, and, every year, may ever more splendid warriors come out of it! And then, let us drink, too, to our own glory, so that our grandchildren and their children shall say that . . . that, yes, there were men once who never let down their friends. So, to our Church, gentlemen, to our Church!"

"To the Church!" shouted those in the front rows. "To the Church!" shouted those behind them and they all drank to the Church.

"To Camp Zaporozhe!" Taras said and raised his hand high over his head.

"To the camp!" the front rows boomed deeply. "To the camp," the old ones said quietly, stroking their gray mustaches. "To the camp!" intoned the young ones, stirring like young hawks. And the voices of the Cossacks drinking to Camp Zaporozhe resounded far afield.

"And now the last, friends—to the glory of every Christian living in the world!"

And all the Cossacks present took the last swig out of their jugs to the glory of all the Christians of the world and for a long time the phrase rolled from troop to troop: "To every Christian in the world."

The wine was gone but the Cossacks still stood with hands raised, and, although their eyes sparkled merrily, they were wrapped in thought. They were not thinking of the possible booty, of pieces of gold, costly weapons, embroidered garments, and Circassian stallions. They were looking into the future like eagles perched high on a rock, scrutinizing the boundless sea with its galleys, ships and vessels of all sorts that look to them like little gulls on the water, seeing the remote narrow coastlines on which the towns show like tiny insects and the trees of the forests like blades of grass. Like eagles, the Cossacks scrutinized their oncoming fate. They saw the whole plain, with its untilled fields and its paths strewn with blanching bones; soon, very soon, it would be drenched with Cossack blood and covered with broken wagons, shattered swords and splintered spears.

And scattered all over would be Cossack heads with their tangled tufts stiff with dried blood and their mustaches drooping; and the eagles would swoop down and claw and peck at their Cossack eyes.

But there is much to be said for a common grave! Not a single noble deed would be lost as a grain of powder disappears in the barrel of a gun. There would come a day when a lute player, his beard waist-long but, perhaps, still full of manhood's fire, would compose strong, resounding words to describe their deeds. And their glory would cross the world like a wild horse and whoever was born in the future would talk about them, for a strong word carries far and wide and is like a church bell into which the maker has put much pure silver so that its clear peals should carry farther and reach towns, villages, hovels, and palaces, calling everyone to join in holy prayer.

Chapter 9

Those in the besieged city did not realize that half the Cossacks had departed in pursuit of the Tartars. The sentries on the city tower noticed some wagons moving into the forest, but they decided that the Cossacks were laying an ambush. The French engineer concurred. In the meantime, the headman proved right when he had said that the defenders would soon be short of food again. As has happened throughout the centuries, the army had underestimated its needs. They tried to make a sortie, but half of those who risked it were slain by the Cossacks and the rest returned empty-handed. Some Jews from inside the city, however, took advantage of the sortie to find out everything: where and why a part of the Cossacks had left, which commanders and which troops, how many men had departed and how many had stayed, what they intended to do. In brief, in a short while, everyone in the city had heard the news. The two colonels cheered up and decided to give battle.

Taras Bulba guessed this from the movement and commotion going on in the city and acted quickly and efficiently. He went around issuing orders and giving instructions. He decided to deploy the troops in three rows, each flanked by wagons as protection; the two remaining troops were sent into ambush and a section of the field was planted with splintered spears, broken swords and sharp sticks—Bulba planned to lure the enemy cavalry over them. A battle formation of this type had always been eminently successful for the Cossacks.

And when all the dispositions were taken, Taras addressed his men. He did so not to cheer them up, not to give them courage, of which he knew they had plenty, but simply to share what he had in his heart:

"I'd like to talk to you, friends, about the ties that unite our brotherhood. Your fathers and grandfathers have told you how greatly respected our land used to be by one and all: our strength was felt by the Greeks, Constantinople had to pay us tribute in gold coin, our cities were prosperous and so were our churches—and our princes were of our own Russian blood, not Catholic heretics. All this the heathen took away from us. We were left orphaned and our native soil was like a lonely widow after her husband has been slain. That, friends, was when we joined hands and that is how our brotherhood originated. There are no ties more sacred than the ties between us. The father loves his child, the mother loves her child, the child loves its father and mother—but it's not the same thing, brothers. A wild beast also loves its young. Only man is capable of a kinship of the spirit, as opposed to blood kinship. There have been faithful comrades in other lands too, of course, but not comrades such as are found on Russian soil. Many of you have spent time in foreign lands. You know the people there are also God's creatures and, on occasion, you can even pass the time with them. But when it comes to matters that touch you deeply, you find it's no good—he may be a sensible man but he's different, a man just like you but not really the same.

"No, brothers, no one can love like a Russian, love not with the head, nor with any one part of him, but with everything that God has given him. Ah, you know!" And Taras waved his hand, twitched his mustache and shook his white head to indicate the absurdity of comparison. "No, I say, no one can love like that! And I say this although I am fully aware of the despicable things that are taking place in our land. There are among us those who think of nothing but filling their barns with grain, owning large herds and keeping a stock of sealed casks of mead in their cellars; those who adopt the devil knows what heretical ways; those who are ashamed of their language, so that, even among themselves, they will not speak their own tongue. There are those who are willing to sell their kinsmen in the market like dumb beasts. The favors of some foreign king—and not even of the king, but of some stinking Polish nobleman, who on occasion kicks them in the face with his yellow boot—is more important to them than brotherhood. But even the lowest of these bastards, even if he's spent his whole life groveling in dirt and subservience—even he has at least a tiny scrap of a Russian heart and one day that scrap will come to life and the miserable creature will beat his breast and tear his hair, and, cursing his villainy, will be prepared to redeem himself through any suffering. So let's let these people know what we mean by the brotherhood of the Russian land! And if we have to die, let 'em realize that none of them will die like us! None, none! Their rabbit's nature prevents it."

And when Bulba was through speaking, he still shook his head, whitened in Cossack campaigns, and everyone around was moved by his strong words. The older Cossacks stood immobile, their gray heads lowered, and many among them wiped away a tear with a sleeve. Then, as if obeying a secret signal, they all stirred, shrugged and shook their seasoned old heads. Probably Taras had stirred in them many a noble feeling, familiar to those who had become inured to sorrow, hardship and adversity. As to the young ones, they understood him instinctively, the way children do, who are an eternal joy to their old parents.

Meanwhile, with drums beating and trumpets blowing, the enemy host emerged from the city gates. The Polish knights, surrounded by large retinues, rode out sitting astride their horses nonchalantly. The big colonel was shouting orders. In tight ranks, the Poles moved on the Cossack wagons, threatening, aiming their pistols, their eyes and their brass armor flashing.

But when they were within pistol range, the Cossacks opened up a continuous fire. The crackling of the shots spread all over the surrounding fields and meadows, merging into one great din. The two forces floated in a cloud of smoke as the Cossacks kept firing without interruption and those behind kept reloading the pistols and handing them to those in the front, completely bewildering their foes who could not understand how the Cossacks managed to fire without reloading. Soon the smoke grew so thick over everything that neither side could see when comrades, one then another, disappeared from their places in the ranks. However, the Poles felt that the bullets were too thick, that it was becoming too hot for them. They moved back out of the smoke and looked around—of their people, many were missing. On the Cossack side, on the other hand, only very few had lost their lives. And they still kept firing without pause. Even the French engineer marveled at this style of fighting which he had never witnessed before. He said out loud, for everyone to hear:

"Wonderful fighters, these Cossacks. Their fighting methods should be emulated by those in other countries." And he advised the Poles to aim their cannons at the Cossack wagons.

A thundering roar came out of the wide, iron throats of the cannons, the earth stirred and shook, the smoke grew thicker than ever and the tang of gunpowder spread across the countryside. But the gunners had aimed too high and the red-hot cannonballs, describing steep arcs, screamed horribly over the Cossacks' heads, and, cutting deep into the ground, hurled columns of black earth into the air. The French engineer tore his hair at the sight of such poor gunnery and went over to aim the guns himself, disregarding a shower of Cossack bullets.

Taras saw from a distance what the cannons would do to the Nezamaikovsky and Stablikiv troops and shouted very loudly:

"Get out from behind your wagons! Everyone on your horses!"

Still, they wouldn't have been able to obey his order in time had it not been for Ostap, who appeared amidst the Polish gunners and struck the fuses out of the hands of six of them. But there were four more gunners and four more fuses which Ostap did not have time to attend to. The Poles succeeded in pushing him back and, in the meantime, the Frenchman himself took a fuse to set to a cannon bigger than any they had seen before. Its monstrous mouth gaped at them horrifyingly and they felt as though a thousand deaths were staring at them straight through it. Then it roared and its incredible thunder mingled with the roars of the other three cannons. The soil trembled and terrible havoc was unleashed. Many a Cossack mother would weep at the news of her son's death, beating her thin chest with her worn hands, and many a Cossack wife from Glukhov, Menirov, and Chernigov became a widow through that blast. But she would not know it and she would rush out every day to the market place, grab the passers-by by their coats, look into their eyes, searching for the one dearest to her; and many, many fighting men would pass through the town and never would she find her loved one among them.

And it was as though one-half of the Nezamaikovsky troop had never existed! They fell like rich, heavy, shiny wheat, flattened by hail in the field, and the Cossacks went mad with fury. They tore forward ferociously to the attack. Kukubenko, the commander of the Nezamaikovsky troop, realizing that better than half of his men lay dead, broke into the Polish ranks, raving and raging, followed by the survivors of his troop. In his anger he cut to pieces the first Pole that he came across as if he were shredding cabbage. Then he upset several horsemen, reaching with his spear for man and beast, and, coming up with the gunners, captured a gun. Turning, he saw that the commander of the Uman troop, Stepan Guska, had already captured the big cannon, so the Nezamaikovsky troop wheeled and barreled back through the Polish ranks, leaving behind them an avenue of corpses. Then they turned to the left and laid out a street. The enemy ranks were noticeably thinning; the Poles were falling like mown grass.

Then up to the attack came Vovtuzenko, from behind the nearest wagons, and Degtyarenko, from those on the far side. Degtyarenko had already speared two Polish noblemen and was trying to do the same to a third, a shifty, stubborn one. The Pole wore rich armor and had with him at least fifty men-at-arms. He was gaining the upper hand against Degtyarenko and finally knocked him off his horse and, swinging at him with his saber, shouted:

"There's not one of you Cossack dogs can overcome me!"

"Here's one to start with!"

It was Shilo. He rushed forward. He was a strong Cossack, a man who had gone through much in his life and had commanded many a Cossack seagoing expedition. He and his men had been captured by the Turks at Trebizond and had been taken as galley slaves, wrists and ankles shackled, with no food and only horrible sea water to drink for two whole weeks. But the poor captives bore it and all refused to renounce their Orthodox faith. That is, all except Shilo, who trampled underfoot his holy faith, rolled an unholy turban around his sinful head, gained the

special trust of the Pasha, and was put in charge of the
captives. The prisoners were sad, knowing that when a
man betrays his faith and joins the oppressors, he becomes
even harsher than any infidel. And this was the way it
turned out. Shilo had them shackled in heavier chains,
three in a row, and he had the shackles made so tight that
their flesh was cut to the bone. And he walked among
them, laying out blows on the backs of their necks. The
Turks were pleased to have found such a servant. They
organized a celebration and, forgetting their religious laws,
drank themselves drunk. Then Shilo took his sixty-four
keys, went down to the hold, handed the keys to the slaves,
who unlocked their shackles, grabbed sabers, rushed out
and slashed the Turks to death. The Cossacks returned
home with a lot of booty and for a long time the lute players celebrated Shilo's exploit. Probably he would have
been elected headman, but he was a peculiar Cossack.
There were times when he could put an operation together
that even the wisest Cossack could not have thought up,
while at other times he would do the stupidest, most ir-
responsible things. He had drunk everything he possessed,
was in debt to everyone, and, worse still, he had committed
a theft as low as that of any street thief: one night he had
crept into a barracks and stolen a harness and all the
equipment of another Cossack, giving it as a pledge to an
innkeeper. So they tied him to the pillar of shame and put
a cudgel at his feet for every passer-by to hit him with as
hard as he could. However, no Zaporozhe Cossack would
lift his hand against Shilo because of his past service.
That's the kind of Cossack Shilo was.

"You'll find that there are men who can wallop you,
you dogs!" Shilo shouted, throwing himself on the Pole.

Then the two swung at each other wildly. Soon their
shoulder plates and breastplates were thoroughly dented
under the blows. The Pole succeeded in cutting through
Shilo's coat of mail and reached his body with his blade.
Shilo's Cossack shirt turned crimson but he paid no attention to the wound, swinging his sinewy arm, famous
for its strength, and striking the Pole a blow on the head.
The brass helmet shattered, the Pole fell stunned, and
Shilo continued to rain down blows on him, slashing him
crosswise with his saber. It would have been better if, instead of finishing off his enemy, he had turned around. But

he did not, and one of the vanquished knight's men buried
a knife deep in his neck. Even so, when Shilo did turn he
would have reached his assailant had it not been for the
thick smoke which enveloped the other. Now the crack
of the guns sounded on all sides. Shilo covered his wound
with his hand; he sensed that it was a mortal one and
shouted to his comrades:

"Farewell, gentlemen, brothers and comrades! May
Holy Mother Russia live forever and may her glory never
pass!"

He screwed up his weakening eyes, and out of his rough
body flew his Cossack soul.

And here Zadorozhny and his men joined the battle and
Vertykhvist and Balaban with their troops were toppling
the Polish lines.

"What do you say, gentlemen?" Taras shouted to his
troop chiefs. "Do you still have plenty of powder in your
flasks? Is the Cossack force still not weakening? Are our
Cossacks still standing firm?"

"There's still plenty of powder, headman, and the Cossacks are as firm and unyielding as ever."

And they thrust forward and wrought confusion in the
Polish ranks. The smallish colonel had the rally sounded
and up went eight bright-colored standards to call together
the widely scattered forces. The Poles rushed toward their
standards, but before they had time to re-form their ranks,
Kukubenko and his Nezamaikovsky troop were in among
them pushing toward the big fat colonel. The fat colonel
was isolated from his men, and Kukubenko's assault was
too much for him. He turned his horse away and Kukubenko chased him across the field, preventing him from
rejoining his men. Stepan Guska watched this chase for a
while and then moved fast on the fat Pole from another
side, his head lowered till it touched his horse's neck, a
rope in his hands. Choosing just the right second, he cast
the noose over the Pole's neck in a single movement. The
colonel turned purple, clutching the rope with his hands,
trying to break it, but a spear, hurled with tremendous
force, drove into his belly, threw him down and pinned
him to the ground. Guska did not have long to live himself—as the Cossacks turned their eyes from the dead
colonel, they saw him raised in the air on four spears. The

poor man shouted: "Death to our foes and long live Russia," and then he breathed his last.

The Cossacks looked around: over on the Metelitsa flank, they were giving it to the Poles, stunning them one after another; and on the other flank Nevylychy at the head of his troop was pushing them back; and by the nearer wagons, it was Zakrutiguba who was on them, while by the farther wagons it was Pisarenko; and, over by the very furthest wagons they were fighting hand to hand, standing on top of the wagons.

And Taras, the acting headman, rode out in front and called:

"Well, gentlemen, have you still enough powder in your flasks? Is there still strength left in your arms? Can the Cossacks still hold out?"

"There's still enough powder, headman, and enough strength; the Cossacks won't give way."

At that moment old Bovdug fell from a wagon. A bullet had struck him under the heart. The old one took a deep breath and managed to say:

"I'm not unhappy to leave this world. No one could wish for a better death and may our Russian land be glorious for ever and ever!"

And Bovdug's soul soared high above the earth to tell those who had died long ago how well the Russians were still fighting, and dying even better, for the Orthodox faith.

And soon after, Balaban, the troop chief, fell. He had received three mortal wounds, one from a spear, one from a bullet, and one from a heavy broadsword. He had been one of the most famous Cossacks and had commanded many a naval expedition, of which the most glorious was his raid on the shores of Asia Minor. They had captured many pieces of gold then, many Turkish fabrics and ornaments and valuables of all sorts. But, on their way home, they had come under the cannons of a Turkish man-o'-war and a salvo had landed among their boats. Half the boats spun wildly around and capsized and many were drowned. But the reeds tied to the sides of the Cossack boats kept them afloat. Balaban ordered the boats rowed as fast as possible and placed in a straight line between the sun and the man-o'-war so that the Turks would not be able to see them. The whole of the following night they spent bailing out with pitchers and hats, stuffing holes, and making sails out of their wide Cossack trousers. And the next morning they managed to lose the fast Turkish ship. And not only did they reach home without further ʻrouble, they even brought with them a gold-embroidered chasuble for the Archimandrite of the Mezhigorsky Monastery in Kiev and a setting of pure silver for the icon of their church in Camp Zaporozhe. And for a long time afterward the successes of this Cossack leader were sung by the lute players. And now he lowered his head in mortal pain and said quietly:

"It seems to me, brothers, that I am dying a proper death. I've slashed seven to death, nine—pierced with my spear, trampled many of them with my horse, and I can't even remember how many of them my bullets have reached. . . . So, may the Russian earth prosper forever!" and off flew his soul.

Cossacks, Cossacks! Do not lose the cream of your army! Now it is Kukubenko who is surrounded. He has only seven men left of his troop and they are finding it hard to stay alive and there is blood on their chief's clothes. Headman Taras Bulba, seeing this, rushed to his rescue. But it was too late: a spear reached Kukubenko's heart before the rescuing Cossacks could get to him and push back the surrounding foes. And he sank into the arms of the Cossacks and his bright young blood streamed out like expensive wine carried from the cellar in a decanter by careless servants who slip and break their precious load by the dining-room door. And the master, seeing the wine all over the floor, holds his head in despair, because he has been keeping this wine for the great day when, in his old age, he would meet a friend of his youth and they'd remember the old days together, when men partook of different and stronger joys. . . .

And Kukubenko half-opened his eyes and said:

"I thank God that I died before your eyes, brothers. May people live after us even better than us and may the Russian land, beloved by Christ, flourish forever. . . ."

And as his young soul left his body, angels took it in their arms and carried it up to heaven. And this soul would be happy there.

"Sit here, on my right, Kukubenko," Christ would say, "you did not betray the brotherhood, you never acted dishonestly, never sold out a comrade, you always upheld and defended My Church."

Kukubenko's death saddened all the Cossacks. Their ranks were thinning terribly. Many, many brave ones had left them, but they still held out.

"What do you think, gentlemen?" headman Bulba inquired of the surviving troop chiefs. "Is there still enough powder in the flasks to go around? Aren't the sabers getting blunt? Aren't the Cossacks exhausted? Can they still hold out?"

"We're all right, headman, there's enough powder, the swords are still sharp enough, the men are not so tired and they can hold out."

And the Cossacks again rushed into the fray as though they'd never suffered a loss. Only three troop chiefs remained alive now. A whole net of scarlet rivers covered the plain and the piles of Cossack and Polish bodies were like bridges over them. Glancing up at the sky, Taras saw a flock of hovering vultures, sensing a feast. And, over there, he saw Metelitsa raised on a spear; and the cut-off head of one of the Pisarenkos spun in the air, its eyelids beating; and then the mangled body of Okhrim Guska fell to the ground.

"Now!" Taras Bulba shouted and waved his kerchief.

Ostap Bulba was waiting for this signal. He leaped out of ambush, and, at a full gallop, he and his men hit the enemy cavalry. The Poles toppled under this fierce assault and Ostap pushed them into the sector of the field where the splintered spears and sharp stakes had been planted. Many of the Polish horses began to stumble, their riders flew over their heads, and Cossacks by the furthest wagons, within range now of the hard-pressed Polish cavalry, opened fire.

The Poles seemed defeated and the Cossacks exulted:

"Victory, victory—we have them!" rang through their ranks and the Cossack victory banner was unfurled while the defeated Poles were still trying to flee and to hide.

"No, no," Taras said, looking at the city gates. "Not quite yet. We haven't finished yet."

And he was right.

The gates opened and out rode a regiment of hussars, the pride of the Polish cavalry. Every horse was a dun-colored Caucasian stallion and at their head rode the handsomest and the boldest rider of them all. As he rode, a black lock escaped from under his shining helmet and lay across his brow; a rich kerchief embroidered by the most beautiful lady in the kingdom fluttered in the wind behind him.

Taras was stunned when he recognized Andrei.

And Andrei, fretting for battle, eager to honor the light scarf tied to his arm, came dashing forward like the youngest, the swiftest, the handsomest greyhound of the whole pack, which, unleashed by the hunter, flies off in a straight line, its feet hardly touching the ground, its body slightly twisted, tossing up the snow as it changes direction, outrunning the hare in a burst of speed.

Old Taras stopped and stared, watching Andrei blast a passage before him, raining blows, slashing right and left, trampling men under his horse.

Suddenly he could stand it no longer and shouted:

"What are you doing? Can't you see, you son of a dog, that you're killing your own people?"

But Andrei no longer knew who were "his people" and who were his foes. He could only see hazel tresses, a swan-like neck and breast, and white shoulders that had been fashioned for his wild caresses.

"Lure him into the wood! Get him over there, lads!" Taras called out to the Cossacks.

And immediately thirty of the fastest Cossacks volunteered. Setting their tall sheepskin caps firmly on their heads, they darted out to cut across the path of the hussars. They hit them from the flank, cut the Polish riders in two and started pressing on the two halves, while Golokopytenko fetched Andrei a blow in the back with the flat of his broadsword. Then, at a signal, the Cossacks turned and galloped off as fast as their horses could carry them. Andrei rose in his stirrups and his young blood rushed to his head. He spurred his horse and flew after the Cossacks without looking back to see how many of his hussars were up with him, not realizing that there were only about twenty of them. And the Cossacks rode at full speed and turned into the wood. Andrei had almost caught up with Golokopytenko when a powerful hand grabbed the bridle of his horse. He looked up and saw Taras.

His whole body began to tremble then and he turned white. He was like a schoolboy who has been hit on the forehead with a ruler by a classmate and, jumping from his seat, red with rage, pursues his frightened friend, preparing to take him to pieces, when he stumbles on the teacher who has just entered the room. Within a second the wild rush stops and the fire of rage goes out. And now it was the same—Andrei's fury disappeared as though it had never existed. And all he saw before him was the terrifying figure of his father.

"What shall we do now?" Taras said, looking him straight in the eye, and Andrei said nothing and just looked down at the ground.

"Where are they now, your damn Poles, son? Why aren't they helping you?"

Andrei said nothing.

"The way you sold out! You sold your religion, you sold your people! Get off your horse!"

Obedient as a child he dismounted, and, neither dead nor alive, stood before Taras.

"Stand still and don't move! It was I who begot you and so it is I who must kill you!" Taras said, stepping back and taking his gun in his hand.

Andrei was white as linen and his lips moved slightly, forming someone's name. But it was not the name of his native land, nor his mother's name, nor the name of one of hi_ _omrades—it was the name of a beautiful Polish lady. And Taras fired.

Like a stalk of corn cut by a sickle, like a young lamb feeling the deadly steel under its heart, Andrei dropped his head on his chest and fell onto the grass without uttering a word.

The murderer of his son stood for a long time looking at the lifeless body. Even in death he was magnificent: his manly face, which only a few minutes earlier had been full of strength and irresistible charm for women, was still incredibly handsome and his black eyebrows framed his pale features like mourning cloth.

"What a Cossack he could've been!" Taras muttered. "So tall and black-browed and with the features of a nobleman and an arm so strong in battle . . . and now, now he's finished, dead ignominiously, like a dog. . . ."

"Pa! What have you done! Was it you who killed him?" Ostap cried, riding up.

Taras nodded.

Ostap looked intently into his dead brother's eyes and was filled with pity for him.

"Let's bury him properly, Pa," he said. "Don't let's leave his body to be jeered at by his enemies or torn to shreds by the buzzards."

"Don't worry about that," Taras said, "they'll bury him without us and he'll have many women to weep and mourn for him."

Nevertheless, for a minute or two Bulba stood there, hesitating whether to leave his younger son's body to be torn by wolves and buzzards or to spare his warrior's honor. But then Golokopytenko rode up at a gallop.

"Bad news, headman, the Poles have been reinforced, a fresh Polish force has arrived to relieve them."

And before Golokopytenko had finished, Vovtuzenko rushed up shouting:

"Things are bad, headman, Polish reinforcements are pouring in."

And then Pisarenko, horseless, came running:

"Where were you, headman? The Cossacks are looking for you. Troop Chief Nevylychy's been killed. Zadorozhny, killed. Chervichenko, killed. The Cossacks are holding but they don't want to die without seeing you, they want you to see them in their last hours."

"Mount your horse, Ostap," said Bulba, in a hurry to get to his Cossacks while they were still alive and to let them see their headman. But even before they were out of the forest, enemy riders armed with spears and swords appeared among the trees around them.

"Ostap, Ostap, don't let them take you," Bulba shouted as he drew his saber and started swinging it right and left.

Six men had suddenly fallen upon Ostap. But soon the head of one of them flew off. Another one toppled over as he backed away. Ostap's spear pierced the flank of a third. The fourth was more daring: rushing forward, he dodged Ostap's bullet, which, however, hit his horse in the chest. It fell, crushing its rider under it.

"Good boy, good boy, Ostap!" Taras kept repeating. "Wait, I'm coming . . ."

And while he kept fighting back his assailants, slashing away, dealing blows to one Polish head after another, he kept an eye on Ostap. And so he saw that about eight of them were on him.

"Ostap, Ostap, don't let 'em . . ."

But now they were overcoming his resistance. Already one of them had succeeded in passing a noose around his neck, already they were tying him up, taking him. . . .

"Oh, Ostap, Ostap!" Bulba howled, trying to make his way toward his son, cutting, slashing everything around him. "Oh, Ostap, Ostap . . ."

But a heavy stone hit Bulba and everything swayed and turned before his eyes. For one second he saw in a haze heads, spears, smoke, sparks, twigs with leaves on them, flashing before his very eyes, and then he crashed to the ground like a felled old oak and a black screen veiled his eyes.

Chapter 10

"I must have slept for a long time," Taras said as he came to his senses. He felt as if he had been in a heavy, drunken sleep and looked around him, trying to recognize things.

He felt a terrible weakness all through his body and could only vaguely make out the walls and the corners of an unknown room. Finally he realized that his friend Tovkach was standing near him, listening intently to his every breath.

"Yes," thought Tovkach, "it looked as if he'd gone to sleep for good." But he said nothing and just shook his finger.

"But will you tell me where I am, after all?" Taras asked, striving to recollect what had happened.

"Keep quiet for God's sake. What else would you like to know?" his friend said roughly. "Can't you see you're all slashed up? We've been riding for two weeks now, and, in your fever, you haven't stopped rattling on—all sorts of nonsense. This is the first time you've fallen properly asleep. So you'd better keep quiet if you don't want to kill yourself."

But Taras kept making desperate efforts to remember.

"But . . . but I was completely surrounded and the goddam Poles were about to grab me. How could I possibly have worked my way out of there?"

"Shut up, I tell you, you offspring of unholy demons," Tovkach shouted at him like a nurse made frantic by an impossible child. "What difference does it make how the hell you got out? The main thing's that you did, isn't it? There happened to be some people who didn't let you down and that should be good enough for you. Besides, we've plenty of night riding to do, because I hope you don't imagine that they rate you as a rank-and-file Cossack. No sir! There's a reward of two thousand pieces of gold on your head."

"Ostap, what about Ostap?" Taras shouted. It had all suddenly come back to him. He tried to rise. He remembered clearly now how they had been binding Ostap before his eyes and he realized that he must be in enemy hands. A terrible despair came over him. He started tearing the bandages from his wounds, throwing them all over the place and then began raving again. Fever and delirium took possession of him and wild speeches flew from his mouth. And his faithful friend stood over him, swearing and reproaching him endlessly for his madness. Finally, Tovkach took him by his arms and legs and swaddled him in bandages like an infant. Then he rolled Taras into a cowhide, picked him up, tied him with ropes to his horse, jumped onto his own and set off once more at a fast gallop.

"Dead or alive, I'll get you back," Taras's friend said to himself. "I won't let the damned Poles insult your Cossack body, tearing it into little pieces and tossing them to the fish one by one. And if it's your fate to have an eagle peck out your eyes, let it be one of our steppe eagles and not a Polish one. Even dead, I'll get you back to the Ukraine."

And Tovkach galloped without rest and brought the unconscious Taras all the way back to Camp Zaporozhe. And there he nursed him patiently back to health with herbs and poultices. He found a Jewish woman who knew about potions and she fed them to Taras for a whole month and at last Taras showed signs of getting better. Whether because of the drugs or his own rocklike constitution, in six weeks he was on his feet and healed and only deep scars bore witness to his terrible wounds.

But he was much gloomier than before. Three deep furrows appeared on his brow and never went away again. And as he looked around the camp, everything seemed different to him. It seemed that all his old comrades were dead. None of those who had gone with him to uphold and vindicate their faith against the Poles were there. Nor any of those who had elected to follow the old headman in pursuit of the Tartars. They too had all perished some time before, some had been killed in open battle, while others had died of thirst or hunger in the Crimean salt marshes.

Others must have died in captivity, unable to bear slavery. And the old headman, too, had been dead for some time. None of Taras's old comrades was still alive and grass grew over what had once been boiling Cossack energy. All Taras knew was that there had been a feast, a noisy feast, that all the glass and hardware had been smashed, that not a drop of wine was left, that the guests and the servants had stolen all the gold and silver goblets and left the sad host standing alone wishing there had never been a feast at all.

In vain did people around him try to cheer him up. In vain did gray-bearded lute players, two, even three at a time, sing to him about his own Cossack feats of arms— he sat there indifferently, staring at the world around him and repeating with his head lowered:

"Ostap, Ostap, my son . . ."

The Cossacks left on a sea raid. They lowered two hundred boats into the Dnieper and Asia Minor got a glimpse of their heads, shaven except for the tuft, wreaking death and havoc on its fertile shores; it saw the turbans of its Moslem inhabitants strewn like flowers over its blood-soaked fields or floating along its coasts. Asia Minor saw many tar-stained Cossack trousers, many muscled arms wielding knouts. The Cossacks ate or destroyed all its grapes; they left mosques heaped with dung and wrapped costly Persian shawls around their soiled coats. For a long time to come, people would find short Cossack pipes along that coast.

The Cossacks sailed back in a happy mood. They were given chase by a ten-gun Turkish man-o'-war and its salvos dispersed their flimsy craft and one third of them perished in the depths. But the rest reassembled and reached the mouth of the Dnieper with twelve barrels of gold sequins.

But Taras was indifferent to it all. He walked off into the steppe as though to hunt, but his gun remained unfired. And he would put it down and sit on the shore and, hanging his head, repeat again and again:

"My boy! Ostap, my son!"

The Black Sea stretched out sparkling all around him. A sea gull screamed in the reeds. Taras's white mustache gleamed like silver as his tears were caught in it one by one.

And finally he could stand it no longer.

"Whatever happens, I must find out whether he's still

alive or if he's in his grave or, even, no longer in the grave.
. . . I must find out, no matter what. . . ."

And within a week he appeared in the city of Uman.
He was on horseback and fully equipped for campaign:
spear, saber, canteen, traveling kettle, powder flask, am-
munition and all. He rode straight to a dirty little house
with windows that could hardly be made out because they
were covered with soot or God knows what; the chimney
was stuffed with a rag and the roof was full of holes and
teeming with sparrows. A heap of refuse was piled up
before the entrance. A Jewish woman in a headdress decorated with discolored pearls appeared in the window.

"Your husband in?" Bulba asked, dismounting and tying
his horse to an iron hook by the door.

"He's in," she said. She disappeared inside the house and
almost immediately re-emerged at the door carrying a
bucket of grain for the horse and a beaker of beer for the
rider.

"Where is he then?"

"He's praying," she said, bowing and wishing Bulba
good health as he lifted the beaker to his lips.

"Stay here and give my horse a drink while I talk to your
husband alone. I have private business with him."

The husband was none other than Yankel. He had been
living there for some time, renting land, running an inn,
and gradually making all the local gentry and aristocracy
dependent upon him by draining them of practically all
their funds, thus making his presence strongly felt in the
area. Not a single house in good repair could be found
within a three-mile radius of Yankel's house; everything
was left to go to ruin and every penny was spent on drink,
until all that was left was poverty and rags as though a fire
or a plague had swept over the place. And had Yankel
remained there another ten years, he certainly would have
succeeded in spreading misery over the entire province.

Taras entered the room where Yankel was. The Jew was
praying covered by a rather stained prayer shawl, and, as
he turned round to spit for the last time as his religion
demanded, his eyes met those of Bulba, standing by the
door. The first thought that rushed to Yankel's head was
of the two thousand gold pieces placed on Bulba's head, but
he was ashamed of his own greed and tried to suppress the

everlasting obsession with gold that torments the Jewish soul.

"Listen, Yankel," Taras said, interrupting him as he greeted him and at the same time rushed to close the door lest anyone see them together. "Remember, I saved your life once; without me they would have torn you to pieces in Camp Zaporozhe. Now it's your turn to render me a service."

"What service?" Yankel said, pursing his lips slightly. "If I can render this particular service, why shouldn't I?"

"Don't say anything to anyone and take me to Warsaw."

"Warsaw? Did you say Warsaw?" Yankel's shoulders jerked up in surprise.

"Don't say anything and take me to Warsaw. Whatever happens, I want to see him once more and say one last word to him."

"Say a word to whom?"

"To him, to Ostap . . . to my son."

"Is it possible, Colonel, that you haven't heard that they . . ."

"I know, I know, there's a price of two thousand gold pieces on my head. What do those stupid fools know about its worth? I'll give you twelve thousand. Here's two to start with. . . ."

And Bulba poured two thousand in gold pieces out of a leather bag.

"You'll get the rest when I'm back."

The Jew seized a towel and threw it over the gold.

"Nice stuff, noble stuff," he kept saying, turning a coin in his fingers, then trying it with his teeth. "I bet the man you relieved of this gold, Colonel, was unable to go on living, deprived of these lovely coins: he must have gone to the river and drowned himself."

"Look, Yankel, I wouldn't have come to you . . . I would perhaps have managed to find the way to Warsaw by myself, but the damn Poles might recognize me and then I am not so good at thinking up clever ways of getting around things, while you Jews, you're just made for it. You can hoodwink the devil himself and you know all the ropes. That's why I came to you. And even if I got to Warsaw, I couldn't get what I want by myself. So hitch up the horses and let's go!"

"Do you really imagine, sir, that I can just harness my

mare and shout 'git up' and take you unconcealed to Warsaw? Is that it, sir?"

"Hide me if you want, put me in an empty barrel or something. . . ."

"Colonel! Do you really think that an empty barrel is such a good place when people expect to find vodka in it?"

"Let them think. . . ."

"What are you saying? Let them think!" the Jew exclaimed, grabbing his side whiskers and pulling them upward with both hands.

"Well, what's come over you?"

"Hasn't it occurred to you, sir, that God created vodka so that it should be tasted by everyone? And around Warsaw, they all know what's good and a Polish squire would be prepared to run behind the cart for five miles to try and steal some by piercing a little hole in the barrel and then, when he saw that nothing came seeping out, he'd say to himself: 'Whoever heard of a Jew carrying an empty barrel around. There must be something hidden in it! Let's grab him, confiscate his money and clap him in prison!' And that's because everything is blamed on the Jew, because the Jew is treated like a dog, because people believe that a human being is not human if he's a Jew."

"All right, hide me in a cartload of fish."

"Impossible, impossible, sir, I swear it can't be done. People all over Poland are hungry as dogs and when they steal the fish, they'll be bound to feel you under it."

"Well, I don't care how, but take me there."

"Listen, listen, Colonel," Yankel said. He stuck his thumbs behind the lapels of his coat, spread out his fingers fanwise and, coming very close to Bulba, said:

"Here's what we're going to do. There's plenty of building going on, fortresses, castles, that sort of thing. French engineers have come from abroad especially for it. And so there's lots of brick and stone being transported all over the place. You'll lie flat on the bottom of the cart and I'll cover you with bricks. You look in good shape, Colonel, and I'm sure you won't mind if it feels a bit heavy. It won't hurt you. And I'll make an opening in the bottom of the cart, for food, you know. . . ."

"Do as you wish, just take me to Warsaw."

And an hour later, a cart loaded with bricks and pulled

by a couple of nags left Uman. On one of the nags sat Yankel, tall and thin as a signpost. His side locks had escaped from his skullcap and bounced up and down as he jogged along.

Chapter 11

At that time there were no guard posts or customs officers on the frontiers such as were later to become the plague of enterprising people, and so anyone could carry around anything he liked. And if by chance someone insisted on inspecting a load, he did so mostly for his own edification and usually because he suspected the load consisted of attractive items and the circumstances were propitious for him to emphasize his personal weight and authority. But few such inspectors were interested in bricks and the cart drove unmolested through the city gates of Warsaw.

Confined in his narrow brick cage, Bulba could hear nothing but the rattling of wheels and the shouts of drivers. Yankel, bouncing up and down on his short, dust-covered nag, chose a roundabout way toward a dark, narrow street known as Muddy Alley or Street of the Jews, because actually it housed almost all the Jews of Warsaw. This street looked very much like a backyard turned inside out. It seemed that the sun never managed to reach the level of the lower floors. Poles stretching across the street, from window to window of the blackened wooden houses, further added to the general gloom. Here and there the red-dish wall of a brick house, gradually turning black, could be seen and now and then the sun would light up the top of a stucco wall which seemed dazzlingly bright amid the surrounding bleakness. The street was littered with chimney pots, rags, vegetable peelings, broken utensils. . . . Whatever was discarded was flung out into the street as an offering to the esthetic feelings of the passers-by. A man on horseback could almost reach the various objects dangling from the poles across the street: the long stockings

Jews wear, their short pantaloons and smoked geese. Sometimes the rather pretty head of a Jewish woman, adorned with discolored beads, would appear in a ramshackle window. Curly-haired children, dirty and tattered, were playing noisily in the dust. A redheaded Jew with freckles all over his face making him look like a sparrow's egg peeped out of a window and immediately got into conversation with Yankel in an incomprehensible tongue, whereupon Yankel turned into a courtyard. Another came in from the street and joined them. All three went into a huddle, talking heatedly until Bulba finally emerged from under his bricks. Then Yankel turned toward him and told him that everything would be done, that Ostap was in the city jail, and that, although it would be very difficult to persuade the guards, he hoped to arrange for Bulba to see his son.

Bulba followed the three Jews into a house. They again started jabbering something and he kept glancing at each of them in turn as he spoke. Something seemed to have snapped Taras out of his deadness and a flame of hope, the hope that sometimes comes to a man driven to despair, appeared in his rough, indifferent face, and his old heart was set beating in the cadence of youth.

"Listen," he said excitedly, "nothing is impossible for you Jews; you can lift a thing from the bottom of the sea and there's even a saying that a Jew can steal himself if he only wants to. Set my Ostap free! Give him a chance to escape from the devil's clutches. I've promised this man twelve thousand gold pieces and now I'll add another twelve thousand, everything I possess, all my costly goblets, all my buried gold, all my houses. . . . I'll sell my last shirt and I'll sign a contract with you by which, as long as I live, one half of everything I bring from the wars will be yours. . . ."

"I'm afraid it can't be done, dear sir," Yankel said with a sigh.

"Impossible," one of the other Jews said.

The three of them looked at one another.

"Still one might try," the third one said. "Maybe, with God's help . . ."

The Jews then started speaking German and try as he might Taras could only make out one word that kept recurring and which sounded like "Mordecai," and nothing else.

"Sir, we must talk it over with a man the like of whom there has never been in this world," Yankel said after a while, turning toward Taras. "He's as wise as King Solomon and if he says he can't do it, no one can. Wait for us. Here's the key. Let no one in."

And they walked out into the street.

Taras locked the door and stood staring out the window onto the dirty street. The three Jews stopped in the middle of it and started another rather heated discussion. A fourth joined them. Then a fifth. Again, the oft-repeated word, "Mordecai, Mordecai," reached Taras's ears. They kept glancing across the street at one of the dingy houses and finally from out of its door there appeared a foot in a Jewish shoe, flashing from under the fluttering skirts of a long coat. A tall, thin Jew, not quite as tall as Yankel but much more wrinkled and with a huge upper lip, approached the group and all of them shouted, "Mordecai!" and started in turns to tell him something. And since Mordecai kept looking toward the little window behind which Taras stood, it was obvious they were talking about him. Mordecai gestured with his hands, listened, spat sideways, lifted the long skirts of his coat to get some trinkets out of his trouser pocket, displaying thus a very shabby pair of trousers. Before long all the Jews were shouting so loud that the one who seemed to be keeping a lookout started making them signs to keep quiet. Taras was already beginning to be concerned for his safety when he remembered that Jews can only discuss matters in the street and that since, anyway, no one, not even the devil himself, could understand their lingo, he had nothing to worry about.

A few minutes later, all the Jews entered his room and Mordecai approached Taras, patted him on the shoulder, and said:

"When we and God decide to do something, don't worry —it gets done."

Taras looked at this new Solomon, the like of whom did not exist in the world, and felt some hope and, indeed, his looks might well have inspired hope: the man's upper lip was simply awe-inspiring, although its thickness was undoubtedly partly due to outside causes. The beard of this Solomon consisted of fifteen hairs and, even so, all of them were on the left side. And his face bore so many marks of the beatings he must have received for the risks he had taken that he himself must have lost count of them and no longer been able to tell them from his birthmarks.

Then Mordecai left, followed by his friends, who were brimming over with admiration for his wisdom.

Left alone, Bulba found himself in an extraordinary situation: for the first time in his life he felt fear. He was in a feverish state. He was no longer his old self, the unbending, unyielding, unmovable oak. He was cowardly and weak. He started at the slightest noise; he started every time a Jew appeared in the street. He stayed there like that till the end of the day: he neither ate nor drank and his eyes never left the window for more than a minute.

It was quite late in the evening when Mordecai and Yankel returned. Taras's heart stood still.

"Well? Did it work?"

He was as impatient as a wild horse. But before they had time to answer him, Taras realized that one of Mordecai's untidy sidelocks was missing. Then the man tried to tell Taras something but Taras could make neither head nor tail of it. As to Yankel, he held his hand over his mouth all the time as though he were suffering from a cold.

"Oh dear, sir," Yankel said finally, "it is quite impossible to do anything now. I swear it's out of the question. Such a vile breed, these people, I'd like to spit in their nasty faces! Let Mordecai tell you. He tried to do what no man has tried, but God was not willing: there are three thousand soldiers to guard them and tomorrow all the prisoners are to be executed."

Taras looked at them and there was no impatience or anger in his eyes.

"If you want to see him, it must be done before sunrise tomorrow. The guards seemed amenable and their officer promised to help. But—may they be unhappy in the next world—what a greedy breed! You won't find the likes even among us. I had to give fifty pieces of gold to each guard and to their officer. . . ."

"All right, take me to him," Taras said, regaining his self-possession.

He agreed to let himself be disguised as a foreign count from the German lands. The provident Jew had already procured clothes for this purpose. Night had fallen. The owner of the house—the freckled Jew—had pulled out a thin mattress covered with a sort of sackcloth and spread it on a bench for Taras. Yankel lay on the floor, on a similar mattress. The red-haired Jew downed a glass of something or other, removed his coat, and, looking somewhat like a chicken in his stockings, climbed with his wife into something that might have been a closet, outside which two children lay down like a couple of puppies. But Taras could not sleep. He sat up, softly drumming on the table with his fingers, smoking his pipe and puffing out so much smoke that one of them kept sneezing in his sleep and pulling his blanket over his nose. And scarcely had the pale forewarning of dawn appeared in the sky, when Taras poked Yankel with his foot and said:

"Come on, get up and give me my disguise."

In a few minutes he was ready. He blackened his mustache and his eyebrows, placed a little dark cap on the crown of his head, and none of his friends would have recognized him. One would hardly have thought him more than thirty-five now, so rosy were his cheeks, and the scars on his face gave him an even more commanding air. The gold-embroidered coat looked very good on him.

The streets were still asleep. There was not a single merchant around with his basket. Bulba and Yankel arrived at a building which looked like a crane sitting on its nest. It was low, wide, and blackened, and on one side of it a sort of tower with a projecting roof jutted upward, the whole thing sticking out like the neck of a crane. This building served many purposes: it was used as a barracks, a jail, and even as a court of criminal justice. Taras and Yankel passed through the gate and found themselves in what was either a vast hall or a roofed courtyard. About a thousand persons were asleep there. Directly opposite the entrance was a little door, next to which two guards were playing a game in which one of them kept flicking his fingers against the other's palm. They paid little attention until Yankel approached and said:

"It's us! Do you hear, gentlemen, it's us!"

"Go ahead," one of the guards said, opening the door with one hand while presenting the other to his colleague to be flicked at.

They entered a dark, narrow passage that took them to a hall similar to the first, with little windows high up under its ceiling.

"Who are you?" several voices shouted at the same time,

and Taras saw armed guards looking at them. "We were told to let no one through."

"But it's us. I assure you it's us, gentlemen!" Yankel shouted.

Still, they wouldn't listen to him. Luckily at that moment a fat man came along. He had all the marks of seniority—that is, he used fouler language than the others.

"But, sir, it's us. You know me already and the count will show his appreciation. . . ."

"Let 'em through, you goddam mother-eating bastards! And don't you let anybody else through, you so-and-sos, and wear your swords and stop making this filthy mess on the floor. . . ." Taras and Yankel didn't hear all the eloquent instructions to the guards, and to everyone they met Yankel kept saying:

"It's us, we're friends, it's us."

When they reached a door at the end of the corridor, Yankel asked the guard standing near it: "All right?"

"It's all right with me," the guard said, "but I wonder whether they'll let you through into the jail itself. Jan has been replaced by another guard."

Yankel moaned softly. "It looks bad," he said to Taras.

"Go ahead," Taras said stubbornly, and Yankel obeyed.

By a door with a pointed top, which led to the dungeon, stood a soldier with a three-storied mustache: the ends of the top story turned upward, those of the second were parallel to his lips and the bottom ones turned down, all of which made him look very much like a tomcat.

Yankel shrank into himself and came up very close to the soldier.

"Your Grace, excuse me, Your Grace. . . ."

"You talking to me?"

"Yes, Your Grace. . . ."

"Hm . . . I'm . . . see, just a soldier," the man with the three-storied mustache said with an amused twinkle.

"I'm sorry, sir, I took you for the Military Governor himself," Yankel said, shaking his head and spreading his fingers wide apart. "You do look like a colonel, sir, I swear, exactly like a colonel! Just a little something, sir, and you'd be exactly like a colonel. Then if they gave you a stallion fast as a fly and regiments to drill . . ."

The soldier smoothed the bottom story of his mustache and his eyes looked very merry.

"What wonderful people, the military," Yankel went on. "What wonderful people! Those gold lacings, those spangles, all those shiny things like sunlight. . . . And the ladies . . . whenever they see a soldier . . . ah, dear me. . . ." Yankel again wagged his head admiringly.

The soldier now gave a twist to the top story of his mustache and let out a sound like the neighing of a horse.

"I would like to ask you for a favor, sir," Yankel said. "You see, this count has come from far away, hoping to have a look at the Cossacks. He has never seen what sort of people the Cossacks are, what they look like."

Foreign counts and barons were no rarity in Poland. They often went there to have a look at that remote, almost semi-Asiatic corner of Europe. They considered Muscovy and the Ukraine as part of Asia itself. And so the mustachioed soldier, bowing rather low, thought it appropriate to put in a few words himself:

"I really don't understand, Your Grace, why you'd want to look at them. They're not human, just a bunch of dogs, and they have a peculiar sort of religion that everyone despises. . . ."

"You're lying, you damn bastard," Bulba said. "You're a dog yourself! How dare you say that our faith isn't respected? It's your heretical faith that isn't."

"Well, well!" the Pole said. "Now I know who you are, friend. You're one of them, one of that lot sitting in there. Just wait while I call our men. . . ."

Taras realized his blunder, but his anger and stubbornness prevented him from trying to retrieve it. Fortunately Yankel managed to come up with something immediately.

"My noble lord," he said, addressing the Pole, "how could you possibly imagine the count to be a Cossack? Supposing he were a Cossack—how could he be dressed like a count, and look like one too?"

"Keep talking," the soldier said and opened his wide mouth to call.

"Your Royal Highness, Your Royal Highness, please, please, quiet," Yankel shouted. "Be quiet and we'll reward you as you've never been rewarded before. We'll give you two pieces of gold!"

"Yes? Two pieces of gold? I'm not interested in two pieces. I give that much to the barber for shaving only one half of my whiskers. Hand over a hundred, Jew!" The soldier gave a twirl to his top mustache and added: "Otherwise I'll start calling."

"Why so much?" Yankel said bitterly, untying his leather purse. Still, he was glad that it did not contain more money and that the soldier couldn't count beyond a hundred anyway.

"Let's go, let's go, quickly," Yankel said to Taras, noticing that the soldier was fingering the money, perhaps regretting not having named a larger sum. "Hurry. What a horrible lot, the people of this country."

"What are you waiting for, you damn Polish swine?" Bulba suddenly said to the Pole. "You took the money all right, do you think you'll get away with not showing us the prisoners? No, you've got to go through with it. Once you've received the cash, you've no right to refuse."

"Get out of here, both of you! Move or I'll report you and then . . . Take yourselves out of here, I tell you!"

"Sir, sir, let's go. Believe me, let's get out of here!" Yankel said, trying to convince Bulba. "The hell with him. May he see horrors in his dreams. . . ."

His head sadly lowered, Bulba slowly walked back along the passage. Yankel trotted behind him, bitterly regretting the wasted pieces of gold.

"What need was there to provoke him! Let the dog swear! These people can't do without swearing. Why is God so kind to some? . . . That pig earned a hundred gold pieces just for kicking us out, while they would tear out a Jew's side locks and push his face in so that nobody'd care to look at him and, have no fear, no one ever offers him a hundred. Oh God, oh merciful God!"

But the failure seemed to have a much deeper effect upon Bulba. There was an all-consuming flame in his eyes.

"Come," he said suddenly, as though trying to snap himself out of a nightmare, "let's go to the square. I want to see how they torture him."

"Why, sir? Why go? We can't help him that way."

"Let's go," Bulba repeated stubbornly and Yankel, sighing like a patient nurse, followed him.

It was impossible to miss the square where the executions were to take place—people were pouring into it from every side. In that savage age, not only the ignorant masses but the aristocracy as well regarded executions as a choice spectacle. Numerous old ladies of great piety, timid maidens and easily frightened women never missed a chance to attend, though throughout the following night gory corpses might obsess them and make them cry out in their sleep using words one would expect only from a drunken hussar. And many of them would scream hysterically that it was horrible and turn away from the tortures and still stay standing there for hours. And some, mouths gaping, arms widespread, looked as though they were about to jump on top of the heads of those around them, to get a better view.

The fat face of a butcher stood out among the ordinary, medium-sized heads. He observed the whole procedure with the expression of an expert and exchanged monosyllabic remarks with a gunsmith whom he addressed as "pal" because they got drunk in the same inn on holidays. Some engaged in heated arguments and occasionally even made bets, but the overwhelming majority were those who gape at everything that happens in the world and go on picking their noses. In the first row, just behind the mustached municipal guards, there stood a young Polish aristocrat, or at least he looked like one. He was dressed in military attire and was wearing absolutely every item he possessed—all that was left in his lodgings was a tattered shirt and an old pair of boots. Two chains, one on top of the other, with some sort of gold coins dangling from them, hung round his neck. He stood there with his sweetheart and kept glancing around to see that no one stained his silky garments. He had explained everything to her so thoroughly that there was definitely nothing to add.

"You see, Juzysya dearest," he said to her, "this whole crowd has come to see the criminals executed. And the one over there, see, dear, the one with the ax and the other instruments, that's the executioner—he's the one who carries out the executions. And when he begins to break them on the wheel and puts them through other tortures, they'll still be alive, but when the head's chopped off, then, sweet, the criminal will die immediately, understand? So at the beginning you'll hear them shout and move but as soon as they chop his head off, the criminal won't be able to shout or to eat or drink, because, of course, my sweet, he won't have any head left."

And Juzysya listened to all this, at once horrified and curious.

The roofs of the houses were teeming with people. Extraordinary mustached physiognomies in what looked like bonnets peeked out of little windows. On the balconies, the aristocracy sat under awnings. The sugar-white hand of a laughing lady lay gracefully on a railing. Majestic and rather fat aristocrats looked around with an air of great dignity. A footman in beautiful livery with flowing sleeves went around with a tray of refreshments. Often some bright, playful thing with black eyes would seize a piece of pastry or perhaps some fruit in her light little hand and toss it into the crowd below. The throng of underfed knights held out their caps to catch the morsel and some tall member of the gentry in a faded red doublet covered with tarnished golden cord, with his head sticking up above the others, would stretch out his arm and, thanks to its length, be the first to snatch it. He would kiss the prize and put it in his mouth. Another spectator was a falcon in a golden cage that hung under a balcony. His beak turned sideways and his claw raised, he too was staring intently at the people.

Suddenly a shiver passed through the crowd.

"They're bringing 'em! They're bringing in the Cossacks!"

The Cossacks' heads were bare, their long tufts swaying in the wind as they walked. They did not look particularly frightened or dejected and there was in their bearing a sort of quiet cockiness. Their coats, made of expensive cloth, were torn and hung in rags. They looked straight ahead without turning their heads toward the crowd. Ostap walked out in front.

What did old Taras feel when he saw his Ostap? Standing among the crowd, he kept his eyes glued on him and the smallest of his son's gestures did not escape him. When they reached the place of execution, Ostap stopped; he had to go through it first. He looked at the other Cossacks, raised his hand and said loudly:

"May God grant that none of the heretics gathered here shall hear a complaint from a tortured Christian! May none of us utter a single word!"

Then he stepped up to the scaffold.

"Good boy! Good, my son!" Bulba said very quietly and hung his old head.

The hangman tore off Ostap's rags. They tied him by

his wrists and ankles onto a frame made especially for the purpose and . . .

But why describe the hellish tortures that make one's hair stand on end? They were the product of that crude, cruel age when men led lives of violence and blood and their hearts were closed to human feelings. In vain did a few exceptional men try to oppose these beastly acts; in vain did the King and some enlightened knights insist that this cruelty would only arouse the Cossacks to vengeance. The authority of the King and of intelligent men counted for nothing, in the chaos of the day, against the arrogant will of the Polish aristocracy, who, through their thoughtlessness, incredible lack of foresight, childishness, and petty vanity, had turned the Polish Sejm into a parody of government.

Ostap bore the tortures and torments like a Titan. No cry, no sound, escaped his lips when they started breaking the bones of his arms and legs, and even when the sinister cracking of his bones was heard in the remotest corners of the square, when the Polish ladies turned away their eyes, he did not let out a moan and his face remained immobile.

Taras stood in the crowd, his head lowered but, at the same time, his eyes were raised and looked with a sort of proud approval at his son, while his lips kept muttering:

"Good boy, you're doing well. Good, son. . . ."

But when they started taking him through the last set of tortures, it looked for on second as if Ostap's strength was coming to an end. His eyes swept around and all he saw, oh God, were strange faces. If only someone close to him could be there as he died. He was longing, not for the desperate sobs of a weak mother nor the hysterical screams of a beloved, tearing her hair and smiting her white breasts—what he was searching for, hopelessly, with his eyes, was a strong, stern man whose calm encouragement would have eased his suffering and helped him to die. His forces were fading and finally he could stand no more and shouted in agony:

"Father! Father! Where are you? Can you hear? . . ."

"I hear, my son!"

The shout rang out in the silence and the whole huge crowd shuddered. Some mounted guards rushed to scrutinize the faces in the crowd. Yankel went deathly pale. But when, after having made certain that there were no guards near, he looked around for Taras, he could not find him. Taras was gone.

Chapter 12

But he was heard of again soon enough. A Cossack army a hundred and twenty thousand strong massed on the border of the Ukraine. This was no small force, no detachment preparing for a profitable raid or setting out to chase Tartars. No, this time the whole nation was up in arms, the patience of the people was at an end. They were thirsting for vengeance—their rights had been flouted, their customs scorned, their faith insulted, their churches desecrated. The savage excesses of alien overlords, the attempts to force allegiance to the Pope, the disgraceful rule of the Jews over a Christian land—all these things had been stored up for long years and had caused fierce hatred to grow in the Cossack people.

Their young and intrepid headman, Ostranitsa, was in command of this vast Cossack force. At his side was Gunia, his experienced friend and adviser. Eight colonels led regiments of twelve thousand men each. Three staff officers rode behind the hetman. The chief standard-bearer carried the principal standard and others fluttered farther back. There were people with all sorts of ranks and functions, quartermasters, scribes, and specialists in transportation. The army had its cavalry and infantry and there were many volunteers in addition to the registered Cossacks. They had come from all the corners of the Ukraine to join—from Chernigov, from Pereyaslav, from Baturin, from Glukhov, from the lower and upper reaches of the Dnieper and from all its islands. Countless horses, wagon trains, and carts stretched over the fields. And among all these Cossack regiments, the crack regiment was led by Taras Bulba. Everything made it stand out from among the others: the age of its commander, his experience in open warfare, and his unmatched hatred. Even his own Cossacks felt that his cruelty and ferocity were at times excessive. His prisoners were doomed to fire and the gallows, and, in a war council, this gray head would always insist on ruthless annihilation.

There's no need to dwell on the battles in which the Cossacks showed their mettle nor to describe the general course of the campaign. All this can be found in the chronicles. We all know what a war in defense of the faith is like in the Russian land. There is no stronger force. It is unmovable and stern like a wild crag jutting out of the unquiet, ever-changing sea, its jagged sides rising to the sky from unfathomable depths. It can be seen from far away, facing unmoved the rolling breakers, and woe to the ship that is hurled against it: splinters fly, everything inside is smashed and crushed, and the startled air is filled with the heartbreaking appeals of the drowning.

The pages of the chronicles describe in detail the flight of the Polish garrisons from the liberated towns, the hangings of unscrupulous Jewish contractors; the helplessness of the numerous Polish force under the King's hetman, Nicholas Potocki. The chronicle tells how, routed and pursued by the invincible Cossacks, many of Potocki's crack troops were drowned in a small river; how the Cossacks then besieged him in a small place called Polonnoye, and how, finding himself driven into a tight corner, the Crown hetman promised under oath that full satisfaction would be given to all Cossack demands by the King and his government and that all their former rights and privileges would be restored. But the Cossacks knew only too well what a Polish promise was, and it is certain that Potocki would never again have been seen swaggering on his Caucasian stallion, valued at six thousand pieces of gold, attracting the eyes of aristocratic Polish ladies and the envy of noblemen, or making so much noise in the Sejm, or giving sumptuous banquets to the senators, had it not been for the intervention of the Russian Orthodox priests.

The Russian Orthodox clergy went out to meet the Cossacks in their gold chasubles, carrying crosses and icons, with the bishop, cross in hand, marching at their head in his miter, and all the Cossacks lowered their heads and removed their hats. To no one else except the king himself would the Cossacks have shown respect at that moment. But they did not dare disobey their church. Hetman Ostranitsa and his colonels agreed to let Potocki go, after he had sworn to let the Orthodox churches practice their faith unmolested, to forget the ancient feud, and to commit no act that could cause prejudice to the Cossack army. Only one of the colonels would not accept this peace. This was Colonel Taras Bulba and he tore a wisp of hair from his head and raised his voice:

"Hetman and colonels! Don't be a lot of old women, don't trust the damn Poles! They'll doublecross you, the dogs!"

And when the scribe presented the treaty and the hetman signed it with his firm hand, Taras unbuckled his costly Turkish saber, drew out the flashing steel blade, snapped it in two like a reed, tossed away the pieces, one to the left and one to the right, and said:

"Good-bye then! Just as these two splinters will never be fused again into one saber, so you and I will never meet again in this life. Remember my parting words. . . ."

Here his voice suddenly grew in volume, rose, acquired an uncanny strength, and all were awed by his prophetic words:

"You'll remember me before you die! You think you've brought peace and quiet? You believe you'll live like squires from now on? Well, I see different things in store for you. You, Hetman, they'll take the skin from your head and stuff it with chaff and for a long time it will travel from fair to fair throughout the country! And you, gentlemen, won't get away with your heads either. You'll perish in damp dungeons, immured within stone walls, if you are not stewed alive like sheep in a caldron. And you, lads," he said, turning to his own regiment, "which of you will die a proper death, not by the stove or in bed like a woman, not lying drunk in a ditch outside an inn, but a true Cossack death, all together, in one field, like newlyweds in their bed? But maybe you're going home to become heretics and let the Polish priests ride on your backs?"

"We're with you, we're with you, Colonel. We'll follow you!" shouted Taras's entire regiment, and many others besides hastened to join them.

"Well, if you're coming, come on then!" Taras said,

pulling his hat down fiercely over his brow and looking defiantly at those who stayed behind. He mounted his horse and shouted to his followers:

"Let no one reproach us or say a slighting word about us! Off we go, lads—let's pay a visit to the Catholics!"

Thereupon he lashed his horse and a hundred wagons moved off behind him and, behind them, many Cossacks on horseback and on foot. Then he turned back once more and threw a threatening look at those who had stayed behind—a look full of wrath. No one moved to stop him. The regiment marched off in sight of the whole army and for a long way Taras kept glancing back threateningly.

The hetman and the colonels stood there greatly disconcerted, sunk deep in thought. It was as though they felt some sinister foreboding. And Taras's prophecy was correct. Everything turned out exactly as he had said. Soon after the treachery of Kanev, the hetman's head was stuck on a pole, as were the heads of many of his foremost lieutenants.

And Taras? Taras swept over Poland with his regiment, burning eighteen villages, about forty churches, and almost reaching Cracow. Many of the Polish gentry were slaughtered. Many a rich and beautiful castle was looted and mead and wines, a century old, were poured out on the ground. They slashed and burned sumptuous clothes and materials and broke and scattered provisions in the larders. "Spare nothing," was all old Taras would say. And the Cossacks did not spare the black-browed damsels either— the white-bosomed, fair-faced maidens could find no safety even by the church altar. And afterward the flames consumed them and their altars. Many a white arm rose toward heaven above the tongues of flame, amidst shrieks for pity which would have touched the damp earth itself and made the steppe grass bow in compassion. But the callous Cossacks heeded nothing—they speared infants in the streets and tossed them into the same flames.

"That's for you, you goddam Poles. A requiem for Ostap," was all Taras would say. And this requiem was repeated in every Polish village and settlement, until it dawned on the Polish government that Taras's exploits were going well beyond the ordinary raids, and they commissioned the same Potocki, at the head of an army of five regiments, to overtake and capture Taras at any cost.

For six days the Cossacks evaded their pursuers, using lanes and byways, and their horses were hard tried by these forced marches. But this time Potocki was equal to the mission entrusted him. He pursued them relentlessly and overtook them on the bank of the Dniester, where Bulba had halted to recuperate in the deserted ruin of a fortress.

The broken ramparts of the fortress loomed above the steep bank of the river. Rubble and broken masonry, strewn along the top of the wall, looked as if they would fall at any moment. At this spot, Potocki concentrated his attack from two sides of the field. For four days the Cossacks fought, struggled, defended themselves with bricks and stones. But their stores and their strength were running low and Taras decided on an attempt to break out. And the Cossacks broke out all right and their swift horses would have carried them away from their foe once more, but suddenly Taras stopped in full gallop and said:

"Hold on, brothers! I've dropped my pipe and my tobacco pouch. I don't want those Polish dogs to get even that much!" And the old chief leaned over and started looking in the tall grass for his pipe, his inseparable companion on sea, on land, on campaign and at home. At that moment, a wave of the enemy swept over them and Taras was grabbed by his heavy shoulders. He twisted his whole body as hard as he could but those who had grabbed him did not fall away as they used to in the olden days.

"Damned old age," he said and began to cry. But it was not a question of old age. Strength was overwhelmed by strength; maybe thirty of them were hanging onto his legs and arms.

"The old crow is caught!" the Poles shouted. "All that's left is to decide how best to honor the dog."

And with Potocki's permission they sentenced him to be burned alive in sight of everyone.

A bare tree that had been struck by lightning stood nearby. They bound him with iron chains and dragged him to it. They nailed him by his hands to the trunk, after lifting him high so that he could be seen from far away. Then they began to build up a fire. But Taras did not look at the firewood and it was not of the fire that he was thinking. He was looking to one side, where the Cossacks were still firing back at the Poles, and from his height he could see everything quite well.

"Occupy it, occupy, occupy the hillock," he shouted, "behind the wood. They won't be able to approach it! . . ." But the wind did not carry his words to them. "My God, they'll be lost for nothing," he said in despair, and looked down toward the gleaming Dniester. Joy gleamed in his eyes. He saw the sterns of four boats sticking up among the reeds and, gathering all his strength, he shouted:

"To the river, lads. Take the path to the left. There are boats hidden there. Take them all, so they can't follow you!"

This time the wind was from the other side and the Cossacks heard his words. But his advice brought him a blow from the blunt end of an ax and everything swayed before his eyes.

The Cossacks raced full gallop downhill with the Poles at their heels. But the path twisted and turned and they saw that it ran parallel to the bank too much of the way.

"All right, brothers, down we go, we've nothing to lose," one of them shouted.

They stopped for a second, raised their whips and whistled. And their Tartar horses detached themselves from the ground, stretched themselves out like dragons, flew through the air, and dropped with a splash into the Dniester. Only two of them failed to reach the river. They fell from the heights hitting the stones, and were lost forever with their horses, without even having time to let out a cry. But the rest were already swimming in the river with their horses and untying the boats. The Poles stopped on top of the precipice, wondering at the incredible Cossack feat and trying to decide whether to leap or not.

One young Polish colonel, with hot, boiling blood, the brother of the beautiful Polish girl who had bewitched poor Andrei, was not long deciding. He threw himself with his horse in pursuit of the Cossacks. Rider and mount spun around three times in the air and were hurled straight upon the jagged rocks. He was torn by the sharp stones and his brain, mixed with blood, bespattered the bushes that grew on the uneven edges of the cliff.

When Bulba came to after the blow, he looked down at the Dniester and saw the Cossacks already rowing away in the boats, while bullets rained down on them from the cliff, missing them. And the eyes of the old chief sparkled with joy.

"Farewell, comrades!" he shouted to them. "Remember me sometimes, and, when spring comes, come back here and have a damn good time! And you, what do you think you have gained, you Polish dogs? Do you think there is anything in the world that'll frighten a Cossack? Wait, the time will come when you'll find out what the Russian Orthodox faith is like! Even today nations far and wide are beginning to feel that a tsar will arise on the Russian land, and there'll be no power on earth that won't submit to him!"

In the meantime, the flames were rising and lapping around his legs and now the whole tree burst into flames. . . .

But are there in the world such fires, such tortures, or such forces as could overcome Russian strength?

The Dniester is no minor river and it has many backwaters, thick reed banks, shallows, and deep pools; the river's mirror glitters, resounding to the ringing cry of swans, and the proud golden-eye skims swiftly over it. There are many snipe, red-breasted sandpipers, and other birds in its reeds and on its banks. The Cossacks rowed swiftly in the double-ruddered boats; steering skillfully, they carefully avoided the shallows, raising frightened birds from the reeds, and talked about their chief.

Afterword

Nikolai Vasilievich Gogol-Yanovski (who later dropped the second part of his hyphenated name) arrived in St. Petersburg in the last days of December, 1828, after a very long and tiresome journey. He had come from the Ukraine, leaving behind, in the family estate of Vasilievka, his widowed mother, then in her late thirties (his father died when he was sixteen), and four sisters, the eldest eighteen and the youngest four. The family estate was of modest size and was appallingly mismanaged. Dearth of money in the family was chronic, but the good Ukrainian earth was so bountiful that little exertion was needed on the part of the masters or of their serfs to provide amply for immediate needs.

Young Gogol (he was not quite twenty when he arrived in the capital) had with him a very small sum of money, a few not very useful letters of introduction, and a diploma earned after eight years in a boarding school in the Ukrainian town of Nezhin. It was a good school by the standards of those days. Gogol's record was not exactly brilliant; he did shine in student theatricals, however, especially in comic parts which he played with notable success. Gogol also brought with him the unfinished manuscript of a rather long narrative poem. This was, for the time being, his secret.

Gogol's purpose in coming to St. Petersburg—at least his avowed purpose—was to enter government service. This he did, quite reluctantly, some ten months after his arrival, spending in government bureaus in all about fifteen months. Before coming to the imperial capital, Gogol had given much thought to service in the government, preferably in the Department of Justice. He would become a great public servant, celebrated by all for his integrity and wisdom. Disillusionment in government service came even before he took his first job. But he had considered other paths to greatness as well. In fact, if he was certain about anything, it was that his destiny was an extraordinary one. Immortality was the young man's main purpose upon entering life. But destiny's call, if it was compelling, did not specify what his glorious mission was to be, what path to greatness he was to embrace.

Some five months after his arrival in St. Petersburg, Gogol's poem had been completed and printed at his own expense (or rather his mother's—a desperate appeal was sent home for three hundred rubles for an urgent, but unspecified, need). The poem was romantic and Germanic. Its title—and the name of its hero—was: *Hans Küchelgarten*. When two reviews, both unfavorable, were published, the author withdrew the unsold copies (the sold copies numbered three) and burned them. He had fortunately used a pen name, and many years went by before Gogol was identified as the author of the poem.

A strange episode followed the *Küchelgarten* debacle. At the very moment when it occurred, Gogol received from his mother a sum of money to pay the interest on the mortgage of the family estate. Instead of paying it, he boarded a steamship sailing for the German port of Lübeck. His letters to his mother were eloquent and full of sentiment, but quite confusing as to the reasons for the sudden departure, or the voyager's future plans. After six weeks in Germany Gogol was back in St. Petersburg.

In Gogol's early letters, written before he moved to St. Petersburg, and in later writings as well, one finds repeated references to at least two plans for his future. One of them was a career in the government; the other one, a dream rather than a plan, but a recurring one, was about leaving his home and his homeland, and going to foreign lands, alone, a pilgrim seeking his way to some unknown shrine, a mysterious altar on which he would offer himself in sacrifice.

This theme is present in Gogol's letters written when he was seventeen, and it is central in his poem whose awkward stanzas tell the story of the young German who leaves the peace and happiness of home and goes, a staff in his hand, on an aimless pilgrimage to distant lands. In the end, however, he abandons his quest for the Absolute. Returning to his home town, the pilgrim marries Fräulein Luise, thus surrendering the ideal to the idyllic.

In 1836, the author of *Hans Küchelgarten* boarded once more the ship sailing from St. Petersburg to the German ports of Lübeck and Hamburg; this was seven years after the first voyage. This time, except for two winters spent in Russia (1839-40 and 1841-42), Gogol stayed abroad for twelve years, returning only in 1848, four years before his death.

During the seven and a half years he spent in St. Petersburg, Gogol served in government bureaus for fifteen months, taught, for three years, in a girls' school (The Patriotic Institute), was appointed adjunct professor of history at the University of St. Petersburg, and, for one year, gave lectures which did not seem to give evidence of especially profound scholarship; and finally, in the course of these years he became a famous writer. Success came some two years after the ill-fated *Küchelgarten,* with two little volumes of Ukrainian stories entitled *Evenings on a Farm Near Dikanka* (September, 1831; March, 1832). They were received enthusiastically and were followed by other successes.

Gogol's first escape to foreign lands in 1829 came after the fiasco of his poem (a poem, one will observe, about an escape to foreign lands). In 1836, seven years later, Gogol's departure followed the first performance of *The Inspector General,* without doubt the greatest comedy ever written in Russian, and one that has never left the Russian stage after its first performance in April, 1836. For its contemporaries the play was controversial, and there was some rather vocal adverse criticism. Gogol, however, spoke of violent and general hostility toward him, in fact so violent and so general that he felt compelled to leave his country.

Did the *Küchelgarten* fiasco have to be re-enacted to justify a renewed escape abroad? With his peculiar disregard for consistency, Gogol added another reason for his departure: he was going to devote himself to a great work in which the whole of Russia would be portrayed; and to complete this *magnum opus* he had to be away from Russia.

This work was *Dead Souls*. Gogol had written the first three chapters of *Dead Souls*, at least in first draft, before leaving Russia. The manuscript traveled with him by sea to Lübeck, thence, across Germany, to Geneva and to nearby Vevey, on the shores of the Lake of Geneva, where the work was resumed. It was continued in Paris, then in Rome where Gogol lived for long periods of time during his years of self-imposed exile.

Dead Souls was completed in 1841 and published in 1842. It was received enthusiastically. Gogol was then thirty-three.

The remaining ten years of Gogol's life were devoted to a sequel to *Dead Souls*. A second volume was begun even before the final revisions of the first were completed; but, dissatisfied with his work, Gogol destroyed the manuscript in 1845 and made a fresh start.

In 1848, after a journey to the Holy Land, Gogol returned to Russia. He had another four years to live. His death in February, 1852, was one of his own making: he imposed upon himself rigorous fasting (it was Lent), then refused all nourishment. His end was hastened by obtuse and overzealous physicians. For many years Gogol had been a typical *malade imaginaire,* complaining of and seeking medical help for symptoms we would now call psychosomatic. This time Gogol had made real his fears of illness and his foreboding of an early end.

On the night of February 11th, ten days before his death, Gogol burned in an open fireplace the manuscript of the second volume of *Dead Souls*.

Beginning with the later stages of his work on the first volume, Gogol came to be dominated by what may be termed a Messianic complex: the notion that he was chosen to deliver a portentous message to his countrymen, a message of truth so compelling that it would bring about Russia's moral regeneration. The image of himself as a great statesman and moral reformer appeared very early in Gogol's life. It receded to the background for a number of years, the years of Gogol's most intense artistic creativity. Now it had come to the surface again, more compelling than ever.

What Gogol sought to accomplish through his great work was a synthesis of the two ideal images, that of the great poet and that of the leader, or statesman, whose power would rest on his genius and his knowledge of the truth. The synthesis, however, was impossible and Gogol spent his creative talent in his efforts to use it as a tool for moral propaganda. As he labored over his *magnum opus* he was more and more often tormented by doubt: had he not erred in believing that he had been chosen for the great mission, and if God had chosen him, why would He not grant him the strength he needed to carry the burden? Or was he unworthy of the choice? He prayed to God that He restore his creative powers, and he would use them in His service. But they were not restored and this was a sign of his unworthiness in the face of God.

It is a plausible conjecture that Gogol's assuming a Messianic role resulted from a deeply buried feeling of guilt. If this was so, his efforts to carry out his mission only brought him new evidence of his guilt and intensified his fears of retribution. He had misread the Divine message. It was his pride that had led him to believe that his book would bring salvation to his countrymen; it had been conceived in sin and must be destroyed. After that only death remained, or rather only life, all he now had to offer in sacrifice.

The works included in this volume were written during Gogol's most productive period, a relatively short period of vigorous and brilliant creativity.

"The Diary of a Madman" was first published in 1835. "The Nose" and "The Carriage" followed in 1836. In 1835 was published an early version of *Taras Bulba* which was later extensively revised and expanded by Gogol for the four-volume edition of his collected works which appeared in 1842. This edition also included "The Overcoat," on which Gogol had been working sporadically for several years.

According to their thematic material, Gogol's works may be divided into three groups related to three geographical areas: provincial Russia, the Ukraine, St. Petersburg. *Dead Souls* depicts provincial Russia; a small town is the scene of *The Inspector General* and of "The Carriage." *Taras Bulba* represents the Ukrainian area and is the most ambitious of Gogol's works based on Ukrainian material. The remaining selections belong to the St. Peterburg cycle. The themes of the St. Petersburg stories found their most complete expression in "The Overcoat," one of Gogol's highest literary achievements.

One could argue that the hero of "The Overcoat" is an overcoat (just as a carriage and a nose are central in the two stories bearing these titles). The central human figure in the story is one Akaky Akakievich Bashmachkin (this being the given name and the family name, with between them, according to Russian custom, the patronymic, a form derived from the father's first name). Akaky Akakievich was employed for many years in a government bureau in St. Peterburg copying official documents (this was the age of the quill pen, long before invention of the typewriter, or even of carbon paper). The life of this lonely, almost speechless, aging, balding little man is reduced to tracing letters, with great care, and some of them, his favorites, even with delight. He goes to his office every morning and returns in the late afternoon to the little room where he eats, sleeps, and does more copying. Twice a day, however, he must walk a few blocks and thus expose himself to the noise and disorder of the crowded street, and even worse, in winter, to the fierce cold, the winds and the blizzards of the northern city. One needs protection from the elements, and Akaky Akakievich did not have adequate protection. He had an old threadbare coat, and one day, when he took it to the tailor's in the hope of having it mended, he heard what sounded to him like a death sentence: the garment was beyond repair, a new one would have to be made. With the tailor's verdict begins the last period in Akaky's life; it is a brief period, but one filled with glory and tragedy. First, the impossible becomes reality: depriving himself of everything, Akaky manages to save enough money to pay the price of the new overcoat, a veritable masterpiece of sartorial art (with a collar of the best cat's fur available, looking very much like marten at a distance). Akaky, who was ignored by his colleagues, or else was made the butt of their practical jokes, is congratulated and welcomed as an equal when he arrives in the office wearing the new coat. The same evening he is invited to a birthday party by one of his superiors at which the glorious garment and its owner are celebrated. Triumph, however, is followed by disaster. Crossing a vast and deserted square on his way home from the party, Akaky is attacked and robbed of his overcoat. No help comes to Akaky, screaming and trembling alone in the night. Nor does help come when he turns to the police. And when he seeks the protection of an "important personage," this worthy, in a thundering display of importance, has him thrown out. In the street he is assailed once more, this time by a snowstorm. This aggression proves fatal for Akaky Akakievich: he contracts a fever and dies within two days.

The story does not end with Akaky's death, but to quote the text, "unexpectedly takes on a fantastic ending." After Akaky's death, street robberies occur nightly in St. Petersburg and a rumor spreads that people are robbed of their overcoats by the ghost of a recently deceased clerk. The constabulary, ordered to "capture the ghost dead or alive," is helpless. The nocturnal attacks cease, however, after one last robbery, when none other than the important personage has his magnificent overcoat dragged off his shoulders. In his assailant the important personage recognizes Akaky Akakievich. Soon thereafter a policeman attempts to arrest the "ghost," but gives up when the "ghost," tall and wearing a formidable mustache, thrusts a huge fist in his face. These features, however, are not Akaky's, but those of Akaky's aggressor, and this identification very subtly brings the "fantastic ending" back to the plane of reality.

One may identify with reasonable certainty three sources of "The Overcoat," three starting points from which Gogol's creative imagination proceeded. The first is a story told in Gogol's presence (the episode has been recorded by a contemporary) about a poor government clerk who after months of privation and overtime work bought a shotgun; as he went shooting wild ducks with it in a little boat, the gun slipped out of his hands, fell into the water, and was lost. The story had a happy ending: a new gun was offered by his colleagues to the luckless Nimrod, who was lying in bed, sick with grief. This is the theme of ardent desire, short-lived possession, and loss.

The episode of the important personage being robbed (supposedly by the "ghost") of his overcoat may be traced to facts, or anecdotes, recorded in the diary of Pushkin, under the dateline of December 17, 1833:

> There is talk in the town of a strange occurrence. In one of the buildings belonging to the Office of the Court Stables, the furniture took to moving and jumping around; the affair was brought to the attention of the authorities—Prince V. Dolgoruki ordered an investigation. One of the officials called a priest, but during the service the chairs and tables wouldn't stand still. Different comments were made. N. said the furniture belongs to the Court and wants it back to the Anichkov (Palace). The streets aren't safe. Sukhtelen was attacked in the Palace Square and robbed. The police, apparently, busy themselves with politics and not with thieves and with the streets. Bludov was robbed last night.

The "jumping chairs" found their way into Gogol's story "The Nose":

> At that time people were prone to fall for supernatural things: only a short time before, experiments with magnetism had caused a sensation. Also, the story about the dancing chairs of Stables Street was still fresh, and people soon began to repeat that Collegiate Assessor Kovalev's nose was to be seen taking a daily walk on Nevsky Avenue at 3:00 P.M. sharp.

As for the street robberies, both victims mentioned by Pushkin were important, indeed very important persons: Count Sukhtelen was a general, and Bludov, also a count, was none other than Minister of the Interior. And since the street robberies took place in the month of December, it is most likely that the two counts were robbed precisely of their overcoats. Pushkin, Russia's greatest poet, was a friend of Gogols, and he may well have told him the story, or Gogol may have heard the bits of town gossip from another source, but it is obviously irrelevant who the immediate source was.

The earliest known version of what later became "The Overcoat" had the title "The Story about a Clerk Who Stole Overcoats." The logic of the development of the plot seems then to have been as follows: a poor clerk has lost his most precious possession; an important person has been robbed of his overcoat; combining the two: he has been robbed by the poor clerk, who (to make the two losses symmetrical) does not drop a shotgun into a pond, but, like the important personage, is robbed of his overcoat. Symmetry on the moral level is vengeance or retribution (an eye for an eye is a symmetrical figure), so the important personage must be made responsible for the clerk's misfortune. He could obviously not be the robber; so he is made responsible, at least indirectly, for the poor clerk's death. Dead, the poor clerk cannot take vengeance, unless the narration were to shift to the plane of the fantastic. It does, but the fantastic is not "really" fantastic: it is generated by rumor and the important personage's troubled conscience. In "actual fact" he is robbed by the same man who robbed Akaky.

One more possible source must be mentioned,* the legend of the sixteenth-century saint of the Russian church, Saint Akaky. St. Akaky was a novice in a monastery, who died after nine years of abuse and humiliation by his elder, which he accepted without murmur. This elder was never at peace with his conscience from then on and was obsessed by the idea that Akaky had not really died. One day he went to his grave and heard his voice which said, "I am not dead, for a man who lived in obedience may not die."

The story of Gogol's Akaky is also a story of humiliation and humility. His humility, however, was not absolute. The making of a new overcoat was imposed upon him by circumstance, as everything was imposed upon him (whatever happens in the story happens *to* him); but when he was forced to recognize the inevitability of a new overcoat, he conceived for it an all-consuming desire. Then he enjoyed possessing it and he enjoyed his brief triumph, the giddiness of being suddenly propelled to a higher social status, one of equality with others. Akaky Akakievich thus violated the law of humility, even if only by accident.

"They receive you according to your clothes, they see you off according to your wits," says a Russian proverb. Akaky never had wits, but for one day in his life he had decent clothes and was received accordingly. The old coat was threadbare, "one could see through it," and in a garment "through which one can see" (through which one can see the wearer), a man is exposed to ridicule and to the

---

* This source was brought to light by the Dutch scholar, F. C. Driessen.

rigor of the elements. He will be laughed at and he will shiver in the winter cold. But is not a garment also a disguise? Is it not deceit to be received according to your clothes, not according to what you really are? Akaky in his new overcoat had no more wit, or virtue, than in the older one. He was welcomed and feted thanks to a travesty. But a garment is always a travesty, and one has to wear a garment. A man dies of exposure if he chooses not to wear one and to be undisguised, to be himself.

It may well be that this paradoxical morality was in Gogol's mind, behind the more obvious one (which it does not necessarily contradict), that Akaky Akakievich suffered injustice and that at least posthumously he found redress when the important personage in his turn became victim of a street robbery.

Many paths lead from "The Overcoat" to Gogol's other stories. To take the one leading to "The Carriage": the hero's giddy ascent comes in this story at the beginning, when landowner Chertokutsky, invited to the general's stag party, mingles with the brilliant, bragging, gambling, and drinking cavalry officers. When the gentlemen are out on the porch after the sumptuous dinner, and the general has his bay mare brought before their admiring eyes, landowner Chertokutsky tells him about the carriage he owns, a veritable masterpiece of Viennese craftsmanship, worth all of four thousand rubles. He then proceeds to invite the whole company to come to his estate the next day for an early dinner and an inspection of the carriage. This, however, is the beginning of his downfall. Arriving home at dawn, the owner of the carriage forgets to mention the invitation to his wife. He is awakened only when the uniformed party arrives. Seized by panic, he grabs his nightgown and rushes to the shed, where he hides in the carriage. It was a poor hiding place indeed; dinner or no dinner, the general, followed by the gentlemen of his party, decides to take a look at the carriage (a very ordinary one, they pronounce) and discovers its owner in a dressing gown under the carriage's leather apron. Thus Squire Chertokutsky is exposed to the eyes of the company, hiding inside the object upon which he had built his fantasy of grandeur, a nude statue suddenly ashamed and hiding in its pedestal. Inside the collapsed symbol of glory, humiliated and de-

fenseless in his nudity, was the man himself. The treasured
object is not lost in this story, but it has lost its power
and is now useless, an "ordinary" carriage that Squire
Chertokutsky dared match against the general's fire-spout-
ing bay mare.

"The Nose" is a story of loss and recovery: a nose is
lost, then recovered by its legitimate owner. Having detached itself from its owner, the nose assumes the identity
of a high-ranking bureaucrat until it is finally restored to
its natural position of an accessory, however important.
A number of literary sources of Gogol's story have been
identified which detract nothing from its originality. Rather
obvious is the phallic symbolism of the nose (its loss suggesting castration, a fairly frequent motif in Gogol).
Humiliation in this story comes before the triumph; the
humiliating loss, moreover, is in the realm of the fantastic,
while the triumph is in a return to the normal order of
things. In an early version the story ended with the hero
awakening to realize that the upsetting adventure was but a
dream. But in the definitive text Gogol deleted the short
epilogue; "it was only a dream" is an easy device for justify-
ing the fantastic and the absurd. In the definitive version
absurdity is pure and unmitigated, and the story stands on
it solidly.

The motif of the garment as symbol of status is present
in "The Diary of a Madman," even if it is only episodic.
"The Diary" is the record of a gradual invasion of its
writer's mind by insanity—more specifically, by delusions
of grandeur. At one point the writer of the diary, another
poor government clerk, discovers that he is none other
than the King of Spain, Ferdinand VIII. For a while he
prefers to remain incognito, but later decides that the time
has come to reveal his true identity. "If only," he medi-
tates, "I could get hold of a royal mantle of some sort. I
thought of having one made but tailors are so stupid. . . .
I decided to make a mantle out of my best coat which I
had only worn twice. . . . I preferred to do it myself. I
locked my door so as not to be seen. I had to cut my coat
to ribbons with the scissors since a mantle has a completely
different style." His first appearance in the "royal mantle"
causes old Marva, the servant, to "let out a yell."

Akaky's overcoat was the attribute of respectability required by society; once it was produced, society granted

him recognition of his human dignity (which he loses together with the overcoat). The writer of the diary, his ego
inflated beyond the limits of the rational, is unable to
produce the requisite attributes. His "royal mantle" de-
ceives no one but himself, and the palace in Spain where
he believes he has been taken turns out to be a lunatic
asylum. The point is, however, that had he maintained his
incognito, had he not worn the mantle to gain the recognition of others, he could have continued to enjoy his regal
status. One may rise to a higher status by changing the real
order of things. Or else (this, however, people choose to
call lunacy) one may decide that the real order is not
"really real" and substitute for this order another reality
in which one is anything one chooses to be. As long as
one's faith in this other reality is strong enough, this is just
as gratifying.

More variations on the themes of status, of rise and fall,
and of different levels of reality are found in Gogol's
famous comedy, *The Inspector General,* and in his novel
(or "poem," as he subtitled it), *Dead Souls.* In the former,
a petty civil servant, stranded in a small town on his way
home from St. Petersburg, is mistaken by the corrupt local
officialdom for a government inspector, traveling incognito.
He thus finds himself in a situation in which, all inhibitions
having been removed, he can give free reign to his wildest
fantasies of grandeur, fantasies that are believed by the
panic-stricken bureaucrats. A reality, or a mode of reality,
has, in other terms, been fortuitously created in which he is
a personage wielding great power and inspiring awe and
admiration ... kaky (young, however, and light-headed)
become an important personage. He is found out, but after
a timely escape, which is also a return to that reality in
which he has no status, nor hardly even an identity.

Chichikov, the hero of *Dead Souls,* is a swindler. The
circumstances in which he is believed to be a man of sub-
stance are not fortuitous, they are of his own making. He,
too, is found out. But the townsfolk are not content with
discovering that in reality he is not a respectable man of
affairs but a swindler. Instead, they modify reality once
more, and in their collective imagination, Chichikov becomes a romantic and dangerous brigand, and it is even
conjectured that he is Napoleon Bonaparte, who has
escaped from the island of St. Helena. This fantasy of

grandeur, going far beyond the image deceitfully created by Chichikov himself, is generated in the collective mind of the community. So was the fantasy that Akaky Akakievich, or rather his ghost, is a dangerous robber. The "Ferdinand VIII" fantasy originates in the deranged mind of an individual and remains subjective; it is incommunicable. In *The Inspector General*, the hero's fantasies of grandeur are shared by the community.

In Gogol's St. Petersburg stories, in his *Inspector* and in *Dead Souls,* the central characters are lonely figures. They have no family, nor do they have any social ties. They live alone in their furnished rooms, they make their way through the crowd to a place behind a desk in some office, they are faceless, and they ruminate, or daydream, or become swindlers, or go insane. One of them, with the help of chance, can daydream aloud, before a credulous and awe-stricken audience, becoming a potentate, if only for a few days. This happens in a comedy, a fantasy of a lonely young man, Nikolai Gogol by name, one of the dwellers of the big city, bureaucratic and impersonal, with its long winters, its gray sky, and its population of many thousands of strangers.

Taras Bulba, the Ukrainian epic, stands in sharp contrast to the moods and the themes of the St. Petersburg stories. The place is Gogol's homeland, the Ukraine; the time is the distant past when the Ukrainian people waged their struggle against their Polish oppressors. The characters are virile, their speech and their costumes are full of color; they are recklessly brave, violent and generous, primitive and poetic. They have families and they love women, but they are stern and unwavering when the moment comes to leave them, to mount their horses and go to battle. They ride across the steppes and fight and die, a compact mass of men, gay and brutal. Old Taras is the bravest of them all, a commander loved and respected by his men. His two sons were worthy of him, or so people believed. But one of them falls in love with a young Polish girl and commits treason. Old Taras will never forgive a traitor, even if he is his son. And the story moves on, propelled by conflicts of violent passion, through scenes of romantic love and fierce battle, treason and retribution,

heroism and adventure, to end in the old warrior's death
and apotheosis.

Taras Bulba is an epic of the romantic period, akin to
the novels of Sir Walter Scott and in some ways to those
of James Fenimore Cooper, a writer greatly admired by
Gogol and by many generations of Russian readers.

Gogol's tale is a work of historical fiction, but one that
attempts to re-create an epoch rather than to present historical facts or characters. Taras and his sons are fictional.
A few real characters are mentioned but left in the background. The most important one is the Cossack leader or
"hetman," Ostranitsa, under whom Taras serves as commander of one of his regiments. Gogol's chronology in the
story is vague; however, the campaign that the Cossacks
waged against the Poles under Ostranitsa took place in
1637. It began with a resounding victory of the Cossack
forces and continued with a series of defeats and Ostranitsa's rather inglorious escape eastward to an area under
the sovereignty of Muscovy. In the Ukraine it was believed
that he had been captured by the Poles and executed.

Gogol had, it seems, a special interest in Ostranitsa,
possibly because the battle he won against the Poles was
fought in the immediate vicinity of Vasilievka, the family
estate where Gogol spent his young years. There is no need
for a biographical explanation of Gogol's interest in the
past of his native Ukraine and especially in those bloody
rebellions against Polish domination that are celebrated in
Ukrainian folk tradition. It may be noted, however, that
his family claimed ancestry from one Colonel Ostap Gogol,
a prominent figure in the struggles of the seventeenth
century. The name Gogol was added to Yanovski by the
writer's grandfather, together with titles of nobility. This
ancestry was doubtful at the very best. One may also note
that in the course of events Colonel Ostap had gone over
to the Poles, surrendering to them an important stronghold.
The fortress was located in the area, perhaps at the very
spot, where Taras Bulba finds a glorious death fighting the
Poles, thus redeeming, if only in fiction, the other colonel's
treasonable act.

It must be added that in the perspective of the seven-
teenth-century wars (the Ukrainian rebellions were followed by Muscovite and Turkish interventions), Ostap
Gogol's act was a matter of political choice; he was most

certainly free to prefer an alliance with Poland to one with Muscovy. But in Gogol's days the policy of allegiance to Muscovy was no longer in dispute; the matter had long been settled. Moreover, the first version of *Taras Bulba* was written in 1834, and at that time, after the Polish national uprising against Russia in 1830-31, strong anti-Polish feelings were rife in Russia. It is in the light of this situation that Taras Bulba's anti-Polish fury must be seen. The political mood of the day was in harmony with the source materials that were available to Gogol: the old Cossack chronicles written in the seventeenth century, then rewritten, with many a dramatic detail added, by one generation after another. These chronicles represented the feelings of the pro-Russian and anti-Polish factions. Gogol followed this tradition, with its mixture of fact and invention, with its cruel and treacherous Poles, its hideous or ludicrous Jews (Jews and Papists alike being enemies of the true faith); he used his sources, perhaps uncritically, because he found in them the color and the drama he needed as a writer of fiction, and because they were in keeping with the official views of the day. And Gogol, a Ukrainian by birth, was a very loyal subject of the Tsar of all Russia.

A note may be added on the plot of *Taras Bulba*. One of the two younger Bulbas, falling in love with a Polish girl, becomes a traitor to his people and also to the manliness that is a warrior's supreme virtue. He perishes. Love, in Gogol's work, is usually presented as a threat to man's very existence, unless it is ridiculed in depictions of matrimonial bliss of this grotesque creature, the average human being.

To Gogol himself, love was alien, whether tragic and destructive or grotesque; he had no experience of sex life.

There are certain established views concerning Gogol and his work. A tradition of literary criticism that was highly influential in Russia until the turn of the century celebrated Gogol as the founder of Russian realism, as a liberal (even if not conscious of his liberalism), a social satirist dedicated to the exposure of the evils of the *ancien régime,* as the writer who was first to portray the "under-

dog" in Russian literature, and who did this with com-
municative compassion.

These views underwent an extensive reconsideration in
the first quarter of this century. Then, in the Soviet period,
they were resurrected and given official sanction and are
no longer subject to dispute.

The official doctrine is demonstrably wrong in most of
its aspects. But there is little need for any such demonstra-
tion. For if the merits of Gogol were those that are officially
recognized, there would be every reason to honor him, but
little reason to read him, whether in Russia or in the West.
There is little reason to read a book if all this book can
do is arouse the reader's indignation over bribery in early
nineteenth-century Russia, or his compassion for down-
trodden office clerks. Nor do we read an author to pay
tribute to his civic or moral virtues.

The reason for reading Gogol is that he is a great writer,
in fact one of the most original, most delightfully and
brilliantly inventive writers of the nineteenth century; one
also whose perception of the world and whose art are
often amazingly modern.

One of the unhappiest among the unhappy race of
creative artists, Gogol is above all an enjoyable writer.
The proof of this, it is hoped, will be found in reading
him. No better proof, at any rate, could be offered.

Leon Stilman
Columbia University

𝒞

SIGNET CLASSICS by Russian Authors